Monotheism and Its Complexities

PREVIOUSLY PUBLISHED RECORDS OF BUILDING BRIDGES SEMINARS

The Road Ahead: A Christian–Muslim Dialogue, Michael Ipgrave, editor (London: Church House, 2002)

Scriptures in Dialogue: Christians and Muslims Studying the Bible and the Qur'ān Together, Michael Ipgrave, editor (London: Church House, 2004)

Bearing the Word: Prophecy in Biblical and Qur'ānic Perspective, Michael Ipgrave, editor (London: Church House, 2005)

Building a Better Bridge: Muslims, Christians, and the Common Good, Michael Ipgrave, editor (Washington, DC: Georgetown University Press, 2008)

Justice and Rights: Christian and Muslim Perspectives, Michael Ipgrave, editor (Washington, DC: Georgetown University Press, 2009)

Humanity: Texts and Contexts: Christian and Muslim Perspectives, Michael Ipgrave and David Marshall, editors (Washington, DC: Georgetown University Press, 2011)

Communicating the Word: Revelation, Translation, and Interpretation in Christianity and Islam, David Marshall, editor (Washington, DC: Georgetown University Press, 2011)

Science and Religion: Christian and Muslim Perspectives, David Marshall, editor (Washington, DC: Georgetown University Press, 2012)

Tradition and Modernity: Christian and Muslim Perspectives, David Marshall, editor (Washington, DC: Georgetown University Press, 2012)

Prayer: Christian and Muslim Perspectives, David Marshall and Lucinda Mosher, editors (Washington, DC: Georgetown University Press, 2013)

Death, Resurrection, and Human Destiny: Christian and Muslim Perspectives, David Marshall and Lucinda Mosher, editors (Washington, DC: Georgetown University Press, 2014)

The Community of Believers: Christian and Muslim Perspectives, Lucinda Mosher and David Marshall, editors (Washington, DC: Georgetown University Press, 2015)

Sin, Forgiveness, and Human Destiny: Christian and Muslim Perspectives, Lucinda Mosher and David Marshall, editors (Washington, DC: Georgetown University Press, 2016)

God's Creativity and Human Action: Christian and Muslim Perspectives, Lucinda Mosher and David Marshall, editors (Washington, DC: Georgetown University Press, 2017)

Monotheism and Its Complexities

Christian and Muslim Perspectives

A Record of the Fifteenth Building Bridges Seminar

Hosted by Georgetown University
Washington, DC, and Warrenton, VA
May 6–10, 2016

Lucinda Mosher and
David Marshall
Editors

Library of Congress Cataloging-in-Publication Data

Names: Building Bridges Seminar (15th : 2016 : Washington, D.C.), author. | Mosher, Lucinda, editor. | Marshall, David, 1963– editor.
Title: Monotheism and its complexities : Christian and Muslim perspectives : a record of the Fifteenth Building Bridges Seminar hosted by Georgetown University, Washington, DC, and Warrenton, VA, May 6/10, 2016 / Lucinda Mosher and David Marshall, editors.
Other titles: Record of the Fifteenth Building Bridges Seminar | Fifteenth Building Bridges Seminar
Description: Washington, DC : Georgetown University Press, 2018. | Includes bibliographical references and index.
Identifiers: LCCN 2017054126 (print) | LCCN 2018013679 (ebook) | ISBN 9781626165854 (ebook) | ISBN 9781626165830 (hardcover) | ISBN 9781626165847 (paperback)
Subjects: LCSH: Monotheism—Congresses. | God—Congresses. | God (Islam)—Congresses.
Classification: LCC BL221 (ebook) | LCC BL221 .B85 2016 (print) | DDC 261.2/7—dc23
LC record available at https://lccn.loc.gov/2017054126

♾ This book is printed on acid-free paper meeting the requirements of the American National Standard for Permanence in Paper for Printed Library Materials.

19 18 9 8 7 6 5 4 3 2 First printing

Printed in the United States of America
Cover design by Debra Naylor.

Contents

Participants in Building Bridges Seminar 2016

Professor Asma Afsaruddin, Indiana University, Bloomington, Indiana

Professor Seyed Amir Akrami, Yale University, New Haven, Connecticut

Professor Muhammad Modassir Ali, Qatar Faculty of Islamic Studies at Hamad bin Khalifa University, Qatar

Professor Ahmet Alibašić, University of Sarajevo, Bosnia and Herzegovina

Professor Najib Awad, Hartford Seminary, Hartford, Connecticut

Professor Dr. Mehdi Azaiez, Katholieke Universiteit Leuven, Belgium

Professor Richard Bauckham, University of St Andrews, Scotland

Professor Yousef Casewit, American University of Sharjah, UAE

Professor M. Shawn Copeland, Boston College, Boston, Massachusetts

Professor Maria Massi Dakake, George Mason University, Fairfax, Virginia

Professor Gavin D'Costa, University of Bristol, UK

President John J. DeGioia, Georgetown University, Washington, DC

Professor Dr. Şaban Ali Düzgün, Ankara University, Turkey

Professor Susan Eastman, Duke University Divinity School, Durham, North Carolina

Professor Waleed El-Ansary, Xavier University, Cincinnati, Ohio

Dr. Brandon Gallaher, University of Exeter, UK

The Rev. Lucy Gardner, St Stephen's House, University of Oxford, UK

Professor Sidney Griffith, Catholic University of America, Washington, DC

Professor Feras Hamza, University of Wollongong in Dubai

Professor Tuba Işık, University of Paderborn, Germany

Professor Paul Joyce, King's College London, UK

Professor Mohsen Kadivar, Duke University, Durham, North Carolina

Professor Veli-Matti Kärkkäinen, Fuller Theological Seminary, Pasadena, California

Professor Daniel Madigan, SJ, Georgetown University, Washington, DC

Professor David Marshall, Duke University Divinity School, Durham, North Carolina

Dr. Jane McAuliffe, Distinguished Visiting Scholar, Library of Congress, Washington, DC

Professor Thomas Michel, SJ, Georgetown University School of Foreign Service in Qatar

Professor Mahan Mirza, Zaytuna College, Berkeley, California

Dr. Lucinda Mosher, Hartford Seminary, Hartford, Connecticut

Professor Martin Nguyen, Fairfield University, Fairfield, Connecticut

Professor Sajjad H. Rizvi, University of Exeter, UK

Professor Abdullah Saeed, University of Melbourne, Australia

Professor Feryal Salem, Hartford Seminary, Hartford, Connecticut

Professor Christoph Schwöbel, University of Tübingen, Germany

Professor Philip Sheldrake, Westcott House, University of Cambridge, UK

Professor Mun'im Sirry, University of Notre Dame, Notre Dame, Indiana

Professor Janet Soskice, University of Cambridge, UK

Preface
Fifteen Years of Construction

A Retrospective on the First Decade and a Half of the Building Bridges Seminar

LUCINDA MOSHER

The inaugural Building Bridges Seminar—an Anglican Communion interfaith initiative born of the sense of urgency following the events of September 11, 2001—was described as an exercise in "appreciative conversation" made possible by "listening with openness and mutual respect" and characterized by "courage, grace, imagination and sensitivity in addressing and retreating from painful issues."[1] More recently, Philip Sheldrake (Wescott House, University of Cambridge), a six-time participant, has called the seminar "an exercise in learning how to listen patiently and receptively to what is 'other' and, through this, to experience a growing solidarity-in-difference." This exercise continues to this day. This essay offers some reflections on the first fifteen convenings of the Building Bridges Seminar—its method, history, and impact.[2]

Building Bridges Methodology

As will become apparent when we review the topics it has taken on, the Building Bridges Seminar has been a flexible enterprise, informed by thoughtful evaluation. Year by year, its planners have maintained a healthy balance between experimentation with the new and return to earlier practice. Its methodology, discernible even in its early years, comprises nine key elements.

1. The Building Bridges Seminar falls within the category of "the dialogue of theological exchange," defined in 1991 by the Pontifical Council of Interreligious Dialogue as a forum in which "specialists seek to deepen their understanding of their respective religious heritages, and to appreciate each other's spiritual values."[3] That is, its participants are scholar-believers: each is either a practicing Christian or a practicing Muslim. Thus, not only is the Building Bridges Seminar

"intellectually stimulating and fun," says five-time attendee Sajjad Rizvi (University of Exeter), it is a conference during which "it is perfectly normal for me to be open about my beliefs." Feras Hamza (University of Wollongong in Dubai) concurs: "The Building Bridges Seminar provides the kind of atmosphere in which participants open up and are happy to articulate and discuss their devotional sensibilities. For those who truly want to understand another religious tradition, there is no substitute for such an encounter."

2. The seminar strives for theological exchange that is *relational* rather than *relativistic.* Daniel Madigan (Georgetown University) explains:[4]

> The risk of all theology, which aims to be a systematic discourse about God, is that *logos* (discourse and system) becomes more important than *theos*, God. And the risk of theological dialogue is that it becomes a defense of our systems of discourse rather than an opening to the divine. The Building Bridges Seminar asserts that the space of theology belongs primarily to God, not to our systems. When we acknowledge that neither of us is the proprietor, but that we are both guests in God's space, something new in theology can emerge. This is the point that the more nervous observers of this process usually begin to speak of as relativism. Yet there is a significant difference between a theology that is *relational* and one that is relativistic. Relativism would suggest that we have different truths and that is fine. A relational theology recognizes that being in search of the one truth means also being in relation to those other seekers of the truth who do not believe as I do. That is a relationship we cannot honestly avoid.

3. Each year's seminar has a clearly demarcated theme—and typically, that theme has three subtopics. Each subtopic sets the agenda for a full day of the seminar.

4. In the interest of ensuring a well-constructed dialogue circle, participation is by invitation only, and those who accept are expected to be present for the entirety of a convening. Always, Muslim and Christian participants are nearly equal in number. Care is taken to balance the circle in other ways as well. Typically, one-quarter of the participants are women. On the Christian roster, most are Anglicans or Roman Catholics, but Orthodox Christians, Lutherans, Methodists, and others have been included as well—thus making it, says New Zealand scholar Douglas Pratt, "an exemplary ecumenical venture."[5] On the Muslim roster, most are Sunnis, but Shiʿites are always included. Effort is also taken to include a few scholars with unique expertise in a given seminar's theme. "While the group of Muslim and Christian participants has varied from year to year," explains Jane McAuliffe (Library of Congress),[6] a participant in twelve Building Bridges seminars, "there have been some of us from each religious tradition who were able to

be there almost every year. This stability proved to be another important factor in freeing the working groups to be as frank and wide-ranging as possible."

5. Preparation is expected. At least a month before a seminar convenes, participants are supplied with an anthology of texts to be discussed, and it is presumed that these will have been read before the first session. All texts are in English translation, but since 2014 all scripture passages are also given in their original language. Several participants are chosen to lecture, and the near-final drafts of those papers are provided in advance to their colleagues.

6. Small-group discussion is crucial to the seminar's style. Thus, each participant is assigned to one of four breakout groups that remain intact for an entire seminar. Each small group is designed with Christian-Muslim balance, denominational variety, the presence of women, and distribution of newcomers in mind. Each group is assigned a moderator—and, some years, a scribe. The seminar schedule provides for significant periods of small-group time devoted to the dialogical close reading of texts (most often, passages from the Bible and the Qur'ān). "It is in these several working sessions each day that we find our own voices and really dig into a generative theological discussion," McAuliffe asserts.

> Knowing that these conversations are not "on the record" allows us to ask each other challenging questions and, on more than one occasion, to offer understandings and interpretations that were preliminary and provisional. The seminar sessions flowed into discussions over lunch and dinner. In these encounters, dialogue becomes a genuine dialectical exchange and we as participants are shaped by the collegial generosity that our mutual engagement generated. Friendships have been formed and our annual gathering has become both a retreat and a reunion.

7. A three-step approach to the conduct of small-group discussion is encouraged. First, the passage under consideration is read aloud. Second, each group member mentions a word, phrase, or sentence he or she finds compelling or puzzling—with only a brief explanation for this choice. Third, after everyone has taken this opportunity, deep discussion of the passage ensues. During a single breakout session, this process may be repeated several times. The moderator keeps the group on task.

8. Plenary sessions set the stage for and facilitate reflection on small-group work. Stage setting takes the form of an exegetical lecture, plus a formal response from an adherent of the other religion. Reflection may include some reporting on points made in one's small group, but at least as often involves free-flowing sharing of insights and lingering concerns.

9. In contrast to some bilateral dialogues, it is not the goal of the Building Bridges Seminar to formulate and issue a formal statement at the conclusion of its meetings.[7] Rather, as a dialogue of theological exchange, the Building Bridges Seminar is as much about exploring difference as it is about finding common ground.[8] In fact, this project has been characterized by both former Archbishop of Canterbury Rowan Williams and Georgetown University Professor Daniel Madigan (past and present convenors, respectively) as an exercise in improving the quality of Christian-Muslim disagreement.[9]

It is this last characteristic that leads five-time participant Brandon Gallaher (University of Exeter) to describe the Building Bridges Seminar methodology as "sympathetic maximalism"—in contrast to the "reductive minimalism" pervasive in other dialogical endeavors:

> Sympathetic maximalism differs from reductive minimalism in that the latter identifies a small core of beliefs that two religions can share in common. Reductive minimalism is afraid of difference, so aims for a bare harmony with no dissonance. When it discovers teachings that are problematic (e.g., the Trinity), then it will do all it can to marginalize and read those teachings in such a way that they no longer can be seen as problematic for the religious Other. This means, of course, that the form of religion that is presented is just an eccentric scholarly construction bearing little resemblance to what is held in the Classic tradition or in any form of orthodoxy. It also ignores the contradictions that exist in any tradition, including in the various forms of orthodoxy.
>
> When, by sharp contrast, sympathetic maximalism is implemented, two traditions meet with no intention of converting one another. They are not asked to assume the truth of the other religion or in any way to step back from the full classic claims of their tradition. Nor are they required to negate the fact that they consider their faith to be absolutely unique and as holding the fullness of the truth. At the same time—and here is the sympathy or co-feeling and thinking—there exists in this methodology in action a pull in the other direction, which is to learn about the other tradition in all its complexity and to share about one's own tradition in all its complexity.
>
> The end result is that traditional, and even conservative, scholars learn about other religious traditions than their own; but, through theologizing across borders, come to a deeper grasp of the essentials of their own tradition and the depths of its truth as illumined precisely through encounter with another religion. Such sustained traditional and constructive interreligious hermeneutic work involving world-class scholars is very rare indeed. Thus, as Christianity and Islam are two traditions that seem to be in a constant violent clash in the public sphere and the political arena, the encounters at Building Bridges seem at certain moments even to be prophetic, offering an alternative vision of living together with better and

> richer disagreements—although, in the midst of them, it may sometimes feel that one is trying to hold a candle alight in a wind storm.

Daniel Madigan would call this mutual theological hospitality:[10]

> Traditionally, theological exchange has tended to be what we might call a boundary discourse—defining, disputing, and policing the borders that separate us. Yet what we experience in Building Bridges is the freedom to allow others into our own theologizing space. As Robert Jenson says [in *A Theology in Outline*], theology is the thinking we need to do between hearing the message and proclaiming it, and this is necessarily a complex and even messy process, with historic disagreements and unresolved issues within our own traditions. We do not normally allow outsiders to see this, but rather offer them creedal formulas and stock phrases that only lead us back to "border disputes." Studying scriptures together patiently over the years, we have inevitably demonstrated for the other the processes we go through between hearing what we take to be the Word of God, in Jesus or in the Qur'an, and expressing that message in a convinced and convincing way. We invite the other into our questioning, not only into our answers.

Building Bridges under Lambeth Palace

"What I particularly appreciate," says Philip Sheldrake, "is the way in which the Building Bridges Seminar has the courage to confront some of the more difficult questions, themes and issues that have been contested throughout our shared history and are inevitably present in contemporary Christian-Muslim encounters." With its methodology in mind, let us review the questions, themes, and issues the seminar has engaged during its first fifteen years.

The first convening, January 2002, titled Building Bridges: Overcoming Obstacles in Christian-Muslim Relations, was exploratory. Some twenty Christian and twenty Muslim scholars and religious leaders—diverse in terms of home base (Europe, the US, Africa, and the Middle East) and denominational/sectarian or theological bent—were invited to Lambeth Palace for two days of deep discussion aimed at broadening interfaith understanding and cooperation. Then–Archbishop of Canterbury George Carey was the host, in collaboration with Prime Minister Tony Blair and His Royal Highness Prince El Hassan bin Talal of Jordan. Professor Gillian Stamp of the Brunel Institute of Organisational and Social Studies served as facilitator. With this conference seen as a first step toward establishment of "new routes for information, appreciation and respect to travel freely and safely in both directions between Christians and Muslims, Muslims and Christians,"[11] the response of its participants to the question of whether such a gathering could be held annually and purposefully was emphatically positive.

When Carey retired in October 2002, plans were well under way for a second Building Bridges Seminar in March 2003. Chaired by Rowan Williams, who succeeded Carey as Archbishop of Canterbury, and held in Doha, Qatar, it was titled Scriptures in Dialogue: Christians and Muslims Studying the Bible and the Qurʾān Together. Clearly moved by his experience there, Williams called this meeting a "seedbed" for future dialogue, in that it had instilled in its participants courage "to believe that it was possible, desirable, and indeed necessary that the conversations which we had begun should be continued."[12]

In fact, the Building Bridges Seminar became a significant priority during Rowan Williams's term as Archbishop of Canterbury (2003–12). The ten seminars under his leadership followed the pattern established in Doha in 2003: Muslim and Christian scholars (some fifteen of each) were invited to meet with the archbishop for three full days of deliberation. Pairs of lectures (some public, others for participants only) would offer Christian and Muslim perspectives on the year's theological theme and its three well-delineated subtopics. At its core, the meeting would entail closed sessions featuring collaborative study of preassigned texts (scripture, usually—but in some years, other material in addition or instead)—most of this taking place in preassigned small groups but with ample opportunity for plenary discussion as well. The proceedings would be published as a paperback book; seminar resources would be shared via an online repository.

The third seminar (2004), held at Georgetown University, Washington, DC, explored Bearing the Word—that is, Christian and Muslim perspectives on the nature of prophecy, the calling of prophets and apostles, prophets and their peoples, the place of Jesus and Muḥammad in prophetic religion, and the completion of prophecy. Building Bridges 2005 (the fourth seminar) took place in Sarajevo, with the city itself lending poignancy and relevance to the theme of Muslims, Christians, and the Common Good. Catholic, Orthodox, and Muslim institutions in Sarajevo were joint hosts for a meeting that focused on several specific concerns raised at the founding seminar in 2002: the interplay of faith and national identity; governance and justice, with attention to the safeguarding of religious freedom; and under the heading "Caring Together for the World We Share," perspectives on addressing global poverty and environmental issues.

In 2006 Georgetown University hosted the Building Bridges Seminar for a second time, this time to consider concerns raised during the inaugural seminar and discussed to an extent in the fourth convening: Christian and Muslim understandings of divine justice, political authority, and religious freedom. Building Bridges 2007 was held at Singapore's National University. The theme was Humanity (thus, theological anthropology), with public lectures and small-group discussion exploring Christian and Muslim understandings of human diversity, destiny, and relationship to the environment. The setting for Building Bridges 2008, Villa Palazzola, an ancient monastery near Rome, had the effect of making the seventh convening more retreat-like, in that its program had no public sessions. Entitled Communicating the Word, it returned to elements of the seminar's third convening, now giving priority to study of the prehistory of revelation, the historical particularity and universal significance of the ultimate revelation, the possibility of continuing revelation, translation of scripture, and passages in which scripture itself reflects on how scripture is to be interpreted. Close reading of excerpts from *Generous Love* (a theology of interfaith relations prepared in early 2008 by the Anglican Communion Network for Inter Faith Concerns) and the final section of *A Common Word between Us and You* (the pan-Muslim call for dialogue issued in October 2007) provoked further conversation around scriptural interpretation and interfaith concerns.[13]

For its eighth meeting, held at Istanbul's Bahçeşehir University, the Building Bridges Seminar took advantage of its coincidence with the two hundredth anniversary of the birth of Charles Darwin—whose legacy, as Rowan Williams reminded participants, "is by no means uniformly hostile to religious faith." To consider Christian and Muslim points of view (past and present) on the interface between science and religion, participants read and discussed excerpts from more than a dozen great thinkers, in addition to germane scripture passages.

The Building Bridges Seminar returned to Georgetown University for a third time in May 2010—having determined to examine Muslim and Christian perspectives on Tradition and Modernity. Writings by such outstanding Christian and Muslim modern thinkers as John Henry Newman, Muḥammad ʿAbduh, Abul Aʿla Mawdudi, Lesslie Newbigin, Alasdair MacIntyre, Seyyid Hossein Nasr, Elisabeth Schüssler Fiorenza, and Tariq Ramadan provided food for thought. Echoing and expanding on the seminar's accomplishments in Sarajevo in 2005, and having been reminded by Rowan Williams that tradition and modernity are not always "natural opposites,"[14] attention was now given to changing patterns in religious authority and different conceptions of freedom.

The project returned to Doha in 2011, but different from 2003, its venue was Georgetown's School of Foreign Service in Qatar (SFS-Q). With prayer as its theme, the 2011 conference brought matters of personal faith, practice, and experience together with scholarly concerns to a degree not typical of past seminars.

For his last time as Building Bridges Seminar convenor, Rowan Williams chose to begin the meeting in London, the site of the project's inaugural meeting eleven years earlier, and then take the group to Canterbury—his seat as the Archbishop in the Church of England who is also the spiritual head of the Anglican Communion—for the remainder. The seminar's approach to its theme—Death, Resurrection, and Human Destiny—was both personal and academic, much in the way the seminar on prayer had been. Texts for study included scriptural and traditional material, funeral liturgies, and excerpts from such literature as al-Ghazālī's *Iḥyāʾ* and Dante's *The Divine Comedy*.

Building Bridges under the Stewardship of Georgetown University

As he anticipated the end of his tenure as Archbishop of Canterbury, Rowan Williams ensured the continuation of the Building Bridges Seminar by ceding stewardship of the program to Georgetown University. In fact, the seminar had been an ecumenical endeavor from its very first convening, and Georgetown had been involved since its second. Among the participants in the 2003 seminar in Doha was the acclaimed Qur'ān scholar Jane Dammen McAuliffe, then a member of the Georgetown faculty. Upon her return to campus, she impressed on Georgetown University president John J. DeGioia the significance and potential of Building Bridges, urging him to consider ways to support it. Without hesitation, he issued an offer to host the 2004 seminar—an offer he repeated in 2006 and 2010. Several Georgetown professors participated in the dialogue under Williams's leadership—as did DeGioia himself. By 2010 Georgetown University's Berkley Center for Religion, Peace, and World Affairs had assumed some of the Building Bridges Seminar's administrative needs. That the relationship between the seminar and the university was deepening became further evident in the choice of its SFS-Q campus as the site for the tenth convening. In 2010 the Rev. Dr. David Marshall, who had been instrumental in the planning of the seminars since their inception,[15] was made a research fellow at the Berkley Center, thus providing him a base from which to continue his service to the project after his role as chaplain to the Archbishop of Canterbury came to an end.

Embrace of a program such as the Building Bridges Seminar was easy for Georgetown University. As DeGioia himself explains, "Since our founding in 1789, Georgetown University has been committed to creating opportunities for dialogue that deepen understanding among faiths, cultures, and peoples. It is within this context—of our tradition, our history, and our commitment to intercultural and interreligious engagement—that [by means of the Building Bridges Seminar] we have brought together a community of individuals dedicated to strengthening understanding across our faith traditions."

So it is that, since 2013, invitations to the Building Bridges Seminar have come from the Office of the President of Georgetown University, with Samuel Wagner, coordinator for Catholic and Jesuit initiatives and interreligious dialogue in the Office of the President, acting as liaison. Daniel Madigan, SJ, Ruesch Family Associate Professor in Georgetown's Department of Theology and a leading Christian scholar of Islam, has assumed the role of chair, working closely with David Marshall, who remains the seminar's academic director. Lucinda Mosher, Hartford Seminary's faculty associate in interfaith studies, has served as the seminar's assistant academic director since July 2012. The university's Berkley Center for Religion, Peace, and World Affairs, directed by Thomas Banchoff, maintains the Building Bridges Seminar website and provides support in other ways as well. Seminar convenings have alternated between Washington, DC, and Doha, Qatar, taking advantage of the existence of Georgetown University facilities and staff in a majority-Christian location, on the one hand, and a majority-Muslim milieu, on the other.

Thus, the twelfth seminar—the first under Georgetown's stewardship, met on the SFS-Q campus—the seminar's third visit to Qatar. Lectures and small-group discussion focused the Community of Believers: its nature and purpose, its unity and disunity, and matters of continuity and change. Quite deliberately, plans called for a return to the practice of studying Bible, Qur'ān, and Ḥadīth texts only. Back in Washington in 2014, the public portion of the thirteenth seminar was limited to a pair of first-day overview lectures on its theme: Sin, Forgiveness, and Reconciliation. Participants were then transported to a conference center in Northern Virginia where their lectures and conversations benefited from an atmosphere similar to the cloistered setting that had served the project so well in 2008. For the fourteenth seminar (2015), SFS-Q was again the venue, with Human Action within Divine Creation as the theme. All texts for study were scriptural, chosen to bring forth Christian and Muslim perspectives on "God's Creation and Its Goal," "The Dignity and Task of Humankind within God's Creation," and "Human Action within the Sovereignty of God." The fifteenth convening found the seminar once again beginning on the Georgetown campus in Washington, DC, then adjourning to the seclusion of rural Virginia for profound engagement with the theme Affirming the Unity of God: Monotheism and Its Complexities, making use of a wide range of texts (scriptural and otherwise), all of which are included in the present volume.

Impact

Significantly, Georgetown University sees itself not just as steward but also as beneficiary of the Building Bridges Seminar. "Georgetown's support of the work of Building Bridges over the past fifteen years—and especially during the past five—has allowed members of our community to engage in reflection and study on issues facing Christians and Muslims, our faiths, and our world," President DeGioia asserts. "The contributions of the scholars and theologians who attend our annual Building Bridges Seminar have a resonance that extends far beyond our gatherings. Their work helps to enrich the extraordinary resources of our faith traditions, our University's Catholic and Jesuit identity, and allows us to build bridges between communities of believers and religious traditions in ways that animate our commitment to interreligious dialogue." If indeed the Building Bridges Seminar has resonance beyond its annual convenings, what impact does it have?

The Building Bridges Seminar is a resource to higher and continuing education. As noted earlier, the Building Bridges Seminar does not craft annual bilateral position statements. It does, however, publish its proceedings—since 2005, with Georgetown University Press. The proceedings have been reviewed by various scholarly journals and have found their way onto undergraduate- and graduate-school syllabi. They also have a robust following beyond the academy. To lift up one example: for nearly a year, the Episcopal Diocese of New York sponsored a project of monthly Christian-Muslim close reading and discussion of one volume of this series. Furthermore, the seminar makes available substantial resources for the study of Christian-Muslim comparative theology by means of its online archives: http://buildingbridges.georgetown.edu. There, portions or a complete copy of each volume of seminar proceedings are available for free download. Also available are videos of some of the seminar's public lectures, biographies of its participants, and other related information. The seminar has been the topic of at least one master's degree thesis. It has been the topic of a growing list of scholarly essays—most recently, Douglas Pratt's "From Edinburgh to Georgetown: Anglican Interfaith Bridge-Building" for the *Anglican Theological Review*,[16] and my "Getting to Know One Another's Hearts: The Progress, Method, and Potential of the Building Bridges Seminar," which is included in a Festschrift for Professor David Thomas (University of Birmingham)—himself a participant in the project's inaugural convening.[17]

The Building Bridges Seminar provides a model and method for dialogical reading. Like Scriptural Reasoning, to which it is often compared, the Building Bridges Seminar has made a priority of dialogical close reading of the Bible and the Qur'ān—which, says Miroslav Volf (Yale University), reflecting on his own experience as a 2003 participant in the seminar, has two strong advantages. First, reading scripture together "brings movement to calcified positions." When scriptures, with their richness and inexhaustibility, are put in the center of dialogue, he says, "deadlock can be avoided. The disputes are now less about us and our opinions and more about something that has a claim on us and to which we give greater allegiance than we do to our own convictions." Putting scripture in the center makes the participants "instruments [rather than agents] of a dialogue whose main protagonists are our respective scriptures." This allows the dialogue participants to remain rooted yet able to "loosen the grip with which we hold onto our own convictions," thus "open to change." Second, says Volf, reading scripture together encourages participants to "enter sympathetically into others' efforts to interpret their scripture as well as listen to how they perceive us as readers of our own scripture." It calls on the participants "to practice interpretive hospitality"—and that, he asserts, "will help us better understand our own and others' scripture, and discourage us from interpreting them in opposition to each other."[18]

More recent Building Bridges participants would concur with Volf. Dialogical reading of scriptures has been called the seminar's "spiritual heart." It has become a Building Bridges truism that for a Muslim to study the Qur'ān with a Christian or for a Christian to study the Bible with a Muslim is a rare occasion; even more so is the opportunity for members of one religious community to wrestle over scripture's meaning in front of members of the other religious community. "The opportunity to study sacred Islamic and Christian Scriptures together in mixed groups provides an awesome venue for mutual learning, enrichment—and respectful challenging of our traditions' views," explains

Veli-Matti Kärkkäinen (Fuller Theological Seminary). "Every time I attend, I learn new things about Christian-Muslim engagement; at the same time I am greatly enriched by friendship and collegiality. I find the whole process so very valuable."

Frequent participants also affirm that dialogical reading of non-scriptural material differs significantly from scripture dialogue. The Christian material is unlikely to be universally familiar to all Christians in the circle or to have equal importance for all of them; likewise, the Islamic material for the Muslims. Yet, some years, the topic simply demands that such material be addressed. Willingness to include as necessary the close reading study of doctrinal statements and excerpts from theological writings from every era differentiates the Building Bridges Seminar from similar dialogical projects.

The value of the Building Bridges Seminar begins with the impact it has on the participants themselves. "In our first years we came together eagerly," Jane McAuliffe recalls,

> but tentatively, unsure what to do or say, not at all convinced that our gathering could serve any significant purpose. Some of us had considerable experience in various forms and forums of Muslim-Christian interaction; others had less familiarity with such efforts. Our initial conversations were a bit stiff and formal. Both Muslim and Christian participants felt an unexpressed concern about religious representation: were we being asked to speak in the names of our respective traditions? Were we to function as de facto spokespersons for either Christianity or Islam? The very idea was both daunting—and inhibiting. It was at this juncture of enthusiasm and unease that the particular power of the Building Bridges format began to reveal itself.

Many participants—Muslim and Christian alike—have shared that taking part in Building Bridges has changed the way they teach. "It has led to greater collaborations with colleagues in theology," says Sajjad Rizvi, "and to a more connected way of presenting theologies in Islam." Brandon Gallaher says it has, in fact, changed the way he *does* theology:

> When I started attending the seminars in 2012, I already did Christian theology ecumenically. I had done my doctorate at Oxford on Trinitarian theology in Orthodoxy, Roman Catholicism and Protestantism and then was working on a post-doctoral fellowship on episcopal authority and secularism in Roman Catholicism and Orthodoxy. Up until then, my encounters with other religions had been mostly non-academic and through family (my niece and nephew are part Moroccan). My introduction to the Building Bridges Seminar's method—and with it, the opportunity to meet Muslim

> scholars open to deep dialogue across theological borders—changed everything for me. Working in my small reading group with the likes of Rowan Williams, Sajjad Rizvi, and Feras Hamza produced a "Eureka moment." I now saw that simply doing theology ecumenically was not enough and even the unity achieved in ecumenism obscured more fundamental religious differences. In an increasingly secularized and globalized world, the theologian was, I discovered, compelled to think through all the loci of Christian dogmatics (Christology, Trinitarian theology, anthropology, etc.) in active and deep dialogue with the religious Other, and, above all, proximate religious "cousins" like Islam. In fact, the changes to my academic work since becoming involved with the Building Bridges Seminar have been marked. Much of my teaching now focuses on inter-religious encounter.

Some frequent participants also remark on the influence the Building Bridges Seminar has on their research and writing. "It has made me more attuned to the need to do history of theology and religion in a more comparative and connected manner," says Sajjad Rizvi, "a manner in which examining the other often elucidates the self." Taking a step further, Asma Afsaruddin notes that "the seminars have established for me the necessity of drawing attention to the importance of interfaith dialogue in my research and publications, whenever relevant." Thus, she says, "in my most recent book, *Contemporary Issues in Islam*, I have devoted a whole chapter to the importance of cultivating healthy and productive interfaith relations in the 21st century."

Given the current, increasingly difficult global climate in which the role of religion in conflict areas cannot be avoided, Philip Sheldrake is appreciative that

> in this context, the kind of Christian-Muslim dialogue promoted by Building Bridges Seminar is not a purely theoretical or academic exercise. It has the potential to be a significant and powerful influence well beyond the participants themselves through the medium of its publications and web pages, but above all through the extensive network of people among whom the seminar participants live or with whom they regularly mix, work or worship. Building Bridges is a voice against polarization and a narrow-minded exclusivism in the world of religion and religiously-influenced cultures.

Ahmet Alibašić (University of Sarajevo) acknowledges "a personal existential motivation" for accepting invitations to attend Building Bridges seminars. Given recent history in his region of the world, dialogue is a vastly preferable alternative to "blood and tears." He sees the project as a unique forum on two counts: first, not only has it sustained itself for fifteen years, it "has survived almost seamlessly change of leadership and other challenges such as wars in its proximity and cancellations of its venues at the last moment; second, its deliberations have been characterized with depth, intensity, and openness rarely seen in such settings."

Where Next?

It is the seminar's custom to spend a portion of its closing plenary brainstorming appropriate topics for the next convening. Even after fifteen years, the possibilities for scripture-driven, Christian-Muslim dialogical study are far from exhausted. "There remain a range of other themes which it might be fruitful to discuss in future years," Philip Sheldrake reminds us, as he reflects on several years of such conversations. Recalling that the focus of the fourteenth Building Bridges Seminar had been human action within divine creation and that of the fifteenth had been "monotheism and its complexities," he first suggests that "further attention could be given to how we understand the on-going *action* of God within the created order, not least in relation to humankind. Is God distant or engaged? In Christian language, is God primarily one who judges and punishes sin and evil or is God one who heals, redeems and loves?" Second, having worked with theological-anthropological topics in 2007, the seminar could take a step into that arena, asking, "How do we understand human identity in relation to God? Is it primarily flawed and sinful or is it primarily defined by being irretrievably united to a God of love?" Third, the problem of human evil in relation to God and God's power could be addressed (including the theodicy question). Fourth, the seminar could ask, "*Within* our respective religions, how do we understand and then handle pluralism—different branches, sects or denominations with differences of practice and even of doctrine?" Finally, Sheldrake suggests that it would be interesting to take up Christian and Muslim perspectives on "leading a religious life": "We addressed the theme of prayer with our 2011 seminar, but there is a broader question of how we understand and approach 'spirituality' and religious practice in Christianity and Islam. This might include some attention to the history, nature and role of 'mysticism' in both religions—including controversies about it!"

The proposals are always wide ranging. As Alibašić puts it, the care with which the seminar has been led since its inception means that "by now no issue or topic is a taboo for this forum, despite the fact that sitting around the table (or rather tables) are people to whom the issues discussed do matter a lot—people who are not sociologists of religion, but rather are believers themselves." No vote is taken, but notes are kept, follow-up conversations are held, a new theme is set—and always, that theme is framed creatively.

"I see us becoming ever more courageous from year to year, now that we have tackled some of the most vexatious of the issues dividing our traditions," says Gallaher.

> The last seminar on God was a watershed as it was a witness to the success of the method I have called sympathetic maximalism and the bonds of enduring friendships. We can tackle the most difficult issues with compassion and wisdom. Now, as we face a political scene in the West ever more hostile to Islam, the world needs to know that experts from Muslim and Christian traditions can have a wise, compassionate and constructive encounter on even the most divisive issue.

Says President DeGioia, "We at Georgetown University are sincerely grateful to the Building Bridges organizers and participants for their efforts to provide a meaningful opportunity each year to engage in scholarship, companionship, friendship—and to deepen our understanding of our faiths, and of one another." The participants are, in turn, deeply thankful for the university's stewardship—thus the gift of continuity. "There is a palpable authenticity about this project," observes Feras Hamza, "instilled in it by those who founded it all those years ago, and constantly replenished by the sincerity of those who attend year after year."

What of the future of this project? This reflection piece was written just weeks before the convening of the sixteenth Building Bridges Seminar—which would examine Christian and Muslim perspectives on divine and human power in a manner that continues to encourage scholar-believers "to know each other's hearts."[19]

Notes

1. Gillian Stamp, "And They Returned by Another Route," in *The Road Ahead: A Christian-Muslim Dialogue*, ed. Michael Ipgrave (London: Church House, 2002), 112.

2. This essay is informed by the published proceedings of the Building Bridges seminars, David Marshall's digest of a 2007 survey of participants in the first five seminars, my own interviewing of a number of participants and seminar staff, and short reflections on the seminar written by several participants at my request. (Quotations from seminar participants and staff are not cited in endnotes.) Earlier forms of the information and reflections presented here include my many public lectures since March 2002 about Anglican Communion interfaith initiatives; my essay reflecting on the Building Bridges Seminar's first five years, published online at http://repository.berkleycenter.georgetown.edu/Mosher-Building-Bridges-Article.pdf; my essay "A Decade of Appreciative Conversation: The Building Bridges Seminar under Rowan Williams," in *Death, Resurrection, and Human Destiny*, ed. David Marshall and Lucinda Mosher (Washington, DC: Georgetown University Press, 2014); and my essay, "Getting to Know One Another's Hearts: The Progress, Method, and Potential of the Building Bridges Seminar," in *The Character of Christian-Muslim Encounter: Essays in Honour of David Thomas*, ed. Douglas Pratt, Jon Hoover, John Davies, and John Chesworth (Leiden: Brill, 2015).

3. "Dialogue and Proclamation," Pontifical Council for Inter-Religious Dialogue, May 19, 1991, accessed February 20, 2014, article 42, http://www.vatican.va/roman_curia/pontif

ical_councils/interelg/documents/rc_pc_interelg_doc_19051991_dialogue-and-proclamatio_en.html.

4. Professor Madigan joined the Building Bridges Seminar in 2003 and has participated in every meeting since then, with the exception of 2009.

5. Douglas Pratt, "From Edinburgh to Georgetown: Anglican Interfaith Bridge-Building," *Anglican Theological Review* 96, no. 1 (Winter 2014): 28. Pratt, a priest in the Anglican Church in Aotearoa, New Zealand, and Polynesia, is professor of religious studies at the University of Waikato, New Zealand, and adjunct professor of theology and interreligious studies within the Department of Old Catholic Theology, University of Bern, Switzerland.

6. McAuliffe, currently director of national and international outreach for the Library of Congress (Washington, DC), is a former dean of Georgetown College, Georgetown University, and President Emerita of Bryn Mawr College (Pennsylvania).

7. An example of dialogue for which issuance of a formal joint statement is the goal is the Joint Commission of Anglican Christians and Sunni Muslims—the result of an agreement between Lambeth Palace and Al-Azhar University—also launched in January 2002.

8. During a given seminar, dialogue between coreligionists is often as intense as that between Christians and Muslims—a point made by Michael Ipgrave in his "Humanity in Context," in *Humanity: Texts and Contexts* (Washington, DC: Georgetown University Press, 2011), xv.

9. Rowan Williams stressed the importance of investigating "what is disbelieved in other religious discourses" as a means for finding "appropriate language in which difference can be talked about rather than used as an excuse for violent separation." See particularly his "Analysing Atheism: Unbelief and the World of Faiths," in *Bearing the Word*, ed. Michael Ipgrave (New York: Church Publishing, 2005), 1–13.

10. See his "Mutual Theological Hospitality: Doing Theology in the Presence of the 'Other,'" in *Muslim and Christian Understanding: Theory and Application of "A Common Word,"* ed. Waleed El-Ansary and David K. Linnan (New York: Palgrave-Macmillan, 2010), 57–66.

11. Michael Ipgrave, *The Road Ahead* (London: Church House Publishing, 2002), 1.

12. Rowan Williams, opening remarks, Building Bridges 2012. See preface to *Death, Resurrection, and Human Destiny* (Washington, DC: Georgetown University Press), 2014.

13. See "Archbishop's Reflections on the 7th Building Bridges Seminar," Dr. Rowan Williams, 104th Archbishop of Canterbury, May 9, 2008, accessed January 19, 2013, http://rowanwilliams.archbishopofcanterbury.org/articles.php/1118/archbishops-reflections-on-the-7th-building-bridges-seminar.

14. Rowan Williams, afterword to *Tradition and Modernity: Christian and Muslim Perspectives*, ed. David Marshall (Washington, DC: Georgetown University Press, 2013), 221.

15. David Marshall, a Christian-Muslim relations scholar, became chaplain to the Archbishop of Canterbury in 2000 and thus was involved in the planning of the initial and subsequent seminars. While he left the Archbishop's office in 2005, he has remained one of Building Bridges' primary planners and has attended almost every annual seminar. He has been affiliate research fellow of Georgetown University's Berkley Center for Religion, Peace, and World Affairs since 2012. He was associate professor of the practice of

Christian-Muslim relations and director of the Anglican Episcopal House of Studies at Duke Divinity School concurrently, 2013–16.

16. Pratt, "From Edinburgh to Georgetown," 15–37.

17. Mosher, "Getting to Know One Another's Hearts."

18. Miroslav Volf, "Your Scripture Meets Mine," *Christian Century*, October 19, 2004, 43.

19. Rowan Williams's description of the Building Bridges Seminar outcome. See his preface to *Death, Resurrection, and Human Destiny: Christian and Muslim Perspectives*, ed. David Marshall and Lucinda Mosher (Washington, DC: Georgetown University Press, 2014), xxii.

Introduction

The Building Bridges Seminar—a gathering of scholar-practitioners of Islam and Christianity—has been convened annually since 2002 for the purpose of deep study of scripture and other texts carefully selected for their pertinence to the year's chosen theme. This book provides a record of the proceedings of the fifteenth such seminar, which met in and near Washington, DC, May 6–10, 2016. As has been the practice since Georgetown University assumed stewardship of this project, Daniel Madigan, SJ, Jeanette W. and Otto J. Ruesch Family Associate Professor in Georgetown's Department of Theology, was the convenor. Georgetown University president John J. DeGioia was present as host and participant. The roster featured a near-equal number of Muslims and Christians—thirty-eight in all, women as well as men, emerging scholars alongside well-known experts, some of them returnees, others attending for the first time. As has long been the case, most Christian attendees were Roman Catholic or Anglican, but some Protestants and one Orthodox scholar were also present. Similarly, the Muslim cohort, while mostly Sunni, did include several Shiʿite scholars.

The very topic of the 2016 convening had an impact on its structure and process. Previous Building Bridges seminars had focused on subjects—for example, prayer, the common good, justice and rights, religion and science, death and the afterlife—that could be addressed by each tradition almost in isolation from the other. Comparisons could be discussed; similarities and differences could be noted. However, on the question of monotheism, Christians and Muslims have been directly and forcefully engaged with one another right from the beginning of the Islamic tradition in the Qurʾān. Therefore, by choosing as our seminar title Affirming the Unity of God: Monotheism and Its Complexities, we strove to avoid setting the Christian doctrine of the Trinity as the starting point. Rather, by beginning with the recognition that, perhaps contrary to appearances, the concern to affirm the unity of God is primary for both traditions, we hoped to move the conversation beyond a simple "yes, we do" / "no, you don't" confrontation about the validity of the Christian claim to believe in only one God. As should be apparent in this book's final chapter, "Dialogue in Northern Virginia," that goal was indeed met.

The 2016 seminar began on the Georgetown University campus with a public session in the university's elegant Riggs Library, during which panelists Richard Bauckham, Asma Afsaruddin, Christoph Schwöbel, and Sajjad Rizvi provided an overview of this year's theme. Seminar participants were then transported to the Airlie Center in Warrenton, Virginia, for four full days of closed meetings in a retreat-like setting. Each morning plenary session laid the foundation for that day's work: one scholar would, by means of a short lecture, introduce the texts preassigned for that day's close reading; another scholar (an adherent of the other religion) would offer a response; for the remaining minutes, plenary discussion would ensue. Participants would then transition to study in one of four predetermined groups that remained constant throughout the seminar for three two-hour sessions of intense discussion of the day's material. An hourlong, pre-dinner plenary offered an opportunity for each small group to share its insights with the others.

The first day's study examined the biblical witness (in the Old Testament as well as the New) to the one God—including the emergence of the recognition of only one God—and the complexity of the attempts in the New Testament to continue to speak in a way that maintains the unity of God at the same time as it is faithful to the experience of God's action in Jesus Christ and the experience of the Holy Spirit. The second day's study brought to the fore critique in the Qur'ān and Ḥadīth of polytheism and of Christian affirmations about God, plus verses that provoked later discussion among Muslims about how to understand the unity of God. Texts chosen for study on the third day of the seminar provided an opportunity to observe the Christian tradition grappling with the complexities raised by New Testament faith, trying to avoid at all costs dividing God up or multiplying divinities—in effect recognizing the very dangers inherent in Christian language about God that the Qur'ān was later to point out. Similarly, texts chosen for the fourth day allowed the seminar to see ways in which the Islamic tradition—not just in *kalām*, but also in *tafsīr*, philosophy and mysticism—has explored the complexities inherent in the affirmation of God's unity. This book's structure reflects this pattern.

In parts 1 through 4, the reader will find transcripts of each pair of plenary lectures, plus the collection of texts that pair of lectures introduces. Thus, in part 1, "The Oneness of God in the Biblical Witness," we have Richard Bauckham's essay "Complexities Surrounding God's Oneness in Biblical Monotheism," in which he explains some of the controversies surrounding this topic among scholars who work on the history of ancient Israel and those who study the Judaism that was the context of Jesus and the New Testament authors. We have also Maria Massi Dakake's Muslim response to Bauckham, "Bridging the Chasm between the Divine and the Human," in which she works with a notion, mentioned during the seminar's opening panel discussion, that a chasm exists between God and everything that is not God—and this has implications for humanity's ultimate vocation. These essays are followed by "Texts from the Bible," which contains the twelve passages from the Old and New Testaments provided to the 2016 seminar participants in their study booklet.

In part 2, "The Oneness of God in the Qur'ān and Ḥadīth," Asma Afsaruddin, in her essay "Monotheism in Islam," discusses selected verses from the Qur'ān that establish the centrality of monotheism as Islam's cardinal tenet, plus verses that mount a critique of belief in multiple deities among the pagan Arabs and of certain Christological conceptions current among contemporary Christians. In his response, Sidney Griffith demonstrates how such passages might be read with a view to discerning some common ground in them even as points of disagreement are identified. In "Texts from the Qur'ān and Ḥadīth" are found the fourteen Islamic scriptural items provided for study.

Part 3, "Grappling with the Unity Question in the Elaboration of Christian Doctrine," includes "The One and the Three in Christian Worship and Doctrine: Engaging with the Question of Divine Unity in the Elaboration of Christian Doctrine" by Christoph Schwöbel. Having asserted that in the course of the history of Christianity "there has rarely been a time when the doctrinal implications of the creeds have not been passionately and controversially discussed," Schwöbel demonstrates how "explicit attention given to Trinitarian matters" actually has functioned. Often, in spite of divergent interpretations, he argues, they served as a bond of unity between a large number of the Christian churches—as can be seen "in forms of the compatibility of important structures of worship in the rich diversity of the liturgical life of the churches." In his response, titled "Of Storytellers and Storytelling," Martin Nguyen explores the implications of looking at the doctrine of the Trinity as a narrative that has undergone "numerous refinements, clarifications, and inflections," giving special attention to "what all this Christian storytelling looks like from the perspective of Muslim storytellers." These two essays are followed by "Texts from the Christian Tradition," which provides the reader with the texts of the Nicene and Athanasian Creeds, plus portions of the writings of theologians from the Early Church Fathers to the present.

Part 4, "Safeguarding Tawḥīd in the Elaboration of the Islamic Tradition," opens with the essay "God Is One but Unlike Any Other: Theological Argumentation on Tawḥīd in Islam," in which Sajjad Rizvi introduces several rich examples of the Islamic intellectual tradition. In her response, "Christianity, Trinity, and the One God," Janet Soskice reminds the reader of the necessity of asking what kind of monotheism a text wishes to affirm, as she explains that, while Muslims and Christians debated their respective understandings of the oneness of God, they were united in rejecting Aristotelian monotheism. "Texts from the Islamic Tradition" presents selections from a range of Muslim authors across the centuries.

Part 5, "Reflections," comprises an essay by Lucinda Mosher. Titled "Dialogue in Northern Virginia," it offers the reader an opportunity to gain a sense of the content and tone of dialogical engagement during the 2016 colloquium.

Readers of *Monotheism and Its Complexities* who wish to look further into this topic might enjoy Miroslav Volf, *Allah: A Christian Response* (HarperOne, 2012); relevant portions of John Renard, *Islam and Christianity: Theological Themes in Comparative Perspective* (University of California Press, 2011); or the lecture given by then–Archbishop of Canterbury Rowan Williams at al-Azhar al-Sharif Institute in Cairo, Egypt, on September 11, 2004.[1]

All dates are CE unless otherwise indicated in the text. Throughout this volume, when not indicated otherwise, quotations of the Qur'ān are from Mohammed Marmaduke Pickthall, *The Meaning of the Glorious Qur'ān* (1930), or are the author's own; likewise, unless indicated otherwise, Bible quotations are from the New Revised Standard Version, copyright 1989 by the Division of Christian Education of the National Council of the Churches of Christ in the USA (used by permission; all rights reserved). Gratitude is extended to Ann Crawford, Hartford Seminary's Director of Library Services for research help in preparing this volume; and to Columbia University Press, Edinburgh University Press, Wm. B. Eerdmans Publishing, Fortress Press, HarperCollins Publishers, Taylor & Francis Publishing, University of Chicago Press, Journal of Reformed Theology, Institute of Ismaili Studies, Muhammad Bin Hama Al Thani Center for Muslim Contribution to Civilization, and Professors James Morris, Muhammad Abu al-Quasem, and Christian Troll for permission to excerpt portions of their publications.

Deep appreciation is extended to Georgetown University president John J. DeGioia for his ongoing support of the Building Bridges Seminar. As for previous seminars, David Marshall (the project's academic director) and Daniel Madigan (its chair) were instrumental in setting the theme, organizing the roster of scholars, and choosing the texts to be studied in careful conversation with the seminar presenters. Many people played a role in the success of the 2016 gathering, particularly Lucinda Mosher, who serves the project as assistant academic director, and Samuel Wagner, coordinator for Catholic and Jesuit Initiatives in the Office of the President, who provides logistical support. Georgetown University's Berkley Center provides a base of operations and online presence for the seminar and has made the publication of this book possible. Finally, gratitude is extended to the staff of Georgetown University Press.

Note

1. The full text and audio of Dr. Williams's lecture is available at http://rowanwilliams.archbishopofcanterbury.org/articles.php/1299/archbishops-address-at-al-azhar-al-sharif-cairo.

PART I

The Oneness of God in the Biblical Witness

Complexities Surrounding God's Oneness in Biblical Monotheism

RICHARD BAUCKHAM

"Monotheism" is a controversial topic among both scholars who work on the history of ancient Israel and scholars who study early Judaism (i.e., the Judaism that was the context of Jesus and the New Testament writers). Many of the former would argue that true monotheism emerged only late in the period from which the writings of the Hebrew Bible come. While many of the latter (including myself) would characterize early Judaism as strictly monotheistic, others would deny that it was truly monotheistic at all, since Jews believed in a plurality of "divine" beings.

We need some definitions and distinctions. I take monotheism to mean "belief in only one God." God, in this sense, belongs to a class of which he is the only instance.[1] Although some scholars use the term "monotheism" (sometimes "inclusive monotheism") for a widespread pattern of religious belief in the ancient world that envisaged a supreme god at the head of a hierarchy of many gods, I find this a misleading use of the term. Such a supreme god is merely the most eminent in the category of gods, not in a class of his own. On the other hand, monotheism does not rule out the existence of many "supernatural" or heavenly beings. Virtually all Jews, Christians, and Muslims before modern times took it for granted that there are vast numbers of such beings (angels and others), but since these were created by and are subject to God, their existence is no more a qualification of monotheism than is the existence of human and other earthly creatures. The key point is that, in true monotheism, a line of absolute ontological distinction is drawn between God and all other reality. In my view, this distinguishes early Judaism and early Christianity from all kinds of ancient polytheism.

No doubt, in ancient Israel, Israel's God, YHWH, was at one time perceived to be one of a class of divine beings. There are linguistic remnants of this view in the Old Testament. For example, according to Psalm 95:3, "YHWH is a great

God, and a great King above all gods." The Old Testament does not usually deny the existence of the gods of the nations, but it does deny that they are truly gods. Once God is defined as the Creator of heaven and earth (and thus of all heavenly and all earthly beings), the absolute distinction between the Creator of all things and all created reality puts both the gods of the nations and the heavenly beings who worship and serve the one God firmly on the "creation" side of this distinction. What we have in the Old Testament is a collection of ancient Israelite literature selected and redacted to be the scriptures of a properly monotheistic religion. Where remnants of more polytheistic beliefs occasionally survive, they should be understood in the context of the monotheizing dynamic of the collection as a whole. For our purposes, it is not the religious history of ancient Israel that is really our concern but the way that these scriptures were understood in both Judaism and Christianity.

The debate about monotheism in early Judaism revolves around the so-called intermediary figures—angels or exalted humans in heaven who are portrayed in various Jewish texts as exceptionally glorious and powerful figures. In the context of a pagan pantheon, these figures would naturally be understood as occupying a very high place on a spectrum of divinity. But when the one God is understood as the Creator and Ruler of all things, as he was in early Judaism, they take their place as eminent creatures and servants of God. In such a context, there is no room for semidivine beings. However highly a figure may rank in the heavenly hierarchy of God's servants, that figure is no closer to *being* God than the lowliest of creatures is. We must bear this point in mind when we consider the exalted status of Jesus Christ in the New Testament.

The *Shemaʿ*: Israel's Confession of the One God

Undoubtedly the most influential text within the Old Testament that states the Jewish and Christian belief in one God is the passage known as *Shemaʿ*, after its first Hebrew word. By the time of Jesus, this text was recited twice daily by devout Jews (following a literal interpretation of Deuteronomy 6:7). It begins, "Hear, O Israel: YHWH our God, YHWH is one. You shall love YHWH your God with all your heart, and with all your soul and with all your might" (Deut. 6:4–5).[2] There are several theoretically possible translations of the crucial statement about God because there is no verb "is" in the Hebrew.[3] But at least by the time of Jesus, it was commonly understood in the way I have just translated it. It is echoed frequently in Jewish literature in the simple form: "God is one." This is also how it is understood and echoed in the New Testament (Mark 12:29, 32; Rom. 3:30; Gal. 3:20; James 2:19). In this reading, the text says that Israel's God, YHWH, is unique. Consequently, what is required of this God's people is the complete devotion of the whole self to him. If cultic worship is seen as the explicit expression of this devotion, then it is clear that monolatry (the worship of one

God) is essential to it, as the first two commandments of the Decalogue were generally understood to require.

So, monotheism defined by this text is no mere intellectual belief that there is only one God. It is a relational matter of heart, mind, and strength. For this reason, some find the term "monotheism" inappropriate for the religion of the *Shema*ʿ. The term originated in the eighteenth century as a way of classifying religions from a disengaged, objective standpoint. Certainly, if we use the term "monotheism" to describe ancient Judaism and Christianity, we must make it clear that it means more than simply belief that there is only one God.[4] On the other hand, such belief is included. The *Shema*ʿ says more than that YHWH is the only God *for Israel*, the only God Israel should worship and serve. It presupposes what is said earlier in Deuteronomy: "YHWH is God in heaven above and on the earth beneath: there is no other" (4:39).

The only echo of the *Shema*ʿ elsewhere in the Old Testament confirms this in an interesting way. Looking to the eschatological future, it foresees that "YHWH will become king over all the earth; on that day YHWH will be one and his name one" (Zech. 14:9). The point is that if, as the *Shema*ʿ states, YHWH is truly the only one worthy of unreserved devotion, then he cannot be so only for Israel. He must prove to be the only one for all the nations. In the end, his uniqueness will not be contested by the nations who call on their own gods by other names. This hope for the universal worship of YHWH as the one and only God is a key aspect of Jewish monotheism that was also of great importance to the early Christians.

The Unique Identity of Israel's God

In what does the uniqueness of Israel's God consist? I find it helpful to think of this primarily in terms of personal identity rather than of nature. Certainly, there are elements of what could be called "divine nature" (such as eternity and supreme power) that the Bible treats as unique to the one God and very importantly so. But the way the biblical writers speak of God relies heavily, though not exclusively, on the analogy of human personality. They are more concerned with *who* God is than with *what* divine nature is. This also means that God is understood primarily in terms of relationship—who he is and what he does in relation to the world. So, he is the God who brought Israel out of Egypt and made them his covenant people. As such, he has a unique personal name, YHWH, that he gives himself so that he may be known by name to his people. His character description (Exod. 34:6–7) lists qualities that indicate the way he relates to people (merciful, faithful, etc.). So far, however, this account of God's uniqueness—as the God of the covenant with Israel—does not necessarily put this God in an ontological category of his own. There could be other gods similarly related to other peoples. So, especially when the uniqueness of Israel's God is asserted against the claims made for other gods, the features that come to the fore are those that relate God to "all things." God is said to be the only Creator of all things and the only sovereign Ruler of all things. These divine roles distinguish the one God from all other reality. He is the only Creator; all other things are created by him. He is the sole Sovereign; all other things are subject to his will. In these terms, the one God is unique not merely in the weak sense that every god in a pantheon is unique (just as every human is unique) but in the sense that he is in a class of his own. He is unique not merely in the way that a supreme god might be more powerful than other gods, but in a way that drives an absolute distinction between him and every other entity, however eminent. We could call this transcendent uniqueness. It is an account of the unique identity of God that I think is everywhere presupposed in the New Testament.

In the ancient world, monolatry was probably the most visible peculiarity of Jewish religion. It presupposes this understanding of the unique identity of the one God. In the ancient world, worship was generally understood to be a matter of degree. One paid appropriate degrees of honor to gods (and humans) of correspondingly differing rank. Early Judaism rejected this pattern and made worship the element of religious practice that represented most emphatically the distinction between the one God and all other reality. The heavenly bodies, for example, might be thought of as personal beings, but they were created and therefore were not to be worshipped. On the contrary, they along with all the heavenly host worship their Creator (Neh. 9:6).

Introduction to Monotheism in the New Testament

If we take the scope of the New Testament as a whole, the overall difference from the Old Testament that emerges is this.[5] While monotheism is strongly reasserted, in all of the principal ways in which it was defined in the Jewish tradition, the texts speak of this one God in three different, though intimately related, ways: as God "the Father" (for whom the term "God" is generally used), Jesus Christ "the Son" (for whom the term "God" is only very occasionally used, but "the Lord" is frequently used), and the Spirit (described both as "the Spirit of God" and as "the Spirit of Christ"). In attempting to understand this novel version of Jewish monotheism, we should note that it is the inclusion of Jesus Christ that determines it. That God is called "the Father" means primarily that he is "the Father of Jesus Christ"; Jesus Christ is the Son of this Father; and the Spirit is defined in relation to him as well as to God the Father. What has changed are the events of the history of Jesus—his life, death, resurrection, and exaltation to heaven—and the consequent outpouring of the divine Spirit on those who believe in him. While God had been known to his people as the God who brought Israel out of Egypt, he is now known as the God of Jesus Christ, the God who has intervened climactically to transform his whole creation. This represents a new kind of divine involvement in the world and its history, and the new threefold way of speaking of God is the way early Christians found they had to speak if they were to do justice to who God was seen to be in this new divine relationship to the world. Their God is unquestionably the same God as was known to Israel in the past, the one and only God, but the identity of this one God had now to be differentiated in a threefold way.

Christological Monotheism in the New Testament

Here we shall briefly consider three texts that take up key monotheistic assertions from the Old Testament and include Jesus Christ in the unique divine identity. Each will provide an occasion also for some more general remarks about Christology and monotheism in the New Testament.

1 Corinthians 8:6

For us there is one God, the Father,
from whom are all things
and for whom we exist,
and one Lord, Jesus Christ,
through whom are all things
and through whom we exist.

In the context, Paul is discussing—in very Jewish terms—the problems that Christians had avoiding involvement in the worship of pagan gods. It is not surprising that he cites the key Jewish expression of monotheism. He provides his readers with a carefully crafted reformulation of the *Shema*ʿ.

Paul has taken all the words of the key statement about God in the *Shema*ʿ ("YHWH our God, YHWH is one") and distributed them between God the Father and Jesus Christ.[6] The word "Lord" (Greek *kurios*) is here, as it is frequently in the Greek Old Testament and New Testament allusions to the Old Testament, a substitute for the sacred name YHWH, the personal name of the God of Israel, which Jews (and so also early Christians) did not pronounce. The word *kurios* refers to the name YHWH while signaling to the reader that only this substitute is to be pronounced. So, Paul uses the word "God" for God the Father but assigns the personal name of this God to Jesus Christ. It is essential to realize that Paul is not affirming the *Shema*ʿ and then adding Jesus Christ as a divine entity distinguished from the God of the *Shema*ʿ. It is inconceivable that Paul could both affirm the *Shema*ʿ and advocate outright ditheism. Rather, for Paul, the unique identity of God, affirmed in the *Shema*ʿ, *consists of* God the Father and the Lord Jesus Christ.

This is made very clear also by Paul's use of the phrase "all things" in relation to both God and Jesus. This is Jewish monotheistic language, distinguishing the one God from all created reality. In Romans 11:36, Paul refers to God (with no apparent reference to Jesus): "from him and through him and to him are all things." Here in 1 Corinthians 8:6, he divides the prepositions between God and Jesus, just as he divides the designations of the God of Israel between them. Exactly how he divides them may not be significant. In Colossians 1:16, he says that "all things have been created through [Jesus Christ] and for him." However, it is noteworthy that Jesus is here assigned a role in the creation of all things. This is remarkable in one of the earliest Christian texts that we have, because, of all the exclusively divine prerogatives, the act of creation most clearly signaled the absolute distinction between God and all other reality. Jews were in the habit of safeguarding strict monotheism by denying that God had any assistants in the work of creation (cf. Isa. 40:12–13, 44:24). Paul must mean that Jesus Christ was not some created assistant to God but himself belonged eternally to the unique identity of the one God. By reformulating the *Shema*ʿ, Paul has expressed this without either denying the distinction between Jesus and God or making Jesus a second god. The result has been called Paul's Christological monotheism.

We may recall that the *Shema*ʿ demands the total devotion of the whole self to God. That Paul here includes Jesus in the *Shema*ʿ is coherent with the ways in which Paul speaks of Christian believers' relationship to Jesus throughout his writings. They are slaves of Christ who serve him and seek to please him. Their lives seem to be focused on Christ, not as an alternative to devotion to God but as the way in which they devote themselves to God.

Philippians 2:9–11

Therefore God also highly exalted him
and gave him the name
that is above every name,
10so that at the name of Jesus
every knee should bend,
in heaven and on earth and under the earth,
11and every tongue should confess
that Jesus Christ is Lord,
to the glory of God the Father.

This is the second half of a very distinctive summary of the story of Jesus, which runs from the act of incarnation (in which the preexistent Christ became human), through death on the cross, to God's exaltation of Jesus to the divine throne, in consequence of which he receives the worship of all creation (not just humans). This part of the text echoes Isaiah 45:22–23, in which YHWH says:

Turn to me and be saved,
all the ends of the earth!
For I am God and there is no other.
23By myself I have sworn,

from my mouth has gone forth in righteousness
a word that shall not return:
"To me every knee shall bow,
every tongue shall swear."

This text from Isaiah is one of the many emphatically monotheistic declarations in Isaiah 40–55. Like the text quoted earlier from Zechariah (14:9), it looks forward to the time when YHWH, the God of Israel and the one and only God, will receive the allegiance of all nations. It expresses the eschatological aspect that was essential to early Jewish monotheism. The Pauline passage implies that it was in order to achieve this universal worship of the one true God that the incarnation and death of Jesus took place. In the self-abasing love of the crucified Jesus, the nations can recognize the deity of the true God. And so, at Jesus's exaltation to the cosmic throne, God bestows on him his own personal name YHWH,[7] and it is to Jesus that every knee shall bow.

Of special interest is the fact that the universal worship of Jesus redounds "to the glory of God the Father." When early Christians worshipped Jesus, they did not see him as an alternative or distinct object of worship alongside God. They included Jesus in their worship of God, much as Paul included Jesus in the *Shema'*. Worship of Jesus did not infringe Jewish monotheism, because Jesus himself belonged to the unique identity of the one and only God. What is envisaged in this passage of Philippians appears in visionary form in the book of Revelation. The crucified Jesus (symbolized by a slaughtered lamb) is seen on the divine throne in heaven, where the myriads of angels sing a doxology to him (a form of praise that Jewish tradition limited to the worship of God). But then all the creatures of every part of creation sing a doxology to God and the Lamb together (Rev. 5:11–13). The praise that the Lamb has won through his redemptive death becomes part of the praise of God. Larry Hurtado calls the worship of Jesus "a significantly new but essentially internal development within the Jewish monotheistic tradition."[8] Christian worship acquires a new shape without ceasing to be monolatrous.

Paul's echo of Isaiah 45:22–23 in this passage is an example of the frequent practice (especially in Paul but also elsewhere in the New Testament) of identifying Jesus with the YHWH of Old Testament texts. In more than twenty citations or echoes of Old Testament texts, Paul takes YHWH in the text as referring to Jesus. It is important to add that in more than twenty citations or echoes of Old Testament texts, Paul takes YHWH in the text as referring to God.[9] So he does not suppose that there are two gods in the Old Testament, one called YHWH and identified as Jesus, the other called God (*Elohim*). He is here as elsewhere including Jesus in the identity of the one God, whose name is YHWH. Paul never or hardly ever uses the word "God" of Jesus, but the word "god" is actually rather ambiguous and could be taken to mean that Jesus was a second god. It is much more significant that Paul can take texts referring to YHWH as references to Jesus. YHWH is the personal name of the one and only God.

In addition to Paul's citations of specific Old Testament texts in this way, Paul also appropriates with reference to Jesus a wide range of stereotyped phrases, including "Lord" (*kurios*), where in the Old Testament this stands for YHWH: "the name of the Lord," "the day of the Lord," "to serve the Lord," "the word of the Lord," "the fear of the Lord," "the glory of the Lord," and "the command of the Lord." This kind of identification of Jesus with the YHWH of the Old Testament is much more pervasive than is generally noticed.

John 1:1–3, 14, 18

In the beginning was the Word,
and the Word was with God,
and the Word was God.
[2]He was in the beginning with God.
[3]All things came into being through him,
and without him not one thing came into being. . . .
[14]And the Word became flesh
and lived among us,
and we have seen his glory,
the glory as of a father's only son,
full of grace and truth. . . .
[18]No one has ever seen God.
It is God the only Son,
who is close to the Father's heart,
who has made him known.

The prologue to John's Gospel begins with the same words ("In the beginning") that begin Genesis, the beginning of the Torah. The correspondence would not be lost on any Jewish reader. John takes his version of the story of Jesus right back to the eternal moment "before" God created the world. He does so, I think, primarily in order to begin where Jewish monotheistic formulations did: with God the only Creator and all things as his creation. He wishes to provide his readers from the start with the insight into Jesus's identity that the characters in his story attain only at the end of the story (cf. John 20:28): that Jesus is God incarnate. He also wants to integrate this insight into a thoroughly Jewish monotheism. In Jewish monotheism, as we have noticed, the belief that God alone was the Creator of all things was critical. No one assisted God in creation, but it could be said that God created all things *by his Word* (Ps. 33:6), a statement that summarizes the narrative in Genesis 1. This creative Word of God was evidently already with God in eternity "before" the creation, but it was not something other than God. It was God's own Word. So, John can say both that the Word was "with God" and that the Word "was God." His careful formulation ("was God" sandwiched between two occurrences of "with God") asserts both a differentiation between

God and his Word and an identification. But in the distinction between God and "all things" created, verse 3, with its seemingly redundant repetition, makes unambiguously clear that the Word belongs on God's side of that distinction. He was God's agent in creation but an agent who belongs to the unique identity of the only Creator.

I have spoken of the Word as "he," and in English the masculine pronoun is unavoidable, but the Greek allows it to be not entirely clear at first that the Word is depicted as a properly personal agent. All the same, verse 1 would be oddly phrased if "the Word" meant no more than the words God speaks (or even God's "reason," an alternative meaning for *logos*). For the Jewish reader, however, the fact that God's Word is often personified in the Old Testament would facilitate the realization that the Word is here a personal subject, both distinguished from and identified with God.

The statement that "the Word was God" is striking for the reader of the New Testament because the word "God" is only rarely used of Jesus (the exact number of instances is disputed). Its use here is obviously very carefully considered, for it unites the beginning and the end of the prologue. (It is now widely agreed that the best textual reading in John 1:18 is "God the only One," which is to be understood as "God the only Son.") In the rest of the Gospel, Jesus is called God only once but, very significantly, in Thomas's confession (John 20:28: "my Lord and my God"), which is the last of the series of confessions of who Jesus is that run through the Gospel. It is the climactic one.

The correspondence between the beginning and the end of John's prologue goes further. It is a correspondence that also makes clear the advance in knowledge of who the Word is that has occurred over the course of the prologue. In verse 1 the Word is both identified with God ("was God") and distinguished from him in close association ("with God"). Also, in verse 18, he is both identified with God ("God") and distinguished from him in close association ("the only [Son] who is on the breast of the Father"). But the colorless image of the Word "with God" is now replaced by the highly interpersonal image of the divine Son in loving intimacy with his Father. The transition to Son-Father language began in verse 14, when the Word became flesh. In the human life of Jesus, in which his disciples saw the divine glory and the divine character ("full of grace and truth"), it became apparent that this Word is related to God as a son to a father. Jesus, by being the Son in his human life, revealed the Father and at the same time the eternal relationship of love between Father and Son. (That the Father-Son relationship did not begin at the incarnation is clear from John 17:24.) In the light of this revelation, it can then also be understood that it was precisely because God's eternal identity comprised the relationship of Father and Son that incarnation was possible for God. The depiction of Jesus as Son of the Father throughout the rest of the Gospel shows that being the Son is a way of being God that can be lived out in a human life.

The Spirit and Trinitarian Monotheism in the New Testament

Jesus Christ most obviously made the difference to the way early Christians understood the one God. The role of the Spirit is not so obvious. There are far more texts that connect Christ with God than there are texts that connect the Spirit with both Christ and God. Moreover, the Old Testament already used the term "Spirit" (literally breath) of God as one way in which to speak of the immanent presence of God in his creation and with his people. Nevertheless, understanding of the Spirit as the Spirit of Jesus Christ gives the Spirit in the New Testament a more distinct profile and integrates the Spirit into the pattern of God's new way of involvement in the world to which the incarnation is central.

The New Testament sees God's new way of involvement in the world as aimed at transformation of the world. God the Creator makes his own divine life available to his creatures to share. Through Jesus and the Spirit believers participate in the eternal life of God. But God's own life is more than eternal life; it is also life in relationship. Through Jesus and the Spirit believers participate in the inner-divine relationship of Father and Son, becoming sisters and brothers of Jesus the Son. The Spirit's role is to be God's presence in human life, and the two most important ways the New Testament defines this is as participation in eternal life and participation in Jesus's relationship as Son to his Father.

Two Pauline texts illustrate how God's three ways of being God enable the participation of humans in God's life:

Romans 8:9–11

> But you are not in the flesh [the old, unredeemed human nature]; you are in the Spirit, since the Spirit of God dwells in you. Anyone who does not have the Spirit of Christ does not belong to him. But if Christ is in you, though the body is dead because of sin, the Spirit is life because of righteousness. If the Spirit of him who raised Jesus from the dead dwells in you, he who raised Christ from the dead will give life to your mortal bodies also through his Spirit that dwells in you.

In this rather involved text, Paul uses the following expressions as essentially synonymous: "you are in the Spirit," "the Spirit of God dwells in you," "[you] have the Spirit of Christ," "[you] belong to [Christ]," "Christ is in you." They are all ways of saying that the divine Spirit enables believers to participate in the divine life by uniting them with the risen Christ who lives the eternal life of God.

Galatians 4:4–6

> But when the fullness of time had come, God sent his Son, born of a woman, born under the law, in order to redeem those who were under the law, so that we might receive adoption as children. And because you are

children, God has sent the Spirit of his Son into our hearts, crying "Abba! Father!"

Abba is the Aramaic word for "father," the word Jesus himself, in his native Aramaic, used to address God his Father. That was so important to the early Christians that the Aramaic word was remembered even in the Greek-speaking world of Paul's readers (few of whom would have known any Aramaic).[10] The Spirit of Christ shares this relationship with believers. They become "adopted" brothers and sisters of Jesus, participating in his relationship with God, a human relationship with God based in the inner-divine relationship of the Son with the Father.

In these two passages from Paul, we can see a "Trinitarian" way of speaking of God emerging. When Paul wishes to speak adequately of the way in which Christian believers are related to Christ, he finds it necessary to speak of God as the Father, as the Son (incarnate as Jesus), and also as the Spirit, whom he calls both the Spirit of God and the Spirit of Jesus Christ. While such a fully "Trinitarian" way of speaking, explicitly naming all three divine persons, is relatively rare in the New Testament, it is found sufficiently widely across most of the key documents in the New Testament to show that it was a well-established practice. The variety of forms that such "Trinitarian" speech takes also shows that it was well rooted in Christian consciousness.[11]

Concluding Remarks

The belief that early Judaism derived from the Hebrew Bible was that YHWH the God of Israel was the one and only God, who created all things, who rules over all things, and who alone is to be worshipped. This Jewish faith in the one God, which required the devotion of the whole person to God, was the context in which the earliest Christians formed their understanding of Jesus Christ. They included him in the unique identity of this one God. He participated in God's creation of all things, he became incarnate as the man Jesus, he lived and died as God's human presence in the world, he was raised from death and exalted to participate in God's unique rule over all things, which he will bring to final perfection. Jesus's relationship to God as his Father was understood as a relationship internal to God's unique identity. When the fresh experience of the divine Spirit was also taken into account, there emerged three distinct, though intimately related ways in which early Christians spoke of God: as God the Father (meaning primarily the Father of Jesus Christ), as Jesus the divine Son, and as the Spirit (known both as the Spirit of Christ and as the Spirit of God). This threefold self-relatedness of God made it possible for God to share his own eternal life with humans and to share them with Jesus's own relationship as child to his Father. Thus, early Christians complexified the Jewish understanding of the unique identity of God while stressing that they remained believers in the one and only God.

Notes

1. I use the masculine gender pronoun for God simply because all of our texts do so.

2. Strictly, this is only the beginning of the *Shema*ʿ, which included more of the text of Deuteronomy, but in the early Jewish period, the exact extent seems to have varied.

3. NRSV has "The LORD is our God, the LORD is one," with three other possibilities in a footnote.

4. James 2:19 points out that even the demons can say the *Shema*ʿ in *that* sense.

5. It is beyond the scope of this essay to enter the detailed nuances of the various New Testament writers and documents.

6. Paul may be reading it as, "YHWH our God is one YHWH."

7. This probably does not mean that Paul thought the pre-incarnate Christ did not bear the divine name. It means that he now bears the divine name as the incarnate one, Jesus Christ. Hence the reference to "name of Jesus."

8. Larry W. Hurtado, *One God, One Lord: Early Christian Devotion and Ancient Jewish Monotheism* (Philadelphia: Fortress Press), 100.

9. Occasionally even the same text can be applied to Jesus in one context, to God in another. In Rom. 14:11, Isa. 45:23 is probably taken to refer to God.

10. Paul uses it also in Rom. 8:15. Mark's Gospel, written in Greek, preserves Jesus's use of this Aramaic word (14:36).

11. See Matt. 28:19; Mark 1:10–11; John 14:26, 15:26; Acts 1:4–5, 2:38–39, 7:55; 1 Cor. 12:4–7; 2 Cor. 13:13; Eph. 2:17–18; 1 Pet. 1:2; 1 John 4:13–14; Jude 1:4–5; Rev. 1:4–5.

Bridging the Chasm between the Divine and the Human

A Muslim Response to Richard Bauckham

MARIA MASSI DAKAKE

Richard Bauckham takes great care in his essay to show the way in which New Testament theology is consciously rooted in the particular monotheistic vision of the Hebrew scriptures. In particular, he explains that Paul drew on various names of God in the Hebrew scriptures and attributed the divine creative act to both God (the Father) and Jesus differentially, but inseparably, as a means of embedding a very new theology within the conceptual framework of Jewish monotheism. This suggests how earnestly New Testament writers conceived of this new theology, not as a radical "break" with Jewish monotheism but as a realization of the fullness and richness of God that was latent—indeed from a Christian theological point of view, eternally present, but not manifest, or at least obscured—in the Hebrew scriptures' conception and description of the one God.

The opening panel discussion of the Building Bridges Seminar 2016 raised the notion that there exists a "chasm" between God and creation or God and the world—or between God and everything that is not God (*Allāh wa mā siwā Allāh*, in Islamic terms)—and explored the way in which both traditions have wrestled with what this chasm means for our relationship with God and for our ultimate human vocation. I thus seek to frame my response to Richard Bauckham in a way that addresses a problem that I think is not only a central one for both traditions but also one on which some common ground—or at least some understanding—might be found.

The Creator and the Created, and the Chasm Between

Richard Bauckham speaks about the Israelite conception of the uniqueness of God; he speaks of God as being in a "class by himself"—and notes that this "transcendent uniqueness" of God is fundamentally rooted in the division between Creator and created. God creates all, and all else is created, forming a seemingly impenetrable divide, with God on one side, and everything else—his creatures—on the other. The notion that God's uniqueness is rooted in singular creative power is similarly and repeatedly affirmed by the Qur'ān. In fact, the idea that God creates and *nothing else creates as God creates* is a key argument in the Qur'ānic rhetoric against idolatry, often presented in the form of rhetorical questions:

> Do they ascribe as partners those who created naught and are themselves created? (al-Aʿrāf [7]:191)
> . . . Or have they ascribed unto God partners who have created the like of His creation, such that that creation seems alike to them? (al-Raʿd [13]:16)
> Is He Who creates like one who creates not? Will you not, then, reflect? (al-Naḥl [16]:17)
> Say, "Have you considered your partners upon whom you call apart from God? Show me what they have created of the earth." (al-Fāṭir [35]:40)
> Were they created from naught? Or are they the creators? (al-Ṭūr [52]:35)

In his essay, Bauckham explains that, given the importance of the creative act as the fundamental basis of the separation between God and everything else, Jesus could not really be conceived of as dwelling on the "God" side of this divide unless he also participated in the act of creating, and Paul and the author of John's Gospel do this by asserting that although God the Father is still the Creator of all things, all things are created "through" Jesus Christ—thus both God the Father and Jesus participate in the creative process, albeit in differentiated ways.

As is well known, the Qur'ān quite explicitly rejects the idea that Jesus dwells on the divine/Creator side of this chasm and does not conceive of a role for him in the creation of the world. I would point out, however, that no prophet in the Qur'ān comes as close as Jesus does to symbolically manifesting the divine creative act in the form of the unique miracles that he is given, for example, when he shapes a bird out of clay that comes to life when he breathes on it—a clear echo of God's creation of Adam. Nonetheless, the Qur'ān quite emphatically states that these tremendous miracles are all done "by God's Leave" (Āl ʿImrān [3]:49; al-Mā'ida [5]:110) and do not represent the independent power of Jesus himself.

If one asserts that Jesus does these things in the sense of serving as the conduit for God's power, then one would have to say that God's power to create is, in these limited instances, operating "through" Jesus, language similar to what we find in Paul. But, of course, in the New Testament conception, Jesus is the one through whom *all things* were created *from eternity*; while in the Qur'ānic passage, these apparently creative acts serve solely as evidentiary miracles (*mu'jizāt*), limited to a particular time and place in Jesus's mission. It is thus quite far from the idea that all things were necessarily and from eternity created through Christ and does not put Christ on the "divine" side of that chasm.

Jesus as God's Word

In his analysis of the prologue to the Gospel of John, Bauckham notes that the identification of Jesus as God's Word furthered this theological work of placing Jesus on the "Creator" rather than "created" side of the existential chasm by hearkening back to Genesis and embedding Jesus in the very Genesis account of creation, where God "speaks" creation into existence with his "words." In the Qur'ān, God also creates through speech or "words":

> When He decrees a thing, He only says to it, "Be!" and it is.[1] (al-Baqara [2]:117)

Given the role of Jesus's identification with the Word of God in Christian theology, it might at first seem quite striking that the Qur'ān also identifies Jesus with God's "word," in a way that is unique among the Qur'ānic prophets. However, while it is true that both scriptures and traditions refer to Jesus as God's "word," the term in relation to Jesus serves quite different functions in the two theologies.

In John's prologue, Jesus is identified as God's Word as a way of understanding his role as an agent in the divine creative act; he is the Word through which all things are brought into being (following Genesis). In the Qur'ān, God also creates through the word; but when the Qur'ān describes Jesus as God's word, it cannot mean that he is the word through which God creates as it does in a Christian theological context, since the Qur'ān asserts elsewhere that Jesus is himself created through God's word:

> She [Mary] said, "My Lord, how shall I have a child while no human being has touched me?" He said, "Thus does God create whatsoever He will." When He decrees a thing, He only says to it, "Be!" and it is. (Āl ʿImrān [3]:47)

So what does the Qur'ān mean when it describes Jesus as God's "word"? The Shiʿite commentator al-Ṭabarsī gives several possible ways of understanding Jesus as God's "word," one of which (which he attributes to the tenth-century Muʿtazilī theologian al-Jubbaʾī) is that Jesus in his person is a guide for human beings (lit. "creation") in the same way that the words of God (*kalām Allāh*)—presumably through scripture—are a guide for human beings in other contexts. This may not initially strike us as a particularly earth-shattering observation (it is quite similar in formulation to the oft-repeated idea in contemporary comparative religious discourse that Jesus is for Christians what the Qur'ān is for Muslims—although al-Jubbaʾī will have to be credited with positing the idea first). But let us keep this observation in mind as we will have occasion to revisit it as we continue our discussion.

Jesus as God's Son

In discussing the prologue to the Gospel of John, Bauckham notes that while the passage begins by speaking about Jesus as the Word, it concludes with speaking of him as God's Son. In Bauckham's words, "The colorless image of the Word 'with God' is now replaced by the highly interpersonal image of the divine Son in loving intimacy with his Father." This transition, it seems to me, is the heart of the Christian theology of revelation in which God reveals himself most fully in the incarnated Word (that is, in the person of Jesus), and what is revealed is not just a set of religious beliefs and prescriptions but a profound relationship of love that defines the nature of God and, by extension, of God's relationship to "the created world."

When we look at the various Qur'ānic critiques of Christian theology, however, we see that one issue on which the Qur'ān is uncompromisingly clear is that God has no child (neither a son nor a daughter) and that claiming as much—whether literally or metaphorically—is a grave and serious matter.

> And they say, "The Compassionate has taken a child." You have indeed asserted a terrible thing. The heavens are well-nigh rent thereby, the earth split asunder, and the mountains made to fall down in ruins, that they should claim for the Compassionate a child. It is not fitting for the Compassionate to take a child. There is none in the heavens and the earth, but that it comes unto the Compassionate as a servant. (Maryam [19]:88–93)

So there seems, at least at first, to be little room for dialogue or even understanding on this particular issue.

Here we may return to the idea that Jesus, as God's Word, does the work in his person that scripture does through the speech or words of God. What is the work that Jesus does as "Word" or as "Son"? Bauckham says that the "sonship" of Jesus is shown in the rest of the Gospel of John to be "a way of being God that can be lived out in a human life." It is, in other words, a way of bridging the chasm between God and all that is other than God; it is a means whereby God crosses from the divine to the created. But the "bridge" that this incarnational act creates is not unidirectional. As Bauckham discusses later, the "sonship" of Jesus also opens up, in Christian theology, a way for those who choose to live as the "sisters and brothers of Jesus the Son" to also participate in this Father-Son relationship. And this whole process is summed up, it seems to me, in the saying of Athanasius: "God became man that man might become God." The bridge that the incarnation sets up over the chasm is not just a path from God to creation but also a path from creation to God.

None of this language regarding Jesus's sonship, or the incarnation, or the filial relationship at the heart of the divine nature can be reconciled with Islamic conceptions of the nature of God and his relationship to the world. But God as conceived of in Islam *does also* cross the chasm between the divine and the created order through "revelation," through the "word"—not the word made flesh, but the word made "sound" or the word recited in the Qur'ān. It is a crossing that is in some ways analogous to the "incarnational crossing" posited in Christian theology—except in this case, the transcendent divine word is "embodied" not in the limitations of human flesh but in the limitations of human language. This mode of crossing the divine-human chasm (as with the incarnation in Christianity) also establishes a bridge, and it is also a bridge that allows traffic in two directions.

If, for Muslims, the divine crosses into the created world through human language, human beings can traverse the same bridge back to God. What else do Muslims do when they recite the Qur'ān in prayer and devotion? They recite God's words back to him and, in so doing, make their way via human language back to God. Let me conclude this point by juxtaposing two deeply similar texts: the *Shema*ʿ (with which Bauckham began his analysis) and Sūrat al-Ikhlāṣ, the Sūra of Sincerity, which sums up Islamic monotheistic belief.

The *Shema*ʿ reads: "*Hear*, O Israel: YHWH your God, YHWH is one." The statement begins with the command to "hear"—that is, to receive, to take in. It indicates communication in one direction: from the divine to the human. When we read the Sūrat al-Ikhlāṣ, however, we note that it begins with a different imperative: "*Say*, 'He, God, is One.'" Not "hear" but "say"! Many passages of the Qur'ān begin with this imperative, traditionally understood (in its singular form) as a command specifically to the Prophet Muḥammad to "say" certain things to his people or to his particular interlocutors on different occasions. But the Prophet Muḥammad is no longer here. So, to whom is the imperative addressed now? Why should contemporary listeners/readers not hear it as addressed to them—indeed to every individual reader and reciter of the Qur'ān—as an invitation not only to hear God's speech but to participate in God's speech, to bear it on their own tongues, to sustain it with their own breath? The verse does not demand that we passively hear God's declaration of his oneness and uniqueness; it demands that we actively speak it back to him. And in this way, it might be said, God speaks his word to human beings in human words so that human beings might speak God's words back to him in human language—the only language available to them.

Note

In this essay, all Qur'ān quotations are according to Seyyed Hossein Nasr et al., eds., *The Study Quran: A New Translation and Commentary* (New York: HarperOne, 2015).

1. Wa-idhā qaḍā amran, fa-innamā yaqūlu lahu kun fa-yakūn.

Texts from the Bible

Deuteronomy 6:4–15

4Hear, O Israel: The LORD is our God, the LORD alone. 5You shall love the LORD your God with all your heart, and with all your soul, and with all your might. 6Keep these words that I am commanding you today in your heart. 7Recite them to your children and talk about them when you are at home and when you are away, when you lie down and when you rise. 8Bind them as a sign on your hand, fix them as an emblem on your forehead, 9and write them on the doorposts of your house and on your gates.

10When the LORD your God has brought you into the land that he swore to your ancestors, to Abraham, to Isaac, and to Jacob, to give you—a land with fine, large cities that you did not build, 11houses filled with all sorts of goods that you did not fill, hewn cisterns that you did not hew, vineyards and olive groves that you did not plant—and when you have eaten your fill, 12take care that you do not forget the LORD, who brought you out of the land of Egypt, out of the house of slavery. 13The LORD your God you shall fear; him you shall serve, and by his name alone you shall swear. 14Do not follow other gods, any of the gods of the peoples who are all around you, 15because the LORD your God, who is present with you, is a jealous God. The anger of the LORD your God would be kindled against you and he would destroy you from the face of the earth.

Proverbs 8:22–31

22The LORD created me at the beginning of his work,
    the first of his acts of long ago.
23Ages ago I was set up,
    at the first, before the beginning of the earth.

24When there were no depths I was brought forth,
when there were no springs abounding with water.
25Before the mountains had been shaped,
before the hills, I was brought forth—
26when he had not yet made earth and fields,
or the world's first bits of soil.
27When he established the heavens, I was there,
when he drew a circle on the face of the deep,
28when he made firm the skies above,
when he established the fountains of the deep,
29when he assigned to the sea its limit,
so that the waters might not transgress his command,
when he marked out the foundations of the earth,
30then I was beside him, like a master worker;
and I was daily his delight,
rejoicing before him always,
31rejoicing in his inhabited world
and delighting in the human race.

Jeremiah 10:6–12

6There is none like you, O LORD;
you are great, and your name is great in might.
7Who would not fear you, O King of the nations?
For that is your due;
among all the wise ones of the nations
and in all their kingdoms
there is no one like you.
8They are both stupid and foolish;
the instruction given by idols
is no better than wood!
9Beaten silver is brought from Tarshish,
and gold from Uphaz.
They are the work of the artisan and of the hands of the goldsmith;
their clothing is blue and purple;
they are all the product of skilled workers.
10But the LORD is the true God;
he is the living God and the everlasting King.
At his wrath the earth quakes,
and the nations cannot endure his indignation.

11Thus shall you say to them: The gods who did not make the heavens and the earth shall perish from the earth and from under the heavens.

12It is he who made the earth by his power,
who established the world by his wisdom,
and by his understanding stretched out the heavens.

Zechariah 14:9

And the LORD will become king over all the earth; on that day the LORD will be one and his name one.

Mark 1:9–11

9In those days Jesus came from Nazareth of Galilee and was baptized by John in
the Jordan. 10And just as he was coming up out of the water, he saw the heavens
torn apart and the Spirit descending like a dove on him. 11And a voice came from
heaven, "You are my Son, the Beloved; with you I am well pleased."

John 1:1–18

1In the beginning was the Word, and the Word was with God, and the Word was
God. 2He was in the beginning with God. 3All things came into being through
him, and without him not one thing came into being. What has come into being
4in him was life, and the life was the light of all people. 5The light shines in the
darkness, and the darkness did not overcome it.

6There was a man sent from God, whose name was John. 7He came as a witness to testify to the light, so that all might believe through him. 8He himself was
not the light, but he came to testify to the light. 9The true light, which enlightens
everyone, was coming into the world.

10He was in the world, and the world came into being through him; yet the
world did not know him. 11He came to what was his own, and his own people did
not accept him. 12But to all who received him, who believed in his name, he gave
power to become children of God, 13who were born, not of blood or of the will of
the flesh or of the will of man, but of God.

14And the Word became flesh and lived among us, and we have seen his glory,
the glory as of a father's only son, full of grace and truth. 15(John testified to him
and cried out, "This was he of whom I said, 'He who comes after me ranks ahead
of me because he was before me.'") 16From his fullness we have all received,
grace upon grace. 17The law indeed was given through Moses; grace and truth
came through Jesus Christ. 18No one has ever seen God. It is God the only Son,
who is close to the Father's heart, who has made him known.

1 Corinthians 8:4–6

[4]Hence, as to the eating of food offered to idols, we know that “no idol in the world really exists,” and that “there is no God but one.” [5]Indeed, even though there may be so-called gods in heaven or on earth—as in fact there are many gods and many lords—[6]yet for us there is one God, the Father, from whom are all things and for whom we exist, and one Lord, Jesus Christ, through whom are all things and through whom we exist.

Galatians 4:4–7

[4]But when the fullness of time had come, God sent his Son, born of a woman, born under the law, [5]in order to redeem those who were under the law, so that we might receive adoption as children. [6]And because you are children, God has sent the Spirit of his Son into our hearts, crying, “Abba! Father!” [7]So you are no longer a slave but a child, and if a child then also an heir, through God.

Philippians 2:5–11

[5]Let the same mind be in you that was in Christ Jesus,
[6]who, though he was in the form of God,
did not regard equality with God
as something to be exploited,
[7]but emptied himself,
taking the form of a slave,
being born in human likeness.
And being found in human form,
[8]he humbled himself
and became obedient to the point of death—
even death on a cross.

[9]Therefore God also highly exalted him
and gave him the name
that is above every name,
[10]so that at the name of Jesus
every knee should bend,
in heaven and on earth and under the earth,
[11]and every tongue should confess
that Jesus Christ is Lord,
to the glory of God the Father.

Hebrews 1:1–4

[1]Long ago God spoke to our ancestors in many and various ways by the prophets,
[2]but in these last days he has spoken to us by a Son, whom he appointed heir of
all things, through whom he also created the worlds. [3]He is the reflection of God's
glory and the exact imprint of God's very being, and he sustains all things by his
powerful word. When he had made purification for sins, he sat down at the right
hand of the Majesty on high, [4]having become as much superior to angels as the
name he has inherited is more excellent than theirs.

1 John 1:1–4

[1]We declare to you what was from the beginning, what we have heard, what we
have seen with our eyes, what we have looked at and touched with our hands,
concerning the word of life—[2]this life was revealed, and we have seen it and testify
to it, and declare to you the eternal life that was with the Father and was revealed
to us—[3]we declare to you what we have seen and heard so that you also may have
fellowship with us; and truly our fellowship is with the Father and with his Son
Jesus Christ. [4]We are writing these things so that our joy may be complete.

Revelation 1:4–6

[4]John to the seven churches that are in Asia:

Grace to you and peace from him who is and who was and who is to come, and
from the seven spirits who are before his throne, [5]and from Jesus Christ, the
faithful witness, the firstborn of the dead, and the ruler of the kings of the earth.
To him who loves us and freed us from our sins by his blood, [6]and made us to be
a kingdom, priests serving his God and Father, to him be glory and dominion for
ever and ever. Amen.

PART II

The Oneness of God in the Qurʾān and Ḥadīth

Monotheism in Islam

ASMA AFSARUDDIN

There is no doubt that a basic introduction to Islamic theology must begin with an emphasis on monotheism, signified by the Arabic term *tawḥīd*. The term connotes belief in the unqualified oneness of the Supreme Being, the Almighty Creator who is named Allāh in Arabic—the one and only deity.[1] The affirmation of divine unity is what demarcates faith/belief (*īmān*) from lack of faith/unbelief (*kufr*), according to Islamic doctrine. It is the first and essential part of the *shahāda*, the basic creedal statement that all Muslims must attest to, through public and private utterance, in their worship and adoration of God, and above all in their heart.

This chapter will discuss selected verses from the Qur'ān that establish above all the centrality of monotheism as the key cardinal tenet of Islam. The other verses discussed mount a critique of belief in multiple deities among the pagan Arabs and of certain Christological conceptions current among contemporary Christians. Among the arguments presented by the Qur'ān in defense of monotheism is that it is a doctrine established by both revelation and reason, capable of being comprehended by the discerning human intellect. Ḥadīths that clearly assert the soteriological efficacy of belief in the one God can be marshaled to underscore the Qur'ānic insistence on the primacy of *tawḥīd* in the Islamic milieu. The paper will conclude by exploring the common ground that is opened up further between Muslims and Christians by engaging closely with the Qur'ānic discourse in this manner and what that portends for the future of interfaith relations.

The Centrality of Monotheism

Numerous verses in the Qur'ān affirm the oneness of God and the centrality of this tenet to the Qur'ānic worldview and conceptualization of the proper, loving relationship between humans and their Creator. Nowhere is this articulated more starkly and powerfully than in the fifth verse of al-Fātiḥa—the first or opening chapter of the Qur'ān. A short chapter composed of only seven verses, it is recited in its entirety by observant Muslims in their daily prayers five times a day. The fifth verse states, "It is [only] You we worship; it is [only] You we ask for help." I add "only" within brackets to Abdel Haleem's translation in order to closely communicate the flavor of the original Arabic emphatic particle (*iyyāka*). Its deployment clearly conveys that no contender to the one and only God may be imagined; God alone is adored by the believer and beseeched for help.

The well-known exegete of the late third/ninth century, Muḥammad Ibn Jarīr al-Ṭabarī (d. 310/923), quotes the famous Companion ʿAbdallāh Ibn ʿAbbās, who glossed "It is [only] You we worship" to mean "It is only You Whom we declare to be one and to hold in awe and in Whom we place our hope—O our Lord, there is none other than you!"[2] As for the next part of the verse, which states "It is [only] You we ask for help," al-Ṭabarī expansively expounds on its meaning thus:

> It is You, O our Lord, Whom we beseech for help in our adoration of only You and our obedience of You in all our matters—there is absolutely none beside You—in contrast to those who do not believe in You and who ask the idols that they worship instead of You for help in their affairs. We however ask You for help in all our matters sincerely dedicating our worship to You.[3]

The Qur'ān insists that God's unicity is absolute. The 112th chapter of the Qur'ān—called the "Chapter on Sincerity and on the Unicity of God," among other names—declares this unambiguously and fittingly reflects the first chapter's emphasis on God's singularity. This chapter—usually termed Sūrat al-Ikhlāṣ in Arabic—also offers a pithy summation of the essential message of the Qur'ān, predicated as it is on the invitation to humans to glorify and supplicate the One God alone. The ḥadīth literature similarly stresses this point and describes the importance of this chapter as succinctly articulating the bedrock essence of the believer's relationship and compact with God. Chapter 112 is therefore declared by the Prophet Muḥammad to be equivalent to a third of the Qur'ān, whose frequent recitation confers untold merit on the believer.[4]

One of the occasions of revelation provided by al-Ṭabarī for Sūrat al-Ikhlāṣ is as follows. According to the Companion Ubayy b. Kaʿb, the Arab polytheists asked the Prophet if he could "provide for us the genealogy of your Lord." In response, the chapter was revealed. Variant versions attributed to Qatāda b. Diʿāma (d. 118/736) and Saʿid b. Jubayr (d. 95/714), among others, state that it was a group of Medinan Jews who asked the Prophet a similar question and further demanded to know that since God had created Creation, who had created God? Al-Ṭabarī comments that in this context, Sūrat al-Ikhlāṣ may be understood to constitute a categorical response to such queries about God's pedigree, his attributes, and his existence. It instructed the Prophet to respond as follows: "He is the one God (Allāh) who is the object of worship of all things; absolutely no one else is worthy of worship but Him."[5]

Many commentators understand the Arabic third-person masculine pronoun *huwa* (he) used in reference to God at the beginning of the first verse in Sūrat al-Ikhlāṣ to indicate the very essence of the Divine Being. The verse continues with the Arabic statement "Allāh aḥad" (God is one). The well-known late sixth/twelfth century exegete al-Rāzī (d. 606/1210) comments that the name Allāh as used here may be understood to signify the totality of positive divine attributes (such as possessing all knowledge and power), while *aḥad* connotes the totality of negative divine attributes (for example, being without corporeal form and substance). The phrase "Allāh aḥad" therefore conveys a full theological understanding of God. As al-Rāzī puts it, "The entire Quran is an oyster, and the pearl is His statement 'Say, He, God is One.'"[6]

The following verse proclaims the self-sufficiency of God by applying to him the epithet *al-Ṣamad*, one of the ninety-nine "beautiful names of God" (*al-asmā' al-ḥusnā*), which occurs only in this one instance in the Qur'ān. Al-Ṭabarī cites the opinion of many early authorities who understood the epithet *al-Ṣamad* to underscore that God does not require sustenance and that nothing emanates from him. This conception is connected to the next two verses of Sūrat al-Ikhlāṣ, which categorically affirm that God does not beget nor is he begotten.[7]

These pronouncements on God's oneness and indivisibility culminate in the last verse, which powerfully asserts that there is absolutely no other being like God. God, by virtue of being God, has no equal and no partner. God the Omnipotent and Almighty (in Arabic *al-Jabbār*, *al-Qahhār*, and other epithets) is in no need of a protector, for there is no limit to his greatness, as further asserted in Sūrat al-Isrā' (17):110–11. These Qur'ānic pronouncements are meant to be a sharp rebuke to the Arab polytheists who believed in multiple deities and ascribed offspring, especially daughters, to God (cf. al-Naḥl [16]:57; al-Ṣāffāt [37]:149–53); this was the interpretation of a number of exegetes. Other exegetes, however, understood the third verse in Sūrat al-Ikhlāṣ to refer instead to Christians and their belief in Jesus as the "Son of God" (cf. al-Nisā' [4]:17; al-Tawba [9]:30; Maryam [19]:35, 91–92).[8] Christian readers may indeed understand this verse to negate the Gospel's reference to Jesus as the "only-begotten Son" (John 1:18). The Qur'ān's references in other verses to Jesus, the Messiah, the son of Mary, as a spirit from God and his Word, who is not ashamed to be a servant of God (Maryam [19]:30), also challenge Christian Trinitarianism.[9] Sūrat Maryam (19):34 proclaims that God is far above the false attribution of progeny to him; he creates ex nihilo and is in no need of a consort. "God is my Lord and your Lord; so serve Him: that is a straight path"—either Muḥammad or Jesus utters this statement, according to the exegetes, since the speaker is not explicitly identified. Nor is it necessary that the speaker in this case be clearly named, for in the Qur'ān both prophets adore and serve the same God and both summon to the straight path of righteousness that leads to glorious success in the hereafter.

In other verses, the People of the Book are specifically admonished not to say "Three" (al-Nisāʾ [4]:171; al-Māʾida [5]:72–73) when referring to God; this admonition is widely understood to be a critique of the standard Christian doctrine of Trinity. But this cryptic Qurʾānic utterance has also instigated discussion among scholars about whether this numerical reference might constitute a critique of specifically tritheism (that is to say, belief in three distinct gods) rather than the orthodox Christian doctrine of the triune God. Al-Ṭabarī's explication of this verse suggests that it is tritheism that is being condemned in the verse. He comments that the verse adjures the People of the Book to believe

> in the oneness of God and His lordship, and [to believe] that He has no son, and to believe in His Messengers who have come to you from God and who have informed you about Him—that He is God the one, the one who has no partner nor consort nor progeny. And "do not say 'three'" means that you should not say, "The lords are three" (*al-arbāb thalātha*).[10]

Recently, Joseph Lumbard, in HarperCollins's *The Study Qurʾān*, has espoused the view that in these verses (al-Nisāʾ [4]:171; al-Māʾida [5]:72–73) the Qurʾān "does not oppose the various forms of orthodox Trinitarian doctrines that have prevailed for most of Christian history. Rather, it appears to oppose crude misunderstandings of it that would lead one to believe that there are three gods instead of one."[11] Such an interpretation may be understood to ameliorate what has traditionally been understood to be practically an unbridgeable chasm between Muslim and Christian conceptions of the Divine Being.

Challenging Anthropomorphism

In Sūrat Ṭā-Hā (20):14, God speaks about himself in the first person to Moses during the event that will be familiar to Christian readers as the burning bush episode in the Hebrew Bible (Exod. 3:2–3). In a powerful theophanic moment, God "reveals" himself to Moses in the sacred valley of Tuwa and proclaims categorically: "I am God; there is no god but Me. So worship Me and keep up the prayer so that you remember Me." To Christian ears, this verse may be heard as echoing the passage in Exodus 3:14 where God similarly reveals himself by declaring, "I am who I am." In his commentary on Ṭā-Hā (20):14, al-Ṭabarī emphasizes the connection between acknowledging God's oneness and making him alone the object of human worship, for as the verse commands, "humans must establish prayer in order to remember and serve God only, forsaking all others."[12] The Andalusian exegete al-Qurṭubī (d. 671/1273) similarly stresses in his commentary on this verse that the believer, after affirming the oneness of

God, must be concerned with the sedulous performance of prayer, for through prayer, he or she can express "proper supplication towards God the Almighty."[13]

God's singularity and sole sovereignty is furthermore established in the Qur'ān because he alone is proclaimed to be the Creator of all things and he alone is in charge of everything (al-An'ām [6]:102). He never sleeps or tires and, while transcendent, can be found everywhere; "To God belong the East and the West, and wherever you turn, there is God's Countenance," declares the Qur'ān (al-Baqara [2]:115). His glorious throne encompasses all of creation, and no one may serve as an intercessor except by His leave, as stated in al-Baqara (2):255. This verse has justly become famous for invoking the ineffable majesty of the Divine Being in incomparably beautiful Arabic. Known in the commentary literature as "the Verse of the Throne" (*āyat al-kursī*), it is recited by Muslims on many occasions in reverential awe of the Almighty and as talismanic protection against the adversities that assail humans in this world. A ḥadīth refers to the Verse of the Throne as the "Mistress of the Verses of the Qur'ān." Al-Ghazālī, in his commentary titled *The Jewels of the Qur'ān*, explains why this verse has achieved such an elevated status. "The Verse of the Throne," he says, is so called because it

> is concerned with the divine essence, attributes and works only; it contains nothing other than these. . . . Now when you reflect on all these meanings [contained in the Verse of the Throne] and then recite all other verses of the Qur'ān, you will not find all these meanings—divine unity, sanctification, and explanation of high attributes—gathered together in a single one of them.[14]

Al-Ṭabarī, in his exegesis of this verse, indicates that early authorities like Ibn 'Abbās and Sa'id b. Jubayr understood "throne" (*kursī*) to be a metaphor for "knowledge" (*'ilm*) so that the verse is understood to affirm that God's knowledge encompasses everything. But other scholars like Al-Ḍaḥḥāk b. Muzāḥim (d. 105/723) understood it to be a reference either to a physical object on which "kings rest their feet" or to the throne itself in which they sit. Al-Ṭabarī himself prefers the metaphorical interpretation of "throne" as "knowledge" here and points to the etymological connection between *kursī* and *kurrāsa*, the latter referring to the "scroll upon which knowledge is inscribed."[15] Al-Rāzī understands "throne" in al-Baqara (2):255 to be a reference to the "majesty of God and His grandeur" and warns against an anthropomorphic reading of this verse.[16]

The Qur'ān's references to God's "throne," his face and hands, and his attributes, however, provoked a lively discussion among Muslim scholars about their proper interpretation. The tension was primarily between God's undisputed transcendence, a doctrinal position that was named in the later literature as *tanzīh*, and his possible anthropomorphization, referred to as *tashbīh*. The Mu'tazila were the most vigorous opponents of a literal understanding of such Qur'ānic locutions that would suggest the corporealization (*tajsīm*) of God's being and thus compromise divine transcendence. They were also highly wary of any concept that might potentially undermine the absolute unity of God; their self-designation after all was *ahl al-ʿadl wa al-tawḥīd* (the people of justice and unity [of God]). Thus, they opposed the understanding of God's essential attributes (*ṣifat al-dhāt/al-nafs*)—such as *ʿālim* (knowing) and *ḥayy* (living)—as "substantive" ones, which would imply that they were eternal "existents" alongside God. The orthodox Sunni position (as articulated by the Ashʿarites) accepts the notion of God's "substantive attributes," which are, however, as they are careful to stress, "neither identical to God nor other than Him."[17] The Qur'ān, after all, states, "There is nothing whatever that resembles Him" (42:11) and "There is none like unto Him" (112:4). The early Ashʿarites were also of the opinion that the seemingly anthropomorphic verses in the Qur'ān should be accepted at face value "without asking how" (expressed pithily in Arabic as *bi-lā kayf*), thus avoiding either a literal or metaphorical interpretation. Later Sunni theologians, like al-Juwaynī (d. 478/1085), however, preferred metaphorical understandings of such verses, construing "hand," for example, to be a reference to God's power and "face" to his essence.

Knowledge and Monotheism

In the Qur'ān, belief in multiple deities is the result of human ignorance and willful disregard for God's self-disclosure through his revealed messages through time. The Qur'ān asserts that those who attribute partners and children to God do so because they have no knowledge (al-Tawba [9]:101) and do not follow divine revelation (al-Tawba [9]:104–6). The Qur'ān in fact invites us to reason our way to monotheism and stresses that belief in a single omnipotent Creator requires no particular leap of faith when we use our faculties of observation. Sūrat al-Mu'minūn (23):91 invites us to ponder the fact that the universe runs smoothly and all of creation is orderly and follows laws of nature that are consistent. Two creators or more would have set in motion different creations at loggerheads with one another. Sūrat al-Furqān (25):1–3 similarly underscores the orderly nature of the heavens and earth, which illustrates God's full and uncontested power over all creation. In a supreme act of irrationality, polytheists worship idols that they themselves fashion with their own hands and "that can neither harm nor help themselves, and have no control over death, life, or resurrection."

In this context, the story of Abraham, recounted in Sūrat Maryam (19):41–50, serves as a powerful affirmation of monotheism as a universally binding theological principle confirmed by both revelation and reason. In these verses, Abraham pleads with his idol-worshipping father to realize the irrationality of his beliefs, for how can a human being endowed with the gift of intellect "worship something that can neither hear nor see nor benefit you in any way?" As opposed to ignorance, which leads to idol worship, Abraham adjures his father to embrace the divinely revealed knowledge (*al-ʿilm*) that he has been given, for in so doing the latter will be guided to "a straight path" (*ṣirāṭan sawwiyan*). Al-Zamakhsharī (d. 538/1144), the Muʿtazilī rational theologian of the sixth/twelfth century, stresses that worship or adoration (*al-ʿibāda*) connotes "the highest magnification" (*hiya ghāyat al-taʿẓīm*), so logically, only a being who is "the utmost in benevolence"; who creates, gives life, and takes it away; who provides for his creation; who is the source of all life's bounties—only such a being is worthy of such glorification. To transfer such glorification to an inert object that is incapable of such acts of benevolence is actually an act of oppression, of going astray, and ultimately of ungrateful denial of God's boundless generosity.[18] Al-Zamakhsharī also emphasizes that when Abraham reasoned with his father about the irrationality of idol worship, he did so with "courtesy, gentleness, compassion and endearing conduct," seeking to provide counsel to his erring father in a pleasing manner befitting of one who had earned the epithet *Khalīl Allāh* (the Friend of God).[19]

God's Universality

Most important for our contemporary fractious period, the God of the Qurʾān proclaims himself to be the one and same God who has communicated with humanity since the beginning of time through his revelations entrusted to and disseminated by his messengers and prophets who went to different communities in different historical periods. Sūrat al-Isrāʾ (17):110–11, which commands humans to "Call on God, or on the Lord of Mercy: whatever names you call Him, the best names belong to Him," clearly implies that God—or whatever name we choose to call him by that emphasizes his beautiful attributes—is the one and the same. Another significant verse reinforces the universality of the one God for Abrahamic believers:

> Say (O Muslims): We believe in God and that which is revealed to us and that which was revealed to Abraham, and Ishmael, and Isaac, and Jacob, and the tribes, and that which Moses and Jesus received, and that which the prophets received from their Lord. We make no distinction between any of them, and to Him we have surrendered. (al-Baqara [2]:136)[20]

In the context of current debates in the American public sphere about whether Muslims worship the same deity as Christians, these verses take on a particularly acute and poignant significance for interfaith relations.

According to the Qurʾān, so critical and foundational is belief in the one God that demarcates the faithful from the unfaithful that there is only one infraction that God will not forgive in the hereafter: the sin of associationism or polytheism (*shirk*) (al-Nisāʾ [4]:48; al-Māʾida [5]:72). Several ḥadīths also underscore the soteriological efficacy of monotheism, the profession of which by itself ensures for the believer entrance into paradise. In these ḥadīths, the Prophet assures his listeners that belief in the one God alone will deliver them from punishment in the next world. One ḥadīth in particular, recorded by Muslim b. al-Ḥajjāj (d. 261/875), further states that the salvific efficacy of belief in the one God is enhanced by confirming Jesus's stature as a completely human prophet.[21] This ḥadīth, then, implicitly denies the Christian belief in the divine nature of Christ.

Scriptural emphasis on the soteriological efficacy of monotheism historically became reflected in the principle of *irjāʾ*, which evolved in roughly the eighth century CE in the Muslim world. The root of the Arabic term *irjāʾ* connotes both "hope" and "deferment." Because of a number of doctrinal schisms that developed in the early period, some Muslim theologians wisely came to see immense virtue in postponing or deferring to God any definitive judgment on the correctness of a particular dogma that was not explicitly referred to in the Qurʾān or ḥadīth. This principle was specifically formulated in contradistinction to the notion of *takfīr* (accusation of unbelief), resorted to by the seventh-century schismatic group the Khawārij. The Khawārij had mutinied against ʿAlī bin Abī Ṭālib, the fourth caliph, when the latter agreed to human arbitration to resolve the dispute between himself and Muʿāwiya, the governor of Syria, over the issue of leadership of the community. The Khawārij (lit. "the seceders") claimed that arbitration was the prerogative of God alone and human arbitration was unwarranted in this case. They considered those Muslims (the overwhelming majority) who disagreed with them to have lapsed from the faith and thus thought they should be fought against until they capitulated—a chilling harbinger of today's minoritarian extremist views.

In contrast to the fissiparous doctrine of *takfir*, the principle of *irja'* stated that any Muslim who proclaimed his or her belief in the one God and the prophetic mission of Muḥammad (that is, affirmed the basic creedal statement of Islam) remained a Muslim, regardless of the commission of even gravely sinful actions, thereby holding out the hope and promise of moral rehabilitation in this world and of forgiveness in the next. A sinning Muslim was liable for punishment for criminal wrongdoing but could not be labeled an unbeliever by his coreligionists. Those who subscribed to such views were known as the Murjiʾa.[22] The principle of *irjāʾ* is being reemphasized by some contemporary Muslims who believe that it is a powerful Qurʾānically inspired principle that can be appealed to as normative and invoked as being in accordance with the spirit of our own, one hopes, more inclusive age.

How should Muslims react when others spurn the Qurʾān's call to monotheism? Sūrat al-Anʿām (6):106 clearly instructs Muslims to "follow that which is inspired in you from your Lord, there is no God but Him," and to "turn away from the idolators." The next verse counsels the Prophet that it is not part of his worldly mission to turn people toward monotheism; his mission is one of preaching the divine message that he was entrusted with that others can embrace or reject, for "we have not made you their guardian, nor are you their keeper." The last verse in this cluster (al-An'ām [6]:108) furthermore categorically establishes a protocol for interfaith conduct and civility in the midst of religious difference that is of particular significance for us today. It states, "Do not revile those [idols] they call upon beside God in case they revile God out of hostility." The verse stresses that it is not for human beings to pronounce on the rectitude of religious doctrines since that leads to dissension and strife in this world. The Prophet Muḥammad himself is clearly warned that it is not among his duties to chastise people for their beliefs contrary to Islam, including idolatry, which represents the polar opposite of cherished Islamic tenets of monotheism and iconoclasm.

A sampling of exegeses of this verse establishes that this fundamental message of non-compulsion in religion was emphasized by the large majority of Qur'ān commentators. The early exegete Muqātil b. Sulaymān (d. 150/767), in his brief exegesis of al-An'ām (6):107, states that if God had so willed, he would have prevented the Meccans from being polytheists. But he did not appoint the Prophet their guardian, nor is he their guardian if they refuse to believe in the one God. As for al-An'ām (6):108, it informs us that the early Muslims used to curse the idols of the Meccans and God forbade them from doing so lest they curse God in their ignorance.[23]

Al-Ṭabarī similarly comments that al-An'ām (6):107 affirms that if God had willed, the people of Mecca would not have disbelieved in God and his messenger, but the Prophet Muḥammad was sent only as an emissary and summoner to people and not as an overseer of their actions or as one who is responsible for their maintenance and welfare. The next verse forbids Muslims from reviling the idols of the polytheists, for that would cause them to revile God in their ignorance.[24] Similar commentaries are given by al-Zamakhsharī, al-Rāzī, and Ibn Kathīr.[25]

The modern exegete Muḥammad 'Abduh (d. 1905) reproduces many of the essential points made by his premodern predecessors in connection with these two verses. But he goes further than his predecessors in asserting that al-An'ām (6):107 makes clear that God, despite being the guardian and overseer of humanity, does not force humans to believe in and obey him. If he were to do so, humans would no longer be humans but would become a different species; that is to say, humans by virtue of their humanness have freedom of choice in religious matters.[26] The implication is that those who heed both reason and revelation are bound to embrace monotheism of their own free and rational volition.

And finally, we come to Sūrat Āl 'Imrān (3):64, a verse that in recent times has received much attention in interfaith circles. This verse states,

> Say: O People of the Book! Come to a common word (*kalimāt sawā*) between us and you: that we shall worship none by God, and that we shall ascribe no partner to Him, and that none of us shall take others for lords

> beside God. And if they turn away, then say: Bear witness that we are they who have surrendered to Him (*muslimūn*).

This verse is concerned primarily with Muslim relations with Jews and Christians. Some of our exegetes reflect on whether this verse deals exclusively with Jews or with Christians or both together and what exactly the Arabic word *sawāʾ* occurring in this verse signifies.

In his brief commentary, Muqātil glosses *kalimāt sawāʾ* as "a word of justice, which is sincerity" (*kalimāt al-ʿadl wa-hiya al-ikhlāṣ*), to be agreed on by Muslims and the People of the Book that they will not worship but the one God and not ascribe partners to him. Muqātil understands this verse to be directed primarily at Christians.[27]

Al-Ṭabarī glosses the term *ahl al-kitāb* in the verse as a reference to both Jews and Christians (*ahl al-tawrāt wa-'l-injīl*; "people of the Torah and the Gospel"), who are summoned to "a just word between us and you." The "just word" signifies that "we should believe in the unicity of God and not worship anyone else; repudiate (*nabrāʾ*) all other beings as objects of worship except Him, and that we should not ascribe any partner to Him." The locution "that any of us should take others as lords besides the one God" is understood to mean that one should not obey any human in matters that contravene God's commandments or one should not exalt another by prostrating before another as one prostrates before God.[28]

Besides referring to "just/justice" (*al-ʿadl*), continues al-Tabarī, the word *sawāʾ* also means "straight/upright" (*mustawīya*). The verse commands the Prophet to exhort the People of the Book to arrive at "a just [word] between us and you." There were others, like Abu l-ʿĀliya (d. ca. 90/708), who maintained that *kalimāt sawāʾ* was a reference to the statement "There is no god but God."[29]

Al-Zamakhsharī similarly points out the different interpretations of *ahl al-kitāb*, variously understood to be a reference to the Christians from Najrān, the Jews of Medina, or both communities. "Common" (*sawāʾ*) refers to what is "[deemed] upright by us and you, regarding which the Qurʾān, the Torah, and the Gospel do not differ." The "word" or "statement" (*kalima*) is elaborated on by the verse itself: "that we worship none but God and not ascribe partners to Him and that none of us should take others as lords besides the one God." If the People of the Book disregard this summons, concludes al-Zamakhsharī, then Muslims are free to assert that they have submitted to God.[30]

The conciliatory nature of this verse directed toward the Christians of Najrān is indicated by the appellation *ahl al-kitāb* for them, says al-Rāzī in the late sixth/twelfth century. He says that this is so because it is the best of appellations and the most perfect of titles, for it has made of them "worthy of the Book of God" (*jaʿalāhum ahlān li-kitāb allāh*). Such an honorific is intended to express respect for those who are so addressed, to cultivate their goodwill, and to persuade people to abandon the path of disputation and obstinacy and embark instead on a quest for fairness or justice. "A common word" is understood by al-Rāzī to refer to "a word which embodies fairness or equality between us," and no one is accorded any preference. *Al-sawa'* is specifically "justice and fairness" (*al-'adl wa-'l-inṣāf*). "A common word" is therefore ultimately a word that is just, upright, and egalitarian.[31]

It is highly significant that in 2007, the Qurʾānic phrase *kalimat sawāʾ* was invoked by 138 Muslim scholars and clerics in a statement addressed to Christian religious leaders of various denominations that became known as the "Common Word" statement. With interpretive creativity, the Muslim signatories to the Common Word statement may be regarded as having distilled these various significations of justice into the pithy commandment "Love God and your neighbor." In our fractious and fragile post–September 11 world, a "common word" must of necessity be a word that unites and creates common ground on the basis of shared beliefs and values. Monotheism is clearly one such shared belief among Muslims and Christians and the cornerstone of our relationship.

Conclusion

ʿAbduh's counsel that we must never denigrate each other's religion is particularly relevant in our troubled world, beset by sectarian controversy as it is. Our survey of both premodern and modern exegeses shows that through a faithful reading of these selective verses from the Qurʾān, we are able to retrieve a broad protocol for conducting respectful and fruitful interfaith and intra-faith conversations that are particularly appropriate for our time. Such mutual respect and affection can exist and continue to be nurtured through our common love for the Supreme Being, even though we may differ in our conceptualizations of him and address him by different names.

Notes

1. Muḥammad ʿAbduh says that the basic meaning of *tawḥīd* "is the belief that God is one in inalienable divinity." See his *Theology of Unity*, trans. Iṣḥāq Musāʿad and Kenneth Cragg (London: George Allen & Unwin, 1966), 29.
2. Al-Ṭabarī, *Tafsīr al-Ṭabarī* (Beirut: Dār al-kutub al-ʿilmiyya, 1997), 1:99. Translation mine.
3. Ibid.
4. Al-Bukhārī, *Ṣaḥīḥ*, ed. Qāsim al-Shammāʿī al-Rifāʿī (Beirut: Dār al-qalām, n.d.), "Kitāb al-Tawḥīd," 8:778, #2176.
5. Al-Ṭabarī, *Tafsīr*, 12:740–41.
6. Seyyed Hossein Nasr, ed., *The Study Quran: A New Translation and Commentary* (New York: HarperOne, 2015), 1578–79.
7. Al-Ṭabarī, *Tafsīr*, 12:742–43.
8. Nasr, *Study Quran*, 1580.

9. For exegeses of these epithets applied to Jesus in the Qur'ān, see Asma Afsaruddin, "The Messiah 'Isa, Son of Mary: Jesus in the Islamic Tradition," in *Nicholas of Cusa and Islam: Polemic and Dialogue in the Late Middle Ages*, ed. Ian Christopher Levy et al. (Leiden: Brill, 2014), 179–201.

10. Al-Ṭabarī, *Tafsīr*, 4:375.

11. Nasr, *Study Quran*, 1779. For Christian groups, often Monophysites accused of tritheism, see *Catholic Encyclopedia (1913)*, s.v. "Tritheists," by Henry Palmer Chapman, last modified March 21, 2015, https://en.wikisource.org/wiki/Catholic_Encyclopedia_(1913)/Tritheists.

12. Al-Ṭabarī, *Tafsīr*, 8:400.

13. Al-Qurṭubī, *Al-Jāmiʿ li-aḥkām al-Qurʾān*, ed. ʿAbd al-Razzāq al-Mahdī (Beirut: Dār al-kutub al-ʿarabī, 2001), 11:161.

14. Al-Ghazali, *The Jewels of the Qur'an: Al-Ghazali's Theory*, trans. Muhammad Abu al-Quasem (Kuala Lumpur: University of Malaya Press, 1977), 75–77.

15. Al-Tabarī, *Tafsīr*, 3:11–12.

16. Fakhr al-Dīn al-Rāzī, *Al-Tafsīr al-kabīr* (Beirut: Dār ihyāʾ al-turāth al-ʿarabī, 1999), 3:13–14.

17. *Encyclopaedia of Islam*, 2nd ed., s.v. "Muʿtazila," by D. Gimaret, accessed October 21, 2017, http://dx.doi.org/10.1163/1573-3912_islam_COM_0822.

18. Maḥmūd b. ʿUmar al-Zamakhsharī, *al-Kashshāf ʿan ḥaqāʾiq ghawāmiḍ al-tanzīl wa-ʿuyūn al-aqāwīl fi wujūh al-taʾwīl*, ed. ʿĀdil Aḥmad ʿAbd al-Wujūd and ʿAlī Muḥammad Muʿawwad (Riyād: Maktabat al-ʿUbaykān, 1998), 4:23–24.

19. Ibid., 24.

20. For a discussion of inclusivist and exclusivist understandings of this verse and of the term "Islam" itself, see Abdulaziz Sachedina, *The Islamic Roots of Democratic Pluralism* (Oxford: Oxford University Press, 2001), 38–40.

21. Muslim, *Ṣaḥīḥ* (Beirut: Dār Ibn Hazm, 1995), "Kitāb al-Īmān," 1:61, #46.

22. For a useful overview of these broad historical trends, see W. Montgomery Watt, *Islamic Political Thought* (Edinburgh: Edinburgh University Press, 1968), 54–63.

23. Muqātil b. Sulaymān, *Tafsīr Muqātil b. Sulaymān*, ed. ʿAbd Allāh Mahmūd Shihata (Beirut, 2002), 1:573.

24. Al-Tabarī, *Tafsīr*, 5:304–5.

25. Al-Zamakhsharī, *Kashshāf*, 2:385; Al-Rāzī, *Al-Tafsīr al-kabīr*, 5:108–11; and Ismāʿīl b. ʿUmar Ibn Kathīr, *Tafsir al-qurʾān al-ʿazīm* (Beirut: Dār al-Jīl, 1990), 2:156.

26. Rashīd Riḍā, *Tafsīr al-qurʾān al-hakīm* (Beirut, 1999), 7:548–49.

27. Muqātil, *Tafsīr*, 1:281.

28. Al-Tabarī, *Tafsīr*, 3:300, 302.

29. Ibid., 3:301–2.

30. Al-Zamakhsharī, *Kashshāf*, 1:567.

31. Ibid., 3:252.

The Complexity of Monotheism in Islam

A Christian Response to Asma Afsaruddin

SIDNEY GRIFFITH

The first article of Islamic faith, readily expressed in the *shahāda*, is "There is no god but the God." Muslim scholars have normally interpreted this confessional phrase in reference to pertinent passages in the Qur'ān, such as "Your God is one God (*ilāh wāḥid*), there is no God but He, *al-Raḥmān al-Raḥīm*" (al-Baqara [2]: 163 passim). This affirmation is regularly expressed in Islamic theology via the shorthand Arabic term *al-tawḥīd*, "to confess one [God]," which is not actually found in the Qur'ān. It is often interpreted in English to mean simply the profession of monotheism. Asma Afsaruddin has provided us with a succinct presentation of Islamic monotheism as we find it grounded in key passages in the Qur'ān, along with passages that bespeak the Qur'ān's criticisms of contemporary Christian statements, mostly about Jesus, that are taken to imperil or even to contradict *al-tawḥīd*. Our task is to study together, we Muslims and Christians, the interpretation of these passages with a view to discerning how we might find some common ground in them even as we identify points of disagreement that we might in turn agree to live with once we understand the rationale behind them.

Reading the selected Qur'ān passages that commend *al-tawḥīd* along with Afsaruddin's discussion of them makes it clear, as she points out, that in the Qur'ān's view, the besetting sin of the unbelievers would be the ungrateful rejection (*kufr*) of monotheism by alleging that God has taken offspring or by assigning associates or partners (*ishrāk* > *al-shirk*) to the one God, seemingly thereby to espouse what one might call polytheism. In the Qur'ān, *al-mushrikūn* seem to this reader almost exclusively to be people who "choose to worship others besides God as rivals (*andād*) to Him, loving them with the love due to God" (al-Baqara [2]:165, Abdel Haleem translation). And that is why the Qur'ān critiques what Christians say about Jesus the Messiah, because what they say about him seems to the Qur'ān to associate the Christians with those who go beyond the bounds in their religion and with the people who went astray in the past (see al-Nisā' [4]:171;

al-Mā'ida [5]:77)—that is to say, the Christians, in effect, make the same mistake as did the ancient scripture-less *mushrikūn*. To make the point, the Qur'ān states in a variety of ways that God has no offspring and no partner (for example, in al-Isrā' [17]:110–11), rhetorically emphasizing it in this verse: "How would He have a son (*walad*)? He has had no female companion *(ṣāḥiba)*" (al-An'ām [6]:101; see also al-Jinn [72]:3).

As it turns out, however, there is considerable complexity in the matter, beyond just the rejection of polytheism, both in the Islamic understanding of *al-tawḥīd*, which is usually taken by Muslim scholars to exclude not only polytheism but all plurality, even notional plurality in reference to God, and in seemingly implied plurality in God talk, including, of course, the Christian understanding of how the one God may in some ways be thought to be treble in being one (see the commentators on Sūrat al-Ikhlāṣ [112]). The history of Islamic thought is replete with complex discussions of how one might reasonably affirm the truthfulness of the multiple divine names and adjectives found describing him in the Qur'ān without affirming any multiplicity in God's being, as the grammatical understanding of the import of these same Arabic names and descriptions *(ṣifāt)* could be taken to imply. Similarly, the evidently anthropomorphic language in reference to God in the Qur'ān, being God's own words, must in some ways also be affirmed as true, and in accord with the logical requirements of the usual understanding of *al-tawḥīd* in Islamic thought, it must also be understood not to bespeak even the possibility of any corporality or composition in connection with the proper understanding of the one God. Afsaruddin's essay opens the door and calls for further discussion of the multiple complexities evident in the ideas of Muslim scholars of various schools of thought concerning the import of monotheism in the Qur'ān and in Islam, extending as it does well beyond just the rejection of any form of polytheism. Then there is the tantalizing issue of the meaning of the predication of "one" itself, be it expressed in terms of *wāḥid* or *aḥad*; much discussion, both Muslim and Christian, has attended this question.

Given the brevity of response to Afsaruddin's paper, I would like to focus most of my attention on passages she cites from the Qur'ān that critique and correct, from its own distinctive point of view, what the Christians within the Qur'ān's purview had to say about Jesus the Messiah and about God. And I would like to say at the outset that, in my view, the Qur'ān's major problem with the Christians is what they have customarily said about Jesus; it is at the root of what is wrong in the Qur'ān's view with what Christians further say about God. And what the Christians (*al-naṣārā*) say about Jesus, according to the Qur'ān, is principally that "the Messiah is the son of God; that is what they say with their lips, which is tantamount to what those had to say who earlier ungratefully disbelieved. May God fight against them; how they have been made to lie!" (al-Tawba [9]:30; see also [9]:29).

As I see it, there are two stages in the Qur'ān's response to Christian claims about Jesus the Messiah. In the Meccan period of Muḥammad's career, the

Qur'ān counters the customary Christian affirmation of Jesus the Messiah as the Son of God by proclaiming him actually to be one of God's messengers and prophets, assigning him the penultimate place in the series of God's messengers and prophets, who is said then to have foretold the coming of Muḥammad (al-Aḥzāb [33]:40), who would be "the seal of the prophets" (al-Ṣaff [61]:6). The Qur'ān's distinctive and determinative prophetology simultaneously then incorporated Jesus the Messiah and his career among the Sons of Israel within its own vision of prophetic history,[1] and in the process, it thereby also effectively removed him from the revelatory parameters within which the Christians in the Qur'ānic milieu perceived him to be the Son of God and the savior of mankind by his passion, death, and resurrection.

In the Medinan phase of Muḥammad's career, when he became more evidently engaged in controversy with Christians in his milieu, the Qur'ān simultaneously and more explicitly voiced its critique of how the Christians within its purview customarily spoke about Jesus and in the process offered a fairly comprehensive statement of what we might call its own "Christology," phrased in the unmistakable terms of its own distinctive prophetology:

> O Scripture People, do not exaggerate in your religion; and do not say anything but the truth about God. The Messiah, Jesus, the son of Mary, is the Messenger of God and His word that He cast into Mary, and a spirit from Him. So believe in God and His Messengers, and do not say "three"; stop it; it is better for you. God is but a single God. Praised be He that He should have a son; His is what is in the heavens and what is on earth. Suffice it to rely on God. (al-Nisā' [4]:171)

In another place, the Qur'ān rhetorically censures what it construes to be the wrongheadedness of Christian teaching about the Messiah:

> They have disbelieved who say, "God is the Messiah, the son of Mary." The Messiah said, "O sons of Israel, worship God, my Lord and your Lord. Whoever accords God associates, God has forbidden the Garden to him; his abode is the Fire and there are none to help the wrong-doers." They have disbelieved who say, "God is one of three" (*thālith thalāthatin*); there is only one God. If they do not stop what they are saying a sore punishment will touch those of them who disbelieve. (al-Mā'ida [5]:72–73)

One sees in these two passages the only explicit allusions to the Christian doctrine of the Trinity to be found in the Qur'ān, and in both places, it seems clear that the topic arises in connection with what the local Christians would have had to say about Jesus the Messiah. In the first instance, the Qur'ān rejects any reason to "say, 'three,'" because the very terms (*God*, "God's word," and "a spirit from him") in which Christians in the Qur'ān's milieu would customarily have spoken of "three" are here personified as names not of the one God but, in accordance with the Qur'ān's own distinctive prophetology, as prophetic titles of Jesus the Messiah. In his very person as God's messenger, he is a word (*kalimah*) that God announced to Mary (Āl 'Imrān [3]:45), and he is a spirit (*rūḥ*) God breathed into her (al-Anbiyā' [21]:91; al-Taḥrīm [66]:12). In the second instance, the phrase *thālith thalāthatin*, as I see it, is best understood as a rendering of the title or the epithet of Jesus the Messiah, "the one of three," or "the treble one," as he was customarily called by local Christians within the Qur'ān's milieu.[2] The Qur'ān rejects anyone saying "God is the Messiah," or "God is one of three," as an obvious blasphemy, even a reductio ad absurdum, and therein lays the rejection's intended rhetorical power. But in fact, no theologically aware, contemporary Christians would have made such a statement; it would imply that God is only Jesus, the Treble One. The Qur'ān seems to suggest as much, arguing that what the Christians actually do say about Jesus—that is, that he is God the Word incarnate—might nevertheless imply the very absurdity that, in its view, they would not want to admit.

As Afsaruddin points out, the Qur'ān has a high regard for Mary, the mother of Jesus the Messiah, reflecting its esteem for her especially in its reminiscences of the Gospel and traditional accounts of Jesus's birth (Maryam [19]:16–36; Āl 'Imrān [3]:36–59). But even in this connection, the Qur'ān records its warning against exaggeration: "[Remember] when God said, 'O Jesus, son of Mary, did you tell people, "Take me and my mother as two gods along with God?"'" (al-Mā'ida [5]:116). Some Muslim and non-Muslim commentators over the centuries, taking this verse together with their understanding of the expression *thālith thalāthatin* in verse 73 of the same sūra, have proposed the unlikely theory that for the local Christians, their Trinity was God, Mary, and Jesus, and not the Father, Son, and Holy Spirit of mainline Christianity. Such an interpretation, in my view, simply misconstrues the evidence. Here is not the place to discuss the historical question about the identity of the Christian communities that would have been known in the milieu of the Ḥijāz in Muḥammad's day. In my view, it makes the best sense to think that the Qur'ān was well aware of what mainline seventh-century Christians in the Aramaic and Arabic-speaking environs of Arabia—the so-called Melkites, Jacobites, and Nestorians—customarily thought and said about Jesus the Messiah, namely, that he is the Son of God.[3] I think the Qur'ān disapproved of what they said about him on the grounds that from the perspective of Qur'ānic prophetology, what the Christians said and thought about Jesus both camouflaged the Qur'ānic truth about him and inevitably led them to talk of "three." That is, speaking of the one God as Father, Son, and Holy Spirit, from the Qur'ān's perspective, offends against the commitment to *al-tawḥīd*. What is more, given the view that the Qur'ān's intention was both to reprove and to correct the Christians in its audience and to call them to speak the truth from its perspective about Jesus the Messiah and about the one God, the reader must recognize that its rhetoric of persuasion included many elocutionary devices, including irony, the deployment of reductio ad absurdum, and a counter-discourse in its own Qur'ānic terms. Interreligious controversy was at the heart of the matter.

As Afsaruddin notes, the Qur'ān's teaching on *al-tawḥīd* is summed up in Sūrat al-Ikhlāṣ, especially in its statement about the one God: "He has not begotten, nor has He been begotten; He has none as an equal" ([112]:3–4). Some non-Muslim scholars, and Angelika Neuwirth in particular, see a counterpoint in these verses to statements in the Christian Niceno-Constantinopolitan Creed, which would have been commonly recited in the Christian liturgies of the seventh century CE.[4] In this connection, it is interesting for our Christian-Muslim conversations in the twenty-first century also to take cognizance of a little-noticed but fortuitous Christian statement about the one God proclaimed in a Western church council. In its rejection of the Trinitarian thought of Joachim of Fiore (ca. 1135–1202), the Fourth Lateran Council in 1215, without any allusion to Islamic thought, declared of God's nature: "That reality [i.e., the divine nature] is neither begetting, nor begotten, nor processing, but it is the Father, who begets, and the Son, who is begotten, and the Holy Spirit, who proceeds; distinctions are in the persons, oneness in the nature."[5] The conciliar statement unawares echoes the line of reasoning taken by many Arabic-speaking Christian thinkers in the days of their now mostly forgotten conversations with Muslim *mutakallimūn* and philosophers in Baghdad and Cairo about Christian monotheism. And as Professor Afsaruddin reminds us, the discussion raises the issue of God's universality, nowadays often expressed in the question, Do Muslims and Christians worship the same God?

The scriptures—the Torah, the Gospel in the Gospels, and the Qur'ān—all identify the one God of whom they speak as the God of Abraham, (Ishmael) Isaac, and Jacob (Exod. 3:6; Matt. 22:31–32; al-Baqarah [2]:133, 136, 140). On this scriptural basis, Muslims and Christians can be said to worship the same God. Christians further believe on scriptural authority that the one God of Abraham, Isaac, and Jacob is Father, Son, and Holy Spirit. (See, for example, Mark 1:9–11; John 1:1–18; and 1 Cor. 8:4–6; other verses could be cited as well.) These same passages testify to Christian faith in Jesus the Messiah as Lord, indeed the Son of the Living God (Matt. 16:16), a confession that, according to the Qur'ān, is a step too far. Professor Afsaruddin quotes in this connection the view that the Qur'ān in these verses (al-Nisā' 4:171; al-Mā'ida [5]:72–73) "does not oppose the various forms of orthodox Trinitarian doctrines that have prevailed for most of Christian history. Rather, it appears to oppose crude misunderstandings of it that would lead one to believe that there are three gods instead of one." This position is attractive from the point of view of interfaith relations, but none of the efforts so far historically to support it have carried much conviction. The problem is that Trinitarian faith is for Christians not just a theologoumenon; it is, in the Christian view, a scriptural revelation about the nature of the one God.

Afsaruddin also cites the much-quoted passage, "Say, O People of the Book, let us come to a common word (*kalimāt sawā'*) between us and you, that we will worship only the one God and not ascribe any partner to Him" (Āl ʿImrān [3]:64). I have a problem with translating the term *sawāʾ* with the adjective "common" in this context, albeit that it is apt in its denotation. In its connotation, however, it suggests something on the order of an invitation to the "People of the Book" to come to a "consensual" or "agreed upon" statement that might be taken to suggest overlooking or bracketing the differences, whereas in its Qurʾānic context (Āl ʿImrān [3]:65–70) it seems to mean something on the order of the "right" or "correct" or "equable" thing to say, meaning what in fact the Qurʾān actually says. So, I wonder if the right interpretation of the verse is not more like this: "Say, O people of the Book, come to a right word between us."

One of the features of interreligious dialogue is that the more it promotes clear, mutual understanding and a measure of rapprochement between those who engage in it, the more it also highlights the differences between them. Christians and Muslims share much in what they say about Jesus the Messiah and about the one God of Abraham, Isaac, Ishmael, Jacob, and the tribes. The challenge to Christians is to discuss how one might reasonably affirm that Jesus the Messiah is the Son of God, thereby also affirming that the one God is Father, Son, and Holy Spirit, just as the challenge to Muslims is still to discuss how one might reasonably affirm the truth of the divine names in affirming that God is one in an understanding that also affirms the strict requirements of *al-tawḥīd*. It is not surprising then that in the culture of the interreligious *majālis* of Baghdad in the tenth century CE, both the Muslim philosopher Abū Naṣr Muḥammad al-Fārābī (870–950) and his Christian student Abū Zakariyyah Yaḥyā ibn ʿAdī (893–974) felt the need to write competing treatises on what it means to say that an entity is "one," *al-tawḥīd*. It remains the challenge here in our own *majlis*.

In this connection, perhaps it may be helpful from a Christian point of view to hear the testimony of the Nestorian Metropolitan Elias of Nisibis (975–1046), herewith appended, who argued in the *majlis* of a Muslim emir in Buyid times that Christians must be considered to be strict monotheists. The reader will notice the virtual pastiche of terms and concepts familiar from Islamic *kalām* texts of the time, woven into the wording of the creed that Mar Elias submitted to the emir in his own hand.

Appendix

Confession of Faith

Elias bar Shīnāyā, Metropolitan of Nisibis (975–1046)
Submitted to the vizir, Abū l-Qāsim al-Ḥusayn ibn ʾAlī al-Maghribī (d. 1027), in July 1026 CE

So says Iliyyā, the Metropolitan of Nisibis:

We, the monotheist (*al-muwaḥḥidīn*) company of Christians (*Naṣārā*) believe in one Lord, there being no God but He alone (al-Baqara [2]:163). He has no associate (al-Anʿām [6]:163) in eternity; there is none like Him in identity (*dhātiyyah*); and there is no match (*naẓīr*) for Him in lordship. He has no companion (*ṣāḥib*) to come to His aid, nor is there any adversary who would oppose Him, nor a peer who would contend with Him. He is without a body, non-composite, nor is He in combination with another, He is impalpable, not situated in space or time, not divisible into parts, and He is unchangeable. So He does not occupy space, nor does He accept an accident; no place contains Him, nor does time enclose Him. He is preexistent, without beginning and abiding without end. He is hidden in His essence; evident in His deeds. He is unique in power, perfection, and solitary in majesty and splendor. He is the source of beneficence, the well-spring of wisdom. He is the originator of everything from nothing, the producer of all existent beings without any [preexisting] material, the maker of creatures at His command, and the One who brings creation into being by His own will. He knows things before their coming to be; He knows secrets before their concealment. He is living, immortal, enduring; He will not pass away, He is strong, He will not change, He is powerful, He will not weaken. He is close-by everyone; He answers anyone who calls upon Him; He goes to the aid of anyone who hopes in Him. He is a sufficient protector for anyone who puts his trust in Him. He is a refuge for anyone who has recourse to Him. He makes blessings last when they are received with thanks (*shukr*); He puts an end to them when they are received with ingratitude (*kufr*). He offers help to the good and He responds to the obedient. He is an enemy of the obstinate, accepting of the penitent, and a helper of those who appeal for help. He is a merciful God, a noble Lord, a wise Creator. He created this world when He wished and as He wished, and He will destroy it when He wants and as He wants. Then He will allow the awakening and the resurrection, and He will revivify those who are in the graves. He will recompense the good by bringing them into happiness, and the bad by putting them eternally in Gehenna. He is one (*wāḥid*) God, one Creator, one Lord, one to be worshipped. There is no God before Him, nor after Him, and no Creator but He, no Lord other than He, and there is no one to be worshipped but He.

We believe that the essence of this Lord, whose descriptive attributes (*awṣāf*) these are (hallowed be His Names), along with His speaking (*nuṭq*) and His life (*ḥayat*), I mean his Word (*kalimah*) and His Spirit (*rūḥ*) are one being/substance (*jawhar*) in three hypostases (*aqānīm*), Father, and Son, and Holy Spirit. To Him, may He be glorified, we declare ourselves acquitted of anyone who believes that this being/substance is like created substances, that these three hypostases are three beings/substances, or that they are three different or equal gods, or three combined bodies, three parts, three opposing accidents, three composite powers, or anything else that could be determined to be positing association (*al-shirk*), apportionment, or division into parts. We also declare ourselves acquitted of anyone who believes that the Creator's "speaking" (*nuṭq*), exalted be He, and His "life" (*ḥayat*), I mean His Word (*kalimah*) and His Spirit (*rūḥ*) are two accidents, or two powers, like the speaking of creatures, and their life. [We also declare ourselves quit] of everyone who believes that this one God has a match (*naẓīr*), or an adversary, or who believes that He is a compound or composite body. [We also declare ourselves quit] of everyone who believes that He occupies space or receives accidents; from everyone who believes that He moves from place to place, or that He is in one direction rather than another, or that He has been seen or will be seen. [We also declare ourselves quit] of everyone who believes that He has married or will marry, has sired anyone or will sire anyone, or that He has taken a female consort. [We also declare ourselves quit] of everyone who believes that He can create a god like Himself, or perform a deed in which there is anything abominable or bad. [We also declare ourselves quit] of everyone who believes that He has a beginning or an ending, and that He created creatures from some preexisting element or material. [We also declare ourselves quit] of everyone who believes that He does not know things before their coming to be, or that He is a nature that manages the world by means of its own [innate] "nature" (*ṭab'*). [We also declare ourselves quit] of everyone who denies prophecy, the appearance of "signs" (*āyāt*) at the hands of the prophets and the righteous Messengers. [We also declare ourselves quit] of everyone who believes that the World is eternal, unoriginated, who denies the resurrection, the sending forth [from the graves], and the hereafter.

So any Christian who believes that our *madhhāb* endorses any of these *madhāhib*, which I have declared ourselves to be quit of, or that we have any scope for believing some of them, let him dispute with me about it.[6]

Notes

In this chapter, Qur'ān translations are the author's own.

1. For more on my ideas about this distinctive concept of "prophetology," see Sidney H. Griffith, "The 'Sunna of Our Messengers': The Qur'ān's Paradigm for Messengers and

Prophets; a Reading of *Sūrat ash-Shuʿarāʾ* (26)," in *Qurʾānic Studies Today*, ed. Angelika Neuwirth and Michael A. Sells (New York: Routledge, 2016), 207–23.

2. On this interpretation of the Qurʾānic phrase, see Sidney H. Griffith, "Syriacisms in the Arabic Qurʾān: Who Were 'Those Who Said, "Allāh Is Third of Three,"' according to *al-Māʾidah 73*?" in *A Word Fitly Spoken: Studies in Mediaeval Exegesis of the Hebrew Bible and the Qurʾān*, ed. Meir M. Bar-Asher, Simon Hopḳins, Śarah Sṭrumzah, and Bruno Ḳi'ezah (Jerusalem: Ben-Zvi Institute, 2007), 83–110; reprinted in Ibn Warraq, ed., *Christmas in the Koran: Luxenberg, Syriac, and the Near Eastern and Judeo-Christian Background of Islam* (Amherst, NY: Prometheus Books, 2014), 119–44.

3. See Sidney H. Griffith, "The Qur'ān's 'Nazarenes' and Other Late Antique Christians: Arabic-Speaking 'Gospel People' in Qur'ānic Perspective," in *Christsein in der islamischen Welt: Festschrift für Martin Tamcke zum 60. Geburtstag*, ed. Sidney H. Griffith and Sven Grebenstein (Wiesbaden: Harrassowitz Verlag, 2015), 81–106.

4. See Angelika Neuwirth, *Der Koran als Text der Spätantike: Ein europäischer Zugang* (Berlin: Verlag der Weltreligionen im Insel Verlag, 2010), 761–68.

5. Heinrich Denziger, *Kompendium der Glaubensbekenntnisse und kirchlichen Lehrentscheidungen*, 40th ed., trans. Peter Hüntermann (Freiburg: Herfer, 2005), 803–8.

6. Translated by Sidney H. Griffith from the Arabic text published in Louis Cheikho and Elie Batarekh, eds., *Trois traités de polémique et de théologie chrétiennes* (Beyrouth: Imprimerie Catholique, 1923), 51–52. The Arabic text was previously published in *Al-Machriq* 20 (1922): 270–72.

Texts from the Qurʾān and Ḥadīth

Al-Fātiḥa (1):1–7

1 In the name of God, the Beneficent, the Merciful.
2 Praise be to God, Lord of the Worlds, 3 The Beneficent, the Merciful. 4 Master of
the Day of Judgment, 5 You (alone) we worship; You (alone) we ask for help.
6 Show us the straight path, 7 The path of those whom You have favored; Not the
(path) of those who earn Your anger nor of those who go astray.

Al-Baqara (2):115

To God belong the East and the West, and wherever you turn, there is God's Countenance. Lo! God is All-Embracing, All-Knowing.

Al-Baqara (2):255

God! There is no God but Him, the Alive, the Eternal. Neither slumber nor sleep overtake Him. To Him belongs whatsoever is in the heavens and whatsoever is in the earth. Who is he that intercedes with Him except by His leave? He knows that which is in front of them and that which is behind them, while they encompass nothing of His knowledge except what He allows. His throne includes the heavens and the earth, and He is never weary of preserving them. He is the Sublime, the Tremendous.

Āl ʿImrān (3):64

Say: O People of the Book! Come to a common word between us and you: that we shall worship none but God, and that we shall ascribe no partner to Him, and that none of us shall take others for lords beside God. And if they turn away, then say: Bear witness that we are they who have surrendered to Him.

Al-Nisāʾ (4):48

Lo! God forgives not that a partner should be ascribed to Him. He forgives (all) except that to whom He will. Whosoever ascribes partners to God has indeed invented a tremendous sin.

Al-Nisāʾ (4):171

O People of the Scripture! Do not exaggerate in your religion nor utter anything concerning God except the truth. The Messiah, Jesus son of Mary, was only a messenger of God, and His word which He conveyed to Mary, and a spirit from Him. So believe in God and His messengers, and do not say "Three"—Cease! (it is) better for you!—God is only One God. Far is it removed from His Transcendent Majesty that He should have a son. His is all that is in the heavens and all that is in the earth. And God is sufficient as Defender.

Al-Anʿām (6):99–108

[99]He it is Who sends down water from the sky, and therewith We bring forth buds of every kind; We bring forth the green blade from which We bring forth the thick-clustered grain; and from the date-palm, from the pollen thereof, spring pendant bunches; and (We bring forth) gardens of grapes, and the olive and the pomegranate, alike and unlike. Look upon the fruit thereof, when they bear fruit, and upon its ripening. Lo! herein verily are portents for a people who believe. [100]Yet they ascribe as partners to Him the jinn, although He did create them, and impute falsely, without knowledge, sons and daughters to Him. Glorified be He and High Exalted above (all) that they ascribe (to Him). [101]The Originator of the heavens and the earth! How can He have a child, when there is for Him no consort, when He created all things and is Aware of all things? [102]Such is God, your Lord. There is no God save Him, the Creator of all things, so worship Him. And He takes care of all things. [103]Vision does not comprehend Him, but He comprehends (all) vision. He is the Subtle, the Aware. [104]Proofs have come to you from

your Lord, so whoever sees, it is for his own good, and whoever is blind is blind to his own hurt. And I am not a keeper over you. [105]Thus do We display Our revelations that they may say (to You, Muhammad): "You have studied," and that We may make (it) clear for people who have knowledge. [106]Follow that which is inspired in You from thy Lord; there is no God save Him; and turn away from the idolaters. [107]Had God willed, they had not been idolatrous. We have not set You as a keeper over them, nor art You responsible for them. [108]Revile not those to whom they pray beside God lest they wrongfully revile God through ignorance. Thus to every nation have We made their deed seem fair. Then to their Lord is their return, and He will tell them what they used to do.

Al-Isrā᾽ (17):110–11

[110]Say (to humankind): Cry to God, or cry to the Beneficent, to whichsoever you cry (it is the same). His are the most beautiful names. And You (Muhammad), be not loud-voiced in your worship nor yet silent therein, but follow a way between. [111]And say: Praise be to God, Who has not taken to Himself a son, and Who has no partner in the Sovereignty, nor has He any protecting friend through dependence. And magnify Him with all magnificence.

Maryam (19):34–50

[34]Such was Jesus, son of Mary: (this is) a statement of the truth concerning which they doubt. [35]It does not befit (the Majesty of) God that He should take to Himself a son. Glory be to Him! When He decrees a thing, He says to it only: Be! and it is. [36]And lo! God is my Lord and your Lord. So serve Him. That is the right path. [37]The sects among them differ: but woe to the disbelievers from the meeting of an awful Day. [38]See and hear them on the Day they come to Us! yet the evil-doers are to-day in error manifest. [39]And warn them of the Day of anguish when the case hath been decided. Now they are in a state of carelessness, and they believe not. [40]Lo! We, only We, inherit the earth and all who are thereon, and to Us they are returned. [41]And make mention (O Muhammad) in the Scripture of Abraham. Lo! he was a saint, a prophet. [42]When he said to his father: O my father! Why did you worship that which does not hear nor see, nor can in anything avail You? [43]O my father! Lo! there has come to me of knowledge that which did not come to You. So follow me, and I will lead You on a right path. [44]O my father! Do not serve the devil. Lo! the devil is a rebel toward the Beneficent. [45]O my father! Lo! I fear lest a punishment from the Beneficent overtake you so that you become a comrade of the devil. [46]He said: Do you reject my gods, O Abraham? If you do not cease, I shall surely stone you. Depart from me a long while! [47]He said: Peace

be to You! I shall ask forgiveness of my Lord for you. Lo! He was ever gracious to me. [48]I shall withdraw from you and that to which you pray beside God, and I shall pray to my Lord. It may be that, in prayer to my Lord, I shall not be unblessed.
[49]So, when he had withdrawn from them and that which they were worshipping beside God, We gave him Isaac and Jacob. Each of them We made a prophet. [50]And we gave them of Our mercy, and assigned to them a high and true renown.

Ṭā-Hā (20):9–14

[9]Has there come to you the story of Moses? [10]When he saw a fire, he said to his people: Wait! I see a fire afar off. Perhaps I may bring you an ember from it or find guidance at the fire. [11]And when he reached it, he was called by name: "O Moses! [12]Indeed! I, truly I, am your Lord, So take off your shoes, for indeed you are in the holy valley of Tuwa. [13]And I have chosen you, so listen to that which is revealed. [14]Indeed! I, even I, am God. There is no God other than Me. So serve Me and perform prayer for My remembrance.

Al-Muʾminūn (23):91

God has not chosen any son, nor is there any god along with Him; otherwise each god would have assuredly championed that which he created, and some of them would assuredly have overcome others. Glorified be God above all that they allege.

Al-Furqān (25):1–3

[1]Blessed is He Who has revealed to His servant the Criterion (of right and wrong), that he may be a warner to humanity. [2]He to Whom belongs the sovereignty of the heavens and the earth, He has chosen no son nor has He any partner in the sovereignty. He has created everything and hs meted out for it a measure.
[3]Yet they choose beside Him other gods who create nothing but are themselves created, and possess no ability to harm or help themselves, nor power over death or life or resurrection.

Al-Ikhlāṣ (112): 1–4

[1]Say: He is God, the One! [2]God, the Everlasting! [3]He begets not nor was begotten. [4]And there is none comparable to Him.

Ḥadīths[1]

. . . Mu'adh bin Jabal related that the Prophet, peace and blessings be upon him, said, "O Mu'adh! Do you know what God's claim upon His servants is?" I said, "God and His messenger know best." The Prophet said, "To worship Him Alone and to join none in worship with Him. Do you know what their claim upon Him is?" I replied, "God and His messenger know best." The Prophet said, "Not to punish them (if they do so)." [*Ṣaḥīḥ al-Bukhārī*: "Book on God's Unity;" *Ṣaḥīḥ Muslim*: "Book on Faith"]

. . . Ibn 'Abbas related that the Prophet, peace and blessings be upon him, used to say, "I seek refuge by means of Your might—there is no god but You, the One Who does not perish even though the jinn and human beings do." [*Ṣaḥīḥ al-Bukhārī*: "Book on God's Unity"]

. . . According to Abu Sa'id al-Khudri, a man heard another man reciting "Say, God He is one" repeatedly. When morning came he came to the Prophet, peace and blessings be upon him, and mentioned that to him while appearing to belittle it. The Messenger of God, peace and blessings be upon him, said, "By the One in Whose hand is my soul, that [verse] equals a third of the Qur'ān." [*Ṣaḥīḥ al-Bukhārī*: "Book on God's Unity"]

. . . Uthman related, "I heard the Messenger of God, peace and blessings be upon him say, 'Whoever dies while acknowledging that there is no god but God will enter heaven.'" [*Ṣaḥīḥ Muslim*: "Book on Faith"]

. . . 'Ubada ibn al-Ṣāmit said, "The Messenger of God, peace and blessings be upon him said, 'Whoever says: I bear witness that there is no god but the one God Who has no partner, that Muḥammad is His servant and His messenger, that Jesus is the servant of God and the son of His bondmaid and His word that He cast into Mary and a spirit from Him, and that Heaven is real and that the Fire is real—God will cause him to enter [heaven] through any one of the eight gates of Paradise that he wishes.'" [*Ṣaḥīḥ Muslim*: "Book on Faith"]

Note

1. Ḥadīth translations have been supplied by members of the seminar.

PART III

Grappling with the Unity Question in the Elaboration of Christian Doctrine

The One and the Three in Christian Worship and Doctrine

Engaging with the Question of Divine Unity in the Elaboration of Christian Doctrine

CHRISTOPH SCHWÖBEL

Christian discourse about the Father, the Son, and the Spirit has from the early church onward played a crucial role in Christian worship, in debates about the content and the constitution of Christian faith within the Christian churches, and in attempts to justify Christian beliefs and practices to those outside the Christian communities. Although one can hardly question the centrality of discourse about the triune God, it has rarely been regarded as something that could be taken for granted. Rather, from the beginning, Trinitarian discourse and Trinitarian patterns of worship required doctrinal elucidation—for catechetical purposes, for theological debate, and in the apologetic endeavors of the Christian communities.

While the conciliar creeds of the fourth century have provided for a long time a framework for confessing the Christian faith in the context of worship, including the proclamation of Christian message and the celebration of the sacraments, there has rarely been a time when the doctrinal implications of the creeds have not been passionately and controversially discussed. The explicit attention given to Trinitarian matters has varied over the centuries, and times of relative Trinitarian forgetfulness have been succeeded by times of emphatic revivals of the doctrine of the Trinity; implicitly it has served, often in spite of rather divergent interpretations, as a bond of unity between a large number of the Christian churches, if not in the form of doctrinal agreement, then in forms of the compatibility of important structures of worship in the rich diversity of the liturgical life of the churches. The Trinity is one of the themes in which in some way the totality of Christian faith and life seems to be under discussion, and theological debates, even those going on today, usually engage with the whole history of Trinitarian debates in the churches, often using labels—both programmatically and critically—that refer to historic debates such as "Nicene," "Arian," "Cappadocian," and "Augustinian."

In view of the wealth, complexity, and often intellectual sophistication of the historic developments and debates, I can point to only some of the major stages of the development and report on some of the issues under discussion in order to try, by clarifying some of the stages in the conversations within Christian theology, to help build bridges of analogical understanding and dialogical exchange with Muslim traditions of worship and reflection. If understanding is always a matter of understanding differences, it is to be kept in mind that the differences we encounter here are not only differences *between* our different faith traditions but also differences *within* our respective faith traditions. They have their significance in that these differences have a referential dimension. They claim to be differences not only between different traditions but between traditions as they refer to God whom both our traditions understand as the source and origin of the life and meaning of our respective traditions as well as the being and meaning of everything. No wonder that these differences matter.

The Functions of Trinitarian Discourse

Christian Trinitarian discourse has its primary functions in expressing the identity of the God Christians worship, in affirming the unity and comprehensiveness of divine action, in relating divine action and divine being, and in safeguarding Christian worship and doctrine against idolatry.

The primary setting on Trinitarian discourse is the communal worship of the Christian churches. In many Christian churches, worship begins with the invocation of the triune name of God. Worship is conducted by gathering the congregation "in the name of God, the Father, the Son and the Holy Spirit," and it concludes with being sent into the world with the blessing of the triune God, often by using the Aaronic blessing (Num. 6:24–26) in which the threefold repetition of "the Lord" is interpreted by Christians as an invocation of the Trinity. Trinitarian speech not only frames Christian worship according to the rhythm of gathering and sending; it also punctuates the liturgy at various places (e.g., "Glory be to Father, the Son, and the Holy Ghost"; the invocation of the Trinitarian persons in the liturgy of the Eucharist). Most prayers are concluded by a Trinitarian formula.

The liturgical use of Trinitarian discourse underlines the significance of the Trinity as the expression of the triune divine name. Addressing God in worship and being addressed in the name of God by scripture being read, the proclamation of the Gospel, and the celebration of the sacraments make the question of the identity of God crucial for the religious life of Christians. In this sense, the triune name is understood as the proper name of God, continuing and modifying the disclosure of the name of God in Israel (Exod. 3:14). Trinitarian reflection has from the beginning the function of prescribing and explaining the proper form of Christian worship.

With the invocation of the triune name of God, the whole range of God's action is represented from the very beginning to the ultimate end. Trinitarian discourse spans the whole of the divine economy, the whole of God's relationship to what is not God, and formulates its primordial ground and eschatological goal. Trinitarian discourse answers in this way to the question of how the unity of the whole of the differentiated structure of God's dealings with the world is to be understood. The answer to the question of how creation, reconciliation/redemption, and the eschatological consummation hang together is framed by Trinitarian discourse. What is at stake here is the unity of the story that is told of the divine economy and of which Christian believers believe themselves to be part, just as everything that exists in the present, past, and future. The structure and unity of the divine economy is usually expressed in the creeds that, in their classical form, present this unity through a Trinitarian structure of the dramatic story narrated and alluded to in their phrases.

Trinitarian reflection is in this way concerned with grasping the unity in the different forms of God's action and interaction with the world. How is the redemption promised in Christ related to creation, what do Christians mean when they speak of both "creation" and "new creation," what is the goal to which God leads the story of creation, and how does God overcome the resistances that stand in the way of the realization of God's purpose?

When this unity is expressed in Trinitarian form, the unity and comprehensiveness of divine action is located in the being of the triune God. Everything God does and the way God does it are understood as rooted in how God *is* in God's Trinitarian being. To answer these questions, the meaning of God's action in time must be related to God's being, which—in a sense to be grasped—transcends the time of creation by being its beginning and its end. Is there a way of rooting God's actions (and passion?) in time (in classical terminology: the *missions*) in a pattern of divine activity in eternity (in classical terminology: the *processions*)? Every form of action (and passion) logically includes relations so that the questions concerning God's relations to what is not God raises the question whether the relations of God to what is not God are somehow grounded in relations within God. This question is closely related to the understanding of divine being. If God becomes relational only as God relates to what is not God, then the external relations contribute to the being of God. What is not God is then in some way constitutive of what God is. But how can that be, if God is truly God in the sense of being categorially distinguished (for instance, as the Creator) from what is not God (the creation)? To avoid suggesting that God is somehow constituted by what God creates, do we have to assume eternal relations in God? And if so, what are the terms of these relations in the one being of God? With these questions, we are already involved in the most foundational questions of the doctrine of the Trinity.

It is one of the intrinsic concerns of Christian faith that in worshipping the triune God, Christians do not commit idolatry by worshipping an entity that is not God. The question of idolatry is first raised with regard to one's own religious practice. How can Christians avoid idolatry when they call on Jesus Christ in prayer or pray "come Creator Spirit"? This is the question that fuels all reflections on Trinitarian discourse, and it is connected to the radical critique of being ultimately concerned with something that is not ultimate, which, in our time, may not only be other religious "deities" but also the "deities" that are worshipped in modern quasi-religions—for example, "the market," "the nation," or even "our religion." Trinitarian discourse is therefore for Christian faith the radical critique of all claims to divinity apart from the one God, the Father, the Son, and the Spirit.

The Roots of Trinitarian Discourse

Christian faith develops on the foundations of Israel's monotheism. Like Judaism, Christianity is committed to the monotheistic principle, which is grounded in the self-identification of God as the one who liberated Israel from slavery in Egypt and is connected to the explicit prohibition to fashion a graven image and to worship anything that is created.[1] The principle includes that God shall be loved with all dimensions of human being in all situations, and this commitment shall be handed on to the next generation.[2] Israel's monotheism is both an "integrative monotheism" and a "differentiated monotheism," embracing various relations of God to creation without compromising the oneness of God.[3]

Early Christian faith, as it emerges in the New Testament, expresses the conviction that the God of Israel has acted decisively in the life, message, death, and resurrection of Jesus of Nazareth. The early Christians understand their life, enabled by the Spirit of God, as lived in a continuing community with the risen crucified One and through him with God, whom they now, following Jesus's example, call the Father. Consequently, they develop means of celebrating their relationship to Christ, through whom they are in relationship to God, in worship, as it is enabled by the Spirit, and of witnessing to it in words and deeds, while avoiding compromising the monotheistic principle.[4]

The primary Christian experience gives rise to forms of coordinating God and Jesus in worship and proclamation and of understanding both as being enabled and empowered by the Spirit. As a response to the way in which the early Christians see themselves addressed by God in Christ and the Spirit and find themselves compelled to respond by worshipping God through Jesus and God and Jesus, we can trace the development of a "prototrinitarian grammar of discourse about God."[5] The identity description of God as the one "who brought you out of the land of Egypt, out of the house of bondage" (Exod. 20:2) is supplemented with new identity descriptions, defining the identity of God through the resurrection of Jesus as "him that raised Jesus our Lord from the dead" (Rom. 4:24). Just as the narrative identification of God in relation to Israel is coordinated with narrative identifications of God in relation to Jesus, so predications that proclaim

God as the Creator and the sustainer of the created cosmos are applied to Christ (Col. 1:16ff.), perhaps drawing on images of the Old Testament wisdom literature (cf. Prov. 8:22–30). The pattern of worship of the one God is Christologically shaped, but the theological explanations of how that is possible already include the Spirit as the one who enables worship of the God in Christ (cf. Rom. 8:26–27). The prototrinitarian grammar that prevents Christian worship from becoming ditheistic or tritheistic is already there in full-fledged form, as in Romans 8:11: "If the Spirit of him who raised Jesus from the dead dwells in you, he who raised Christ Jesus from the dead will give life to your mortal bodies also through his Spirit that dwells in you."

Defeating Gnosticism and Unity of the Divine Economy

The discussions of the second century manifest something like an experimental stage in the development of Christian teaching. In the debates with Gnosticism that are characterized by postulating a higher knowledge of a variety of mediating spiritual beings that are there to liberate human beings, who possess a spiritual core, from their entanglement in matter, Christian theologians had to defend the connection of creation and redemption so that redemption can be understood not as liberation from the world but as the liberation of the world. In counteracting the almost limitless internal differentiations of the Divine Being in Gnosticism so that it included a host of mediating entities, Irenaeus of Lyon (ca. 135–ca. 202 CE) construes a "Trinitarian" account of the unity of the divine economy confessing the almighty God-Father, the Creator of heaven and earth; Jesus Christ, the Son of God who became incarnate for redemption of humanity; and the Spirit, who expresses the unity of the work of salvation in prophecies.[6] The unity of the divine economy can also be expressed by stating that God works through his "two hands," the Son and the Spirit.[7]

Central for the quasi-horizontal historical construction of the activity and the being of God is the recapitulation of all things in Christ (*anakephalaiosis*) so that the narrative has its plot in its center, the person and work of Christ. In arguing against the schools of Noëtus and Praxeas, who had emphasized God as the one ground of being (*monarchia*) with the effect of making God the Father suffer in the suffering of Christ (Noëtus) and had interpreted God as Spirit so that only Christ's humanity suffered (Praxeas), Tertullian (after 150–after 220 CE) anticipates the orthodox formula of one substance, three persons, but without any clearly developed metaphysical understanding of these terms.

More influential was the school of the so-called Logos theologians who interpreted Christian faith as the "true philosophy" and imported the common language of Hellenistic philosophy into their elaboration of the plausibility of faith. They interpreted the biblical language of God the Father in terms of the negative theology of philosophical reflection. God is understood as unoriginate, uncreated, without beginning and end, imperishable, immortal, perfect, unmoved, incomprehensible, and inconceivable. The Logos, who breaks forth from the one God before all time, becomes the mediator between the one God and the many of creation. The monotheistic principle can be preserved in a metaphysical form. The Logos can be seen as a "second God" (Justin, *Dialogue with Trypho* 56.4), but he is also understood as "created" as the origin of all God's ways (*Dialogue with Trypho* 61.3; *Apology* 1.21). As the mediator between the One and the many, the Logos belongs to both spheres, either successively or simultaneously.

Ideas like this form the background of the first great systematic thinker of Christianity, Origen (d. 254 CE), who both laid the foundations of "scholarly" (i.e., methodologically reflected), Christian exegesis and presented Christian faith as a comprehensive metaphysical system. To bridge the gap between the One, the Father, who is beyond being, without origin, and incomprehensible, and the material universe, Origen postulates two mediating principles: the Logos, who is eternally begotten from the Father, the mediator of the first creation of rational beings, and the Spirit, who as the first being created by the Logos is the origin of the world of transcendent, pneumatic angelic beings. Before the creation of the material world, there is the creation of an immaterial world of rational beings (*logikoi*) that turn away from the contemplation of the Logos and fall. To contain this primordial fall, God creates the material universe and sends the Logos and the Spirit to bring back and unite the whole of the cosmic creation with God. The creation before the creation and the fall before the fall serve as the metaphysical matrix or the explanatory metaphysical theory for everything that exists and occurs in the material world. For the development of the doctrine of the Trinity, Origen introduced a plurality of hypostases in the Divine Being who are distinct from the completely transcendent One, the Father. Instead of the horizontal divine economy of Irenaeus, we have here a quasi-vertical hierarchical order in which every event and every being can have a place. The differentiation of the one being of God in three hypostases (or rather, the One and two hypostases) implies their subordination. The oneness of God can be preserved only through a carefully "stepped" order of subordination.

Councils and Creeds

Many of Origen's ideas became influential only much later. In principle, his metaphysical scheme provides the conceptual tools for what is later defined as orthodoxy (by supplying the notion of eternal generation) and for what is later defined as heterodoxy (by interpreting it in the sense of an ontological gradation involving subordination). With the beginning of the fourth century, we encounter two major options for conceiving of the relationship between the Father, the Son, and the Spirit: one that is more cultivated in the West and the other that is explored in a deeper and sophisticated way in the East. It is surely wrong to perceive of the contrast as the West started from divine unity and moved to a differentiation of "persons" whereas the East started from the plurality of divine hypostases so that all Eastern theologians tried to conceive the unity from this perspective. However, there are and have remained different emphases and sensibilities. One of these different emphases concerns the question, Should the issue of divine unity and plurality be understood primarily in the context of an explanatory theory of the world or in the context of the practice of worship? Does the way in which Christians understand the relationship of the Father, the Son, and the Spirit primarily relate to how the One God relates to the many of creation, or is it concerned with securing a way in which the sacrifice of praise of believers can be brought to the eternal Father in the intercession of the Son and the Spirit?

While the West leaned toward modalism, understanding Father, Son, and Spirit as different, successive, and transient modes of appearance of the one God, the East tended toward a form of ontological subordinationism. Both ways of thinking are concerned with reconciling Trinitarian worship with the monotheistic principle, inherited from the Old Testament and strengthened by the philosophical systems understanding the whole of reality as modifications of the One beyond being. The modalistic tendency was unable to account for the communicative interaction between Father and Son, for example, in Jesus's prayer to God the Father, and inadvertently postulated a fourth behind all the modes of manifestation as the true God. The subordinationist tendency interpreted the difference between Father and Son as an ontological division and so was at risk of blurring the question of who is the subject of redemption.

The significance of the "Arian crisis" and the response to it at the Council of Nicaea (325 CE) bring all these questions together and emphasize their shared soteriological significance.[8] The teaching of Arius sharply underlined the question, Where exactly should the dividing line between the being of God and the being of the world be drawn? The ease with which the Logos theologians of the second century could place the Logos either on the divine side or on the side of the world, depending on which aspect of the mediation should be spoken of, appeared no longer tolerable. Arius and his followers defended a monotheism in which God, the perfect and purely transcendent monad, first creates one divine being (with reference to Prov. 8:22), the Logos, who is created from nothing in time, has a mutable free will, and is therefore also in need of redemption. The Father ascribes to him the dignity of being God by grace, and in following the example of the Logos incarnate, believers are brought to God the Father. The reply to this view concentrated on the question of *who* can be the agent of creation and of our salvation and *how* this involves the whole of human nature, which in the state of sin can be healed only by being reunited with the Creator.

The answer given in Nicaea, with the unscriptural and therefore, by both sides, much criticized concept of homoousian, asserts two things: The agent of our salvation can only be God. If the Father is God, because the Father is the God Christians worship, then the Son must be conceived as not originating outside the

Father's being, but internal to the Father's being. To be one God is to be internally relational. To be the Son, therefore, means to be in this eternal relation to the Father. The word "begotten," not "made," excludes any kind of ontological gradation in the Divine Being. That this "one Lord Jesus Christ" "for us and our salvation came down from heaven and was incarnate" means that the one who is eternally of one being with God the Father is not only the agent of creation but also the subject of the story of the Gospel that ends with his ascension to heaven and his sitting at the right hand of the Father until he comes again to judge the living and the dead. To be God, therefore, includes being relational, giving being (the Father) and receiving being (the Son) and although eternal, being the subject of a temporal history. Being God is not being absolutely monadic; it is not being exclusively giving and in no way receiving; it is not being timeless and therefore incapable of living in temporal relations. The whole set of attributes of God that necessitates the cataract of mediating beings is redefined so that there need not be any mediating beings, because the only-begotten Son of God, who is of one essence with the Father, is also the one who "was incarnate" and "was made man."

The relationship between the Father and the Son explains both the relationship between the one and the many and the way we in Christ can through him bring our praise and intercession to God. Rowan Williams is certainly right when he describes the creed of Nicaea as "a first step in the critical demythologizing of Christian discourse."[9] The homoousian abolishes the need for mediatorial entities, be they demigods or supermen or superwomen, both as part of an explanatory theory of the cosmos and as part of liturgical worship. Is this a factor that contributed to the fact that by the end of the fourth century the pagan temples of the Roman Empire were largely empty?

Distinguishing *Ousia* and Hypostasis: The Cappadocian Contribution

If the *homoousios* has such a significance, how exactly is it to be understood? And how does the Spirit fit into this scheme? While it was clear what the formula achieved critically in rejecting Arianism, it was largely unclear what precisely it affirmed. The complex developments after Nicaea often present the image of a formula in search of a convincing explanation so that its impact is only retrospectively fully recognized. Even Athanasius, whose theology provided the most convincing theological basis for understanding the homoousian, only adopted the formula constructively years after the council. Furthermore, the doctrinal position of the different factions was inextricably bound up with the dynamics of the imperial politics of finding a way of securing a basic consensus for the conflicting religious parties. The decisive new step appeared only in the seventies of the fourth century with a new generation of theologians who were keen to refute the *pneumatomachoi*, the "Spirit fighters" who challenged the divinity of the Holy

Spirit, and to provide a persuasive metaphysical account of oneness and threeness in God. The question of the Spirit was crucial since it concerned the heart of Christian worship as it was offered *in* the Spirit *through* the Son *to* the Father. Is it therefore right to worship the Spirit as the Son and the Father are worshipped? Can one address worship also to the Father *and* the Son *and* the Spirit?

Basil of Caesarea, starting from the observation that the critics of the divinity of the Holy Spirit merely tried extending the Arian view of Christ now to the Spirit, argued that if one applied a strict distinction between the being of the Creator and created being, the Holy Spirit clearly belonged on the side of the Creator. Furthermore, it has to be acknowledged that in God's action every divine work begins in the Father, is executed by the Son, and is perfected in the Spirit. If the Spirit is in this way constitutive for Trinitarian divine agency, then the Spirit belongs ontologically with the Father of the Son. If they all have the same essence in equal measure, how are their particularities to be understood? How is the particular (*idion*) related to that which is common (*koinon*)? Here Basil introduces a conceptual distinction that has been interpreted as a "revolution in Greek philosophy."[10] He distinguishes between *ousia* (essence) and hypostasis (lit. "that which underlies"; "substantia") and interprets hypostasis as the individual mode of existence of the one *ousia*.[11] While individual human beings share in the same human nature—but only in an incomplete form, because no individual being actualizes the whole concept of humanity—the Father, the Son, and the Spirit share completely in the divine essence. They are therefore *homoousios*. How then do they differ? Basil's answer is that "how" they actualize the same divine essence constitutes the difference. This "how" can be described only with regard to the originating relations among the three. The Father begets the Son, the Son is begotten; the Spirit proceeds from the Father. Now we can locate difference in the eternal Trinity and not only in the external modes of being. This is achieved by understanding relations not only as external attributes that contribute nothing to the particular being of something (e.g., being to the right of, being to the left of) but as the particularity of being (begotten, proceeding). The individually identifying characteristics of the three persons are the relations they have with one another, precisely with regard to the way in which they share in the Godhead.

The next step is to identify the hypostasis with the concept of the person (*prosopon*). This concept had formerly been understood in terms of social functions or legal responsibilities. Now it is understood ontologically and becomes a logically and metaphysically primitive concept. It cannot be derived from another concept. This now opens a way out of an old dilemma. If Father, Son, and Spirit are neither attributes of the same substance (modalistic monism) nor three substances having one common attribute of being divine (tritheism), then the oneness in God and the threeness in God must be understood as equally foundational. From this follows that "God" cannot be predicated of three logical subjects. "God" can be predicated only of the divine activity toward us, and since every divine action begins with the Father, is present through the Son, and is perfected in the Spirit, the name of the action cannot be divided among three agents. The divine *ousia* is, therefore, exactly what is communicated by the inner-Trinitarian relations. It is neither independent of the relations between the Father, the Son, and the Spirit, nor can it be identified positively apart from the Father, the Son, and the Spirit in their relations. After the Council of Constantinople (381 CE), this was summarized in the formula *mia ousia–treis hypostaseis, una substantia/essentia–tres personae*, which can perhaps be rendered as one essence, three personal identities.

It is important to note that for Christians of the fourth century, the doctrine of the Trinity was not a problem; the problem was the solution, how their forms of worship were reconciled with their commitment to the one God, to monotheism. What the doctrine of the Trinity has achieved is that the oneness of God is not determined through the contrast to what is not God, to the many of the world, but in relation to God alone. Similarly, the infinite that is contrasted to the finite and so limited by the finite cannot be true infinity—as Hegel said almost 1,500 years later—because the true infinite comprises the finite within itself.

Augustine's *De Trinitate* and Its Consequences

The Western church received the doctrine of the Trinity as it had been elaborated in the Eastern church. The conceptual differentiations, which the Cappadocians had introduced, had as their background the differentiation of the hypostases in the Origenistic tradition. In contrast, the Western tradition worked from a background of metaphysics in which the statement that God is one substance (*una substantia*) defined the common ground. Theologians like Ambrose of Milan and Hilary of Poitiers and philosophers like Marius Victorinus tried to translate the distinction between *ousia* and hypostasis into Latin, which in the case of Marius Victorinus led to creating the new term *subsistentia* as a Latin equivalent for hypostasis. The work that has shaped the discussion of the Trinity in the Latin West until today is Augustine's *De Trinitate.*[12] With regard to Trinitarian theology, the discussion in the West can be described as a series of footnotes on Augustine's *De Trinitate.* It was the textbook from which theologians developed their own Trinitarian thinking either by knowing it directly or through excerpts in the textbooks of scholasticism. Some of the most radical differences of opinion that one encounters today concern the interpretation of this work and the evaluation of its effects in Christian theology. Some of the moves that Augustine introduces have, however, become the standard form of Trinitarian reflection in the West, and new attempts to grapple with the Trinitarian question inevitably start from a discussion of Augustine.

Augustine's skepticism about the distinction between *ousia* and hypostasis—after all, both terms could be rendered as *substantia* in Latin—led him to prefer the term "essence," instead of "substance," for the unity in God because it emphasizes the connection to *esse.* Talking of essence also prevents one from being immediately entangled in the question of the relationship between a substance and its accidents (its mutable attributes), which cannot be applied to God. Instead, Augustine analyzes statements about God in two respects: propositions about God *ad se* (in relation to Godself, i.e., *secundum substantiam*) and propositions *ad aliquid* (in relation to something other, i.e., *secundum relativum*). The result this grammatical rule for theological propositions has with regard to Trinitarian language is not entirely unproblematic. The concept of "person" does not pass the test. If one sees it as an expression for the relation, it seems contradictory to apply it to only one term of the relation, for example, "the Father is a person," because it implicitly involves the Son. If one applies the concept "person" *ad se*, one ends up with either only one ("Father, Son, and Spirit are one person") or three substances ("Father, Son, and Spirit are three persons"). The problem is that the term "person" is applied in conciliar teaching to God in relation to Godself (*ad se*) and nevertheless is to be understood in a relational sense, as specified by the relations of origin (*ad aliud*). If, however, "person" is in effect deconstructed by Augustine's rule with respect to the three in the one, how should one come to a better understanding of the one in three?

The new approach that Augustine tries out with regard to Trinitarian language, the approach through the *vestigia Trinitatis*, the footprints or traces of the Trinity in the human mind, produces many examples of how three are related in such a way that each term is relatively distinct and nevertheless implied in the other two. However, if one looks at the whole of the argument, it seems doubtful whether Augustine's teaching on the Trinity is indeed a "psychological doctrine of the Trinity."[13] In many passages, it reads like an account of theological anthropology based on an image relation between the triune God and the human mind. A further question is whether the triads that Augustine develops help to see the structured three-in-one of divine action and being in the divine economy or whether the triads of the *vestigia Trinitatis*, in effect, replace the divine economy and provide an alternative access to the understanding of the triune God. While this remains contentious, and one could offer arguments for both sides, it is clear that the Father, the Son, and the Spirit always act undivided (*inseparabiliter operari*), not only in the divine economy but also in the inner-Trinitarian relations (Augustine, *On the Trinity* 1.8). If the Spirit is now understood as the love that binds the Father and Son together, this must be so from eternity. Therefore, one can neither state that only the Father is the origin of the Spirit nor that the Son sends the Spirit in the divine economy. Rather, since the Spirit is posited, once Father and Son are posited in their relationship of love, one must say that the Spirit eternally proceeds from the Father and the Son (Augustine, *On the Trinity* 15.45–47; "*ex patre filioque*").

When the text of the version of the creed accepted at Constantinople became known in the West, the phrase that the Spirit proceeds from the Father (alluding to John 15, 26) was, perhaps already in the fifth century, supplemented with the addition "and from the Son" (*filioque*). Since the Eastern church regarded the text as sacrosanct because of its importance in the Christological debates following the Council of Chalcedon (451 CE), it found this insertion wholly unacceptable. It has since then been *the* contentious issue between the East and the West and led to the great schism of 1054 CE. One can understand the seriousness of this divergence only if one puts it in the context of the question of monotheism. For the Eastern church, saying that the Spirit proceeds from the Father and the Son immediately invokes the danger that there might be two archai, two origins in the Trinity. However, that violates the *monarchia* and smacks of polytheism. Conversely, if the Spirit as the bond of love between the Father and Son is already there when the Father and the Son are in relation, then it would, for the Western church, violate the principle of monotheism if the Spirit would not proceed from the Father and the Son eternally.

The standard form of Trinitarian teaching bridging the debates in late antiquity and medieval times is the third creed *Quicumque vult*, erroneously ascribed to Athanasius, which can be only roughly dated in the sixth century. This text presents the Trinity for the first time not in three parts, dedicated to the Father, the Son, and the Spirit, but affirms the unity of substance before turning to the distinction of the persons. This confession played a very important role in the theological education of clerics. It was sung as a canticle, usually at the first Sunday office, and it is the confession traditionally recited on Trinity Sunday. Its structure of first affirming the unity of God and then the Trinity, following the rule that we are "neither to confuse the persons nor divide the substance," forms the matrix of Trinitarian confessional formulas such as in Luther's confession of 1528 CE and the Augsburg Confession (1530 CE).

Medieval Debates on the Doctrine of the Trinity

The medieval debates in the West can mainly be understood as a continuation of reflection along the lines of Augustine's conception of the Trinity. The theory of the Trinity articulated by Anselm of Canterbury (1033–1109 CE) in the *Monologion* is based on the Augustinian triads, but Anselm offers a different justification for the internal differentiation of the divine unity. The decisive difference is that of the divine speaking (*locutio*), which is based on divine reason (*ratio*). Since the Son proceeds from the Father, the structural similarity to the order of *ratio* and *locutio* is clear. Anselm expresses that through the first two elements of the Augustinian triad, *memoria* and *intellegentia*. However, he replaces the third element, which was in Augustine the will (*voluntas*), with love (*amor*). If love unites the Father and the Son, it must proceed from the Father and the Son. The problem that occurs if the characteristics of the persons are expressed in this way is that it becomes difficult to show that they are in fact to be attributed to the persons and not to the divine essence. We must therefore, according to Anselm, speak of a threefold unity and a unitary trinity (*trina unitas et una trinitas*).[14] It is interesting that Anselm responds to the possible challenge that this position is heretical by referring to Augustine's difficulties with the adaptation of the Greek Trinitarian terminology.

The problem that presents itself if particular attributes are associated with one of the persons becomes clear in Abelard's *theologia summi boni.* Abelard (1079–1142 CE) posits the triad of power, wisdom, and benevolence (*Potentia–sapientia–benignitas)*, arguing that in God as the highest good, each of the elements cannot be thought of without the other two. Abelard's indefatigable enemy, Bernard of Clairvaux (1090–1153 CE), quickly identified the problem: Does this construction not relativize the power of the Son and the Spirit? Abelard's doctrine was thus condemned at the Synod of Sens in 1140. Abelard's counterargument that the persons could not be reduced to these characteristics, that they were merely meant to *identify* their particularity and not describe each of them exclusively, did not lead to a revision of the condemnation, since he died in 1142 on the way to Rome to defend himself before the pope.

These debates illustrate quite clearly where the problem of Western Trinitarianism is located. Can the particularity of the persons be identified in such a way that it does not reduce their coequal possession of the one divine essence and that it does not turn the persons into three substances? One of the most intriguing proposals for the solution of the problem is offered by Richard of St. Victor (d. 1173), who saw the need for revising the concept of the person developed by Boethius, which had been most frequently used in Trinitarian debates and according to which a person is *naturae rationabilis individua substantia.* If the "substance" of the Trinity is indivisible (*individua*), then the Trinity must be the person. If the substance is divisible, then the person participates in a divisible divine nature. To avoid the dilemma, Richard introduces the concept of *existentia* instead of *substantia. Existentia* has two main characteristics. It defines a particular identifying quality and that from which it stands out (as Richard explains *ek-sistere*), its origin. While Father, Son, and Spirit share in one being that is beyond substance because its accidents cannot be predicated of it (*supersubstantiale esse*)—a new definition of *ousia*—they nevertheless are distinct because of their different origins. They have an existence that cannot be communicated to another and also cannot be possessed by another. The person is in this sense *existentia incommunicabilis*, an "incommunicable existence." Richard tried to corroborate this conception by demonstrating that love as that which is most perfect achieves this perfection only when the love between two can be directed to a third. While Richard found a new way of differentiating between essence and person and emphasized that relations must constitute real terms of a relation (so that fatherhood is not the Father), this argument is based entirely on a priori considerations. Is the divine economy—as some interpretations of the slogan of the Augustinian tradition that the works of the Trinity *ad extra* are undivided would seem to suggest—irrelevant for identifying the particular being of the persons?

Joachim of Fiore (ca. 1130–1201/2 CE) put this question again on the agenda. The three persons in the one substance of the triune God have their unity because their activity constitutes the one economy of salvation, he argues in a book devoted to showing the concordance between the Old Testament and the New (*Liber Concordiae Novi ac Veteris Testamenti*). We must therefore distinguish between a period, or kingdom, of the Father (from creation to Jesus), a period or kingdom of the Son (from Jesus to Joachim's present), and a period of the Spirit, which Joachim sees beginning in his lifetime, characterized by direct Spirit experiences that replace the role of Holy Scripture. Only if we construe the relationship of the three persons as a temporal succession, Joachim argued, can we avoid suggesting that the divine essence becomes a fourth reality, somehow lurking behind the persons of the Father, the Son, and the Spirit. The Fourth Lateran Council condemned his teaching in 1215, but the question Joachim had raised has remained a live issue ever since.[15]

Thomas Aquinas's (1225–74 CE) theology of the Trinity has for a long time been the paradigm of Roman Catholic teaching on the Trinity. From the time of the Reformation, when the *via antiqua* proved to be victorious in the "contest of the ways"—the debate between the *via antiqua* of Thomism and the *via moderna* of Nominalism, not least through Cardinal Cajetan de Vio's commentaries on Thomas's work—the *Summa Theologiae* replaced the commentary on *Sentences* by Peter Lombard as the main textbook in all Catholic institutions of theological learning. However, Thomas's teaching on the Trinity has also been blamed for the division of the doctrine of God into two treatises, "On the one God" (*De Deo uno*) and "On the threefold God" (*De Deo trino*), in the theological manuals. According to Karl Rahner, this division is at least in part responsible for the fact that many Christians are, in Rahner's view, mere monotheists.[16] More recently, Thomas's doctrine of the Trinity has again come to the center of a debate that focuses on the question of whether the concept of divine simplicity has a controlling function in Christian discourse of the Trinity or whether Thomas's concept should be interpreted in a personalist and not an essentialist way.[17] Thomas has offered different explications of the doctrine of the Trinity, from his early *Commentary on the Sentences* to the unfinished *Summa Theologiae*. In all his works, Thomas distinguishes his approach sharply from theologians, from Anselm to Bonaventure, who believe that belief in the Trinity can be demonstrated by necessary reasons. Trying to demonstrate the Trinity by reason alone would, in Thomas's view, make the Trinity the laughingstock of nonbelievers. Reason, Thomas insists, has for the Trinitarian faith an explicatory and a constitutive function. The Trinity must be understood on the basis of God's revelation, attested by the authority of scripture. Thomas first distinguishes between a procession that creates something external to God (creation) and a procession that occurs immanently within the Divine Being (i.e., the begetting of the Son). This immanent procession is to be understood similarly to mental acts of understanding and communication (*verbum cordis*) (Aquinas, *Summa Theologiae* Prima

Pars, q. 27, a. 1). The next distinction refers to what is common to the three persons and what is characteristic for each of the three. The procession in God, Thomas states, must be understood as a mental emanation (*emanatio intelligibilis*) that is neither the bringing forth of an effect that is (ontologically) different from the cause (Arianism) nor the transition from the cause into the effect (Sabellianism). With regard to the relations, Thomas distinguishes between the ontological status (*esse*) and the particular character (*ratio*). Relation is not an internal characteristic of a subject (like quality or quantity) but denotes a relationship to another (*ad aliud*). With regard to the *esse*, the relation must be identical with the divine *esse* because there are no accidents in God. With regard to the particular character (*ratio*), the relation expresses an operation with respect to the origin: fatherhood, sonship, and being breathed (*spiratio*). Therefore, the relations are really distinguished by their particular character but not by their ontological status. The concept of the person unites these two elements for Thomas: the unity of essence as hypostatic subsistence in the one essence of God and the personal particularity of each person. From Boethius's definition of the person as an individual substance of a rational nature, Thomas takes these three elements: individuality (the particular characteristic), substantiality (existence through itself), and rationality (as the capacity of free agency). These three marks make the person the most perfect in nature. The definition of the person protects the coequal Godhead of the three persons. While this protects Thomas's formula against Arianism and modalism, the danger of tritheism is not yet completely averted. This Thomas achieves by interpreting the concept of the person as a subsistent relation (*relatio ut subsistens*, or *relatio per modum subsistentiae quae est hypostasis*), which takes up the two determining elements of a relation (Aquinas, *Summa Theologiae* Prima Pars, q. 29, a. 4). According to its ontological status (*esse*), the person subsists in the divine essence with which it is identical. According to its proper characteristic (*ratio*), the person has its specific identity in the relation to another but no independent principle of being. This defines for Thomas the tri-personalist Christian monotheism. It can be shown against critics of Thomas' doctrine of the Trinity that the three persons of the Trinity, on the basis of their proper characteristics (*proprietates*), have a specific role in the unitary but not undifferentiated work of the Trinity to what is external to God (*ad extra*).

The Trinity in Reformation Theology

For the Reformation, the Trinity was not one of the doctrines for which there existed differences with the teaching of the Catholic Church. Only at the time of the second-generation Reformers (like John Calvin) did the so-called scripture principle (*sola scriptura*: scripture is the sole rule of all doctrine) provide the background for the anti-Trinitarian teaching of Michael Servetus (1509/11–53

CE) and Fausto Sozzini (1539–1604 CE), whose name—whether with justification or not—identifies the anti-Trinitarian movement of Socianism in Eastern Europe. Luther based his Trinitarian theology in its various literary genres (catechetical and exegetical writings, sermons, academic disputations and hymns) on the classical creeds of the early church. In some of his writings (e.g., *Of Councils and the Church,* 1537), he recounts the history of the ecumenical councils and justifies the condemnations of the early church. There are two differences in his approach from medieval theology that become normative for the theology of the Reformation.[18]

The first characteristic is that all Trinitarian discourse must be based on the witness of scripture because it is only through scripture that we can discover the reality of the Trinity (*res*) and so reconstruct the meaning of the terms (*vocabula*) of Trinitarian theology. Luther was convinced that the reality of the Trinity is present in scripture in a variety of forms, although the doctrinal formulas cannot be found there. However, since all concepts receive a new signification in Christ that discloses again the meaning of all things in God's original creative speaking in creation, this new meaning can be expressed where God confirms the Trinitarian self-manifestation of God in scripture for us by his Holy Spirit. With the help of the thesis of the new signification, Luther can speak of the Father as the *Grammatica*, the Son as the *Dialectica*, and the Spirit as the *Rhetorica* of all divine speaking.[19] An example of this new meaning is the interpretation that Luther gives to the term "relation." While in created things relations are external to the "things" (*res*), it must be maintained that "with regard to divine things the relation has being, it is a hypostasis and subsistence" (In divinis relatio est res, id est, hypostasis et subsistentia). The relations among the persons must in this sense be understood as internal, constitutive relations. They constitute the persons within the one divine substance.

This conceptual re-formation on the basis of scripture corresponds to the connection that Luther establishes between the Trinity and the doctrine of the justification of the sinner by grace alone, as it is witnessed in a normative sense by scripture, and as it is to be received by faith. In its Trinitarian form, the whole creed expresses how God has disclosed himself and has revealed the deepest abyss of his fatherly heart and of inexpressible divine love in all three articles. The Trinity is in this way not one doctrine that is to be believed alongside other articles of the creed. Rather it is the frame in which all articles of the creed have to be understood. The Trinitarian form of discourse expresses the logic of divine self-presentation by connecting the being of God, God's self-disclosure, and God's self-authentication in the Holy Spirit. The Trinity in this way expresses the unity between the author, the content, and the effect of God's self-presentation for faith. Luther tries to express this with the logic of divine self-giving. Divine self-revelation is Trinitarian insofar as it is triune self-giving: The Father gives us everything that is in heaven and on earth, and even more than that, he also gave us his Son and the Spirit, through which he brings us to himself. Without Christ, who is a mirror of God's fatherly heart, we would see only an angry and terrible judge, but through Christ, we can recognize the Father's favor and grace. We could not know Christ without the Holy Spirit, who reveals Christ to us.

Epistemically, knowledge of God proceeds from the Spirit, who makes the witness of scripture certain for us, to Christ, who is the revelation of God the Father's heart, and so to God. This mode of knowing is knowledge by acquaintance. Knowing God in this way brings us to God. According to the *ratio essendi*, we can now understand how the Father reveals himself through the Son in the Spirit. Ontologically, this is grounded for Luther in the Trinitarian conversation that God is. In this way, the so-called *particulae exclusivae* of the Reformation (only scripture, only through Christ, only by grace, only in faith) are explained and justified in their relationship to the Trinitarian *fundamentum fidei.* Because it has this integrative function for the whole of Christian faith, which appears as completely grounded in the Trinitarian self-manifestation of the triune God, the doctrine of the Trinity is for Luther "the highest article in faith on which all other others hang" (Luther, 7.215.28).

The connection that Luther maintains between the soteriological promise of Christian faith and the constitution of God's tri-personal being was at first not shared by all Reformers. Melanchthon, in his 1521 *Loci Theologici*, claimed that it is better to adore the mysteries of the Godhead than to investigate them. This may have been a reaction to the alleged oversophistication of scholastic treatments. However, a few years later, when he was writing the *Augsburg Confession*, Melanchthon included a formal summary of the conciliar teaching on the doctrine of the Trinity as the first article. From 1525 onward, the new editions of the *Loci* include an extensive treatment of the doctrine of the Trinity. The latest edition, the *Loci praecipui* of 1559, includes not only an extensive treatment, based on the scriptural witness, but also reflections that continue the Augustinian tradition of trying to grasp the inner-Trinitarian relations through the *vestigia Trinitatis*, the traces of the Trinity in the human mind.

Calvin's *Institutes of the Christian Religion*, especially in the last edition of 1559, which Calvin oversaw, presents a systematic exposition of the whole of Christian doctrine according to the insights of Reformation theology. The *Institutes* was meant as an introduction to the interpretation of scripture. Much of the discussion has the form of deriving conceptual distinctions from scripture, always informed by the ecclesial tradition, but this conceptual apparatus is meant to be applied again in the exposition of scripture. Many distinctions have therefore the function not only of presenting a metaphysics of faith but also of serving as grammatical rules in the interpretation of scripture. Heretical teaching is therefore teaching based on a misconception of scripture, and it leads in its application to the proliferation of heresy in the exposition of scripture.

This, for Calvin, is the ultimate danger for Christian teaching—if heretical thoughts are presented with the authority of scripture. If the Son is "the express image of his person" (i.e., of the Father), this must be guarded against an understanding that would deny the hypostasis of the Son so that he is merely a form of appearance of the Father. Calvin through scriptural exegesis introduces the classical terminology of the doctrine of the Trinity. He interprets the person as a subsistence in God's *esse*, which possesses in its relations to the other Trinitarian persons an incommunicable character (Calvin, *Institutes* 1.13.6; *quae ad alios relata, proprietate incommunicabili distinguitur*). The understanding of any relation implies at least two terms of the relation, which apart from subsisting in the one divine essence must have a distinguishing and incommunicable character (*proprietas*). The divine essence, which Calvin sees as the one and simple being of God, subsists in three persons. In every divine act, the three persons are coordinated in such a way that the Father is the principle of all action, the fount and origin; the Son is wisdom, counsel, and the ordered dispensation of the activity; and the Spirit is the power and efficacy in action (Calvin, *Institutes* 1.13.18). This is the basis of a number of grammatical distinctions. If we talk indefinitely (indefinite) of God, we mean the one simple being of God in three persons. If we talk about the Father and the Son, a relation comes into play (*in medium venit relatio*), and we have to talk definitely about the persons with their characteristics. The persons with their characteristics, however, must be understood in a certain order. The Father always comes before the Son and the Spirit. Does that mean that the Son has his divinity from the person of the Father? This view, often associated with Basil, would introduce an ontological priority of the Father into the Trinity. Would that be a hidden form of subordinationism?

Calvin denies that because it is the nature of the Godhead to exist absolutely from itself. If the Son is God, and if the Spirit is God, their Godhead must in each case be from itself. Christ's *divinity* does not have a beginning or principle, and therefore, the name of God (*kyrios*) may properly be used of Christ. However, if we talk about his *person*, then his person has its beginning in the Father since he is begotten from the Father. This provides a rule for talking about the priority of the Father, not in the sense of an ontological priority but in the sense of a reasonable order of the Trinitarian relations.

What are the implications of this? We may not be able to approach the question of the divine essence directly, but if each of the Trinitarian persons possesses the divine in its absoluteness, then the way we encounter God in revelation—that is, in the three persons in their relations—is the way we really encounter the divine essence. As in Luther, it is the link that is established among God's being, the revelation of God's being, and certainty concerning the truth of the revelation of God's being that is the point of the construction. In each case, the point consists in emphasizing that God alone makes God knowable (God is known only by God), God alone discloses God (God is known only where God makes himself known), and God alone can create certainty concerning the knowledge of God that is constituted by God alone in this way (God alone can create faith). This is the version of Christian Trinitarian monotheism that is characteristic of Reformation theology. Its hallmark is the Trinitarian integration of personal experience of faith, the narrative of God's action in history as witnessed in scripture, and reflection on the ultimate constitution of reality.

The Enlightenment: The God of Natural Religion and the Trinity

This exclusive knowledge of God as Trinity, as it is formulated in Reformation theology, is bound to the historical revelation of God in Christ and the personal vindication of the truth of that revelation through the internal testimony of the Holy Spirit. It was the link to particular historical contingent events, to the action of God in Israel and in Jesus Christ, that was the target of Enlightenment criticism. It is not easy to give an accurate overall description of "the Enlightenment" since the regional and cultural differences produce very different images. Moreover, the "historical Enlightenment" is rather different from the stereotype of the Enlightenment that floats through current public debates.[20]

It is perhaps most helpful to understand the Enlightenment as connected to a particular religious tradition and to pay attention to the characteristic cultural differences in different contexts. The Enlightenment employs the images and forms of expression of religious traditions (most notably in the pneumatological and Christological image of light) but interprets them with a conscious disregard for their theological foundations. In fact, *not* asking for a theological foundation constitutes much of the Enlightenment's programmatic rhetoric. For European Christianity, one of the characteristics is the disjunction of reflection on the ultimate principles of reality, the historical events of God's revelation in history, and the personal experience of the certainty of faith. The personal experience of faith is no longer understood as constituted for humans by the illumination of the Spirit. Rather, it becomes the illumination of the human mind by its own capacities. The historical events witnessed in scripture are no longer the events of God's interaction with his creation but become the data of historical research. The triune God confessed by the church becomes an ultimate monistic principle of explanation for reality based on human reason alone. The pneumatological and Christological elements of a Trinitarian understanding of God are extrapolated so that there remains a divine monad, an absolutely simple principle of rational explanation or moral obligation. The second and the third person of the Trinity are transformed into a first-century teacher of wisdom and morality and the autonomy of human reason. The understanding of God is that of a single divine *subject* that is transcendently pitted over against the world, a God who thus becomes an *object* for the human knowing subjects. This understanding of God, which is emphatically celebrated as "monotheistic" with the new term "monotheism," which was coined by the Cambridge Platonist Henry More, is often developed in terms of a Deistic understanding of God.[21] The problem becomes God's involvement in the contingencies of history, in the rule-governed structures of nature, and in the workings of the human mind. Forms of philosophical theism attempted to solve the problems by postulating God's occasional interventions in the natural processes of the world. The explanation of miracles becomes one of the chief topics of philosophers engaging with religion in this way. For the Deists, the monadic God, the supreme primordial artisan or watchmaker, sets up the regularities of the processes of the world and then takes early retirement. While this understanding of God might still be understood as monotheistic, it is a highly reductive form of monotheism. Understanding monotheism in this way turns history, nature, and the human mind into the arena of atheological explanations. The rise of modern atheism must be understood as the reaction against this kind of reductive monotheism.

The Recovery of the Trinity by the Philosophers: German Idealism and Its Theological Heirs

The rediscovery of the Trinity over against these interpretations of God in the Enlightenment is in both its most spectacular versions—that of Georg Friedrich Wilhelm Hegel (1770–1831) and that of Friedrich Wilhelm Joseph Schelling (1775–1854)—a conscious attempt to see the Trinity as the key to understanding the whole of reality. It was Hegel who put the problem of the Trinity again on the agenda of Protestant theology.[22] For Hegel, the Trinity is not a doctrine that needs to be interpreted. Rather, it is the fundamental dynamic structure of reality itself. This is constituted as a process in which the eternal tri-unity, the Father, distinguishes himself so that the Son is posited as the principle of difference over against the simple identity of the Father.[23] The self-emptying of the general in the particular history of the world makes the world of the many not a reality external to God but includes it in the movement of the divine Spirit. The self-manifestation of the universal divine Spirit occurs in the incarnation of the Spirit in the empirical and historical reality of Jesus of Nazareth. Jesus's death on the cross is insofar both the extreme self-emptying of the general in the particular and the negation of the negation of the particular as particular over against the universal, so that identity and difference are reconciled as identity in difference, sameness and otherness are reconciled in the Spirit. Hegel can describe this process as the movement of the absolute Spirit through its self-opposition to the final reconciliation, which embraces both the process of the objective Spirit (culture) and of the subjective Spirit (the human mind). The process is twofold: The self-manifestation of the infinite Spirit and the interiorization of this process by the finite Spirit are both constitutive for the process as a whole. Hegel views this process retrospectively from its goal that the absolute Spirit exists as the community of believers. The eschatological aim has been reached, and from this perspective, the preceding stages are reconstructed.

It is important to note that for Hegel religion is not just one expression of this process among others. Rather, this process occurs in the history of religions until it reaches its goal in Christianity. As a revealed religion, it is also the revelatory religion in that in Christianity the historical reality of religion, Hegel claims, corresponds to the concept of religion. The history of religions is in this way construed by Hegel as the history of the emergence of true monotheism. True monotheism is reached when the oneness of God is not defined over against the many of the world. True monotheism comprehends the many in the one in three, just as the true infinite can be infinite only if the finite is not posited outside the infinite, so that the infinite would be limited by the finite and could therefore not be infinite. Rather, the finite must be comprehended as finite within the infinite, which only in this way can be understood as true infinite.

Of course, there can be many questions raised to challenge this conception of the Trinity as the matrix for the understanding of the history of God and the world. Is God not only at the end of this process the true Trinity? How does that fit with the classical notion that God is triune from eternity? Does Hegel's philosophy (and perhaps the Christian view of the divine economy) call for a new interpretation of the relationship of time and eternity? How can God's freedom be affirmed in a system that by its own logic moves through the different stages of simple identity and difference to identity in difference? Does the whole process not come to stand under the dictatorial rule of the end, which—as Hegel believed—had already been reached? However one wants to respond to these questions, it seems clear that Hegel anticipates in his philosophy the most significant thesis of twentieth-century theology. Karl Barth's view of the unity of God as revealer, revelation, and revealedness can easily be found in Hegel, just as one can find Rahner's thesis "the 'economic' trinity is the 'immanent' trinity and vice versa." Although both Barth and Rahner would deny being influenced by Hegel, the structural similarities are evident. From being a marginalized doctrine of only historical significance in the Enlightenment, the Trinity is, for Hegel, simply what reality is and becomes—for God as well as for the world.

Revivals and Critiques

While the nineteenth century is the age of Trinitarian renaissance in philosophy, the twentieth century brings in its second half the renaissance of Trinitarian theology. Karl Barth and Karl Rahner programmatically called for a reassessment of the role of the doctrine of the Trinity. The core of their respective proposals is the conjunction of the doctrine of the Trinity and the doctrine of revelation. The Trinity is, along very Hegelian lines, understood as the self-revelation of God so that the Trinity is God in his revelation.[24] If that is correct, the doctrine of the Trinity cannot be one doctrine of material dogmatics among others. It becomes the framework in which all other doctrines must be developed. If all doctrines rest in God's revelation, and if God's revelation is self-revelation in the precise sense—characterized by the unity of the author of revelation, the content of revelation, and the effect of revelation—then all doctrines developed in this framework must be developed in a Trinitarian way. The way in which both Barth and Rahner presented the constructive development of their doctrines could not yet be seen as the fulfillment of the program they had themselves announced. Barth's emphasis rests on the point that God's relationship to creation in creation, reconciliation, and atonement is grounded and prefigured in the relationship of the three modes of being (a term Barth uses to avoid the concept of the person). God reveals himself as he really is in the divine Trinity.

Rahner laments that owing to the discussion of the unity of God *before* the Trinity in traditional dogmatic theology, the realities of salvation do not contribute anything to the Christian understanding of God. However, if the Trinity is the mystery of the origin of Christianity, the Trinity must structure the exposition of the reality of salvation in all parts of dogmatics. This can be achieved only if the "missions" of the three persons in salvation history are properly appropriated to the persons so that they are not only appropriations but proper *proprietates*, genuine particular characteristics. In this sense, Rahner can formulate his foundational axiom: "The 'economic Trinity' is the 'immanent Trinity' and vice versa." The program of Trinitarian theology as Barth and Rahner had envisaged it could be carried out only when the restrictions that Barth and Rahner imposed for a full development of the mutuality of the personal identities of Father, Son, and Spirit and of the relational unity of the one divine essence were no longer observed. The concept of the person had to be recovered over against Barth's preference for the language of "modes of being," and the notion of otherness had to be posited against the dominance of the reflexive self-relation in Rahner's theology.

The program of Trinitarian theology was first put into practice in Jürgen Moltmann's *The Trinity and the Kingdom of God* (1980). This book inaugurated the new phase of Trinitarian theology. There are several features that the different versions of engagement with Trinitarian theology had in common.[25] It was strongly influenced by the different strands of the ecumenical liturgical movement with its rediscovery of historic Trinitarian liturgical modes of discourse and rites. Furthermore, the Trinitarian renaissance is an ecumenical movement to which theologians from different confessional and denominational churches contributed, bridging otherwise very pronounced differences between theologies oriented to the official teaching of the churches and theologies that would identify themselves as liberationist. It is characterized by a strong interchange between Eastern and Western traditions of Trinitarian theology. While Trinitarian theology was first especially prevalent in modern systematic theology in new constructive approaches (Moltmann, Jenson, Pannenberg, etc.), it has since led to an engagement with the rich history of Trinitarian thought and draws on resources from the early church, medieval theology, Reformation theology, and modern and postmodern philosophy and theology. In recent phases, it has also led to a new engagement with Trinitarian theology in the context of interreligious dialogue.[26] Many of these areas of Trinitarian theology are characterized by a lively debate between systematic and historical theologians. During the first phase, beginning in the 1980s, there was a thoroughgoing emphasis on the questions of Trinitarian relationality, a new reflection on divine unity and communion and on the interrelationship among Christology, ecclesiology, and the Trinity, or even the wider concerns of the understanding of human society and culture. Similarities that appear between the different approaches concern precisely the points that Daniel Migliore has underlined in the text in our selection of readings:

- an affirmation of the personal being of the triune God as a unity of "'persons' in the bond of love";
- an emphasis on the communal character of the life of the triune God that transcends all understandings of human "sociality"; and
- an understanding of the triune life of God as "self-giving love," which includes vulnerability and thus provides a bridge between Christian faith and the Christian life.

In the way in which these points are presented, we can also find an emphasis on the way in which biblical witnesses describe the relationship between Father, Son, and Spirit, even if they sometimes do not easily fit into the traditional concepts of the doctrine of the Trinity. This move from the formal structure of the Trinity to the narrative acting out of the relationship among God, Jesus, and the Spirit often involves the acknowledgment that their relations cannot be restricted to relations of origin but must be understood as reciprocal and mutual relationships.[27] In most Trinitarian theologies, there is a conscious link between the Trinity and the eschatological rule of God that leads to the social implications of the doctrine. In other proposals, there is a strong emphasis on the modes of spirituality, which are seen as corresponding to knowledge and worship of the triune God.[28]

One can perhaps distinguish a new phase in the debates of Trinitarian theology. It is characterized by a return from an orientation toward constructive theology to a new engagement with the classical conceptions of Trinitarian theology in the history of Christian thought. This is a field that is at the moment highly contested. Are the views held by systematic theologians of the Trinitarian teachings of, for instance, the Cappadocians, Augustine, Thomas Aquinas, or Luther really in accordance with the findings of historical theologians when they reconstruct the original settings of these teachings and the spaces of discourse in which they were first formulated? This debate has in recent years been very much influenced by the interest the classic creedal doctrines of Christianity have found in the work of Christian philosophers, very often with a background in analytic philosophy.[29] Here the interest is not so much in the way these doctrines came to be formulated, as historical theologians normally ask, and not so much in how they can plausibly be presented in our different contexts in church and society, as systematic theologians would normally ask. Rather, the interest is in how the meaning of Trinitarian propositions is to be construed and how the truth claims Trinitarian propositions make can be supported or refuted by rational arguments. The most ardent defenders of social views of the Trinity or of Latin Trinitarianism can today be found in the camps of analytic Christian philosophers. Similarly, the most decisive criticisms of the doctrine of divine simplicity, which has found new proponents among Christian theologians, come from the camp of Christian analytic philosophers.[30] Most recently, a new group of theologians and philosophers has formed under the name of "analytic theology," trying to facilitate dialogue between philosophers and theologians on the rational warrants for Christian beliefs, not least in the Trinity.[31] Another development that, in my view, is urgently needed is based on the observation that if we look closely, we cannot write the history of Christian thought without paying attention to the fact that in their original settings, in the West and the East, these theologies are based not only on conversations only among Christian theologians but also on the engagement with thinkers of other religious convictions in medieval times and, during the Reformation and afterward, on exchanges, both critical and constructive, with Jewish and Muslim thinkers (Luther, 7.214.28). The fact that the thought of Thomas Aquinas, who was recommended as the normative teacher of the Catholic Church in the 1879 encyclical letter *Aeterni Patris* by Pope Leo XIII, worked in an intellectual paradigm that was defined in Baghdad, and that most of his theological arguments cannot really be understood without paying attention to the ways in which he responded to Ibn Sina (980–1037 CE) and Moses Maimonides (1135/38–1204 CE), has not really transformed the way in which the history, meaning, and truth claims of Christian theology are discussed. The prospect that such an understanding of important periods holds is to better understand not only the respective other traditions but also our own traditions.[32]

And the Question of Monotheism?

During the first phase of the renaissance of Trinitarian theology, there were proposals not to connect the formulation of a Trinitarian theology to the principle of monotheism, but rather to see Christian theology as critique of a "political" and "clerical monotheism." Jürgen Moltmann has in this sense written, "Strict monotheism obliges us to think of God without Christ, and consequently to think of Christ without God."[33] The development of Trinitarian theology, which I have tried to sketch in its barest outlines, seems to me to point in another direction. It is the principle of monotheism, inherited from the Old Testament and reaffirmed in a Christological mode in the forms of worship and theology we find in the New Testament witnesses, that pushes the development of Christian doctrine toward the affirmation of the coequality of Christ and the Spirit with God the Father with regard to the divine essence at the Council of Constantinople in 381 CE. The brief overview of the development of Trinitarian theology in medieval times offers plenty of examples of strenuous attempts to show that the newfound formula *treis hypostaseis–mia ousia* may be neither interpreted in the sense that three individuals form a common essence nor seen as construing the Father, the Son, and the Spirit merely as three transitory modes of appearance or as three attributes of one divine essence. A new stage is reached when in Reformation theology, the tri-unity of God is interpreted in such a way that it is God alone in his Spirit who grants certainty of faith concerning the truth of the Gospel that Christ is the only source of salvation by God the Creator. The exclusive particles of Reformation theology that believers are saved only by God's unconditional grace; only through Christ, God's grace in person; only in faith; and only in unconditional trust in God alone can be interpreted to offer a radicalization of the monotheistic principle. According to this interpretation, the commandment "you shall love the Lord your God with all your heart, and with all your soul, and with all your might" (Deut. 6:5) can be kept only when God in his Spirit creates the faith that enables such love, when Christ is understood as the liberation from all that separates believers from God once and for all, so that we can find communion with God, solely by God's grace. God is one in being the Creator of faith by his Spirit, of salvation in Christ, and of being and meaning as the Father. If the Spirit, the Son, and the Father together are in three persons the one God, then the oneness of God constitutes the being, meaning, and end of everything there is. H. Richard Niebuhr has distinguished such a form of monotheism that is rooted in Being Itself from "henotheism," represented in modern times, for example, by nationalism, and from "polytheistic pluralism," in which, as Niebuhr writes, "an unintegrated, diffuse self-system depends for its meaning on many centres and gives partial loyalties to many interests."[34] The monotheism that can overcome these forms of orientation toward one (partial) God or the many gods Niebuhr calls "radical monotheism." In my view, the development of Trinitarian theology documents not a reduction in commitment to monotheism but rather a process of the radicalization of monotheism in which monotheistic faith is ultimately grounded in the triune self-manifestation of God. In this sense, I tried to formulate as a principle for Christian theology a number of years ago that "only a radically monotheistic theology can be a proper Trinitarian theology, and only a proper Trinitarian theology can be a radically monotheistic theology."[35] If I understand the development of the interpretation of *tawḥīd* in Islamic theology correctly, it documents a similar concern for radical monotheism, which is for this reason, critically and constructively, of the greatest importance for Christian Trinitarian theology.

Notes

1. "I am the Lord your God, who brought you out of the land of Egypt, out of the house of bondage. You shall have no other gods before me. You shall not make for yourself a graven image, or any likeness of anything that is heaven above, or that is in the earth beneath, or that is in the water under the earth; you shall not bow down to them and serve them; for I the Lord your God am jealous God." (Exod. 20:2–5a)

2. "Hear, O Israel: The Lord our God is one Lord; and you shall love the Lord your God with all your heart, and with all your soul, and with all your might . . . and you shall teach them diligently to your children, and shall talk of them when you sit in your house, and when you walk by the way, and when you lie down, and when you rise." (Deut. 6:4–5, 7)

3. Christoph Levin, "Integrativer Monotheismus im Alten Testament," *Zeitschrift für Theologie und Kirche* 109 (2012): 153–75.

4. Cf. the magisterial work by Larry W. Hurtado, *One God, One Lord: Early Christian Devotion and Ancient Jewish Monotheism*, 3rd ed. (London: Bloomsbury T&T Clark, 2015). An accessible introduction to the debate is Larry W. Hurtado, *At the Origins of Christian Worship* (Grand Rapids, MI: Eerdmans, 2000). See also the seminal article by Richard Bauckham, "The Worship of Jesus in Apocalyptic Christianity," *New Testament Studies* 27 (1980–81): 322–41.

5. I have first used this description in "Christology and Trinitarian Thought," in *Trinitarian Theology Today: Essays on Divine Being and Act*, ed. Christoph Schwöbel (Edinburgh: T&T Clark, 1995), 113–46. On the rules of this grammar, compare to my article "The Trinity between Athens and Jerusalem," *Journal of Reformed Theology* 3 (2009): 22–41. The grammatical rules are, in fact, quite simple:

- The one God of Israel can be referred to by the three proper names "the Father," "Jesus Christ," or "the Son" and "the Spirit," which denote different identities in the one reality of God but no gradation of divine being.
- These identities are ordered by their relations in such a way that the Father is the ultimate "point of origin" of all relations between the Father, Jesus Christ / the Son, and the Spirit. All activities of Christ and the Spirit can be related to their origin in God the Father, although the mode of agency is particular to the Father, the Son, and the Spirit.
- Because of their one "point of origin" in the Father, being related to Christ or to the Spirit implies being related to God the Father. In this way, "being in relation with Christ" is an incomplete expression of "being in relation through Christ with the Father." The same applies to the Spirit.
- In these relationships, the Father is both the initial "point of origin" and the ultimate "terminus of all relationships" "who activates all [activities] in everyone" (1 Cor. 12:6), and so the beginning of everything refers to the same God who in the end "may be all in all" (1 Cor. 15:28).
- These identities (Father, Son / Jesus Christ, Spirit) form one ordered relational unity, which is clearly distinguished from everything that has its created existence from God.

6. Irenaeus of Lyon, *Adversus haereses* 1.10.1. Throughout this essay I refer primarily to texts from the history of Trinitarian theology reprinted in this volume. Full docu-

mentation of the sources discussed can be found in my writings on the Trinity, which I quote for this purpose.

7. Cf. Christoph Schwöbel, "God's Two Hands: Beyond Fundamentalism and Spiritualism," in *Word and Spirit: Renewing Christology and Pneumatology in a Globalizing World*, ed. Christoph Schwöbel and Anselm K. Min (Berlin: de Gruyter, 2014), 13–27.

8. The fullest account of the discussion around Nicaea to date is Lewis Ayres, *Nicaea and Its Legacy: An Approach to Fourth-Century Trinitarian Theology* (Oxford: Oxford University Press, 2004). For the debate after Nicaea, see Frances Young, *From Nicaea to Chalcedon: A Guide to the Literature and Its Background* (London: SCM Press, 2010). For the contemporary relevance of these debates, see Frances Young's Bampton lectures: Frances Young, *God's Presence: A Contemporary Recapitulation of Early Christianity* (Cambridge: Cambridge University Press, 2013).

9. Rowan Williams, "The Nicene Heritage," in *The Christian Understanding of God Today: Theological Colloquium on the Occasion of the 400th Anniversary of the Foundation of Trinity College, Dublin*, ed. James M. Byrne (Dublin: Columba Press, 1993), 45–48.

10. John D. Zizioulas, *Being as Communion* (Crestwood, NY: St. Vladimir's Seminary Press, 1991), 36. For Zizioulas's interpretation of the Cappadocians, see "The Doctrine of the Holy Trinity: The Significance of the Cappadocian Contribution," in Schwöbel, *Trinitarian Theology Today*, 44–60.

11. Cf. Andrew Radde-Gallwitz, *Basil of Caesarea, Gregory of Nyssa, and the Transformation of Divine Simplicity* (Oxford: Oxford University Press, 2009).

12. The discussion today focuses on Lewis Ayres, *Augustine and the Trinity* (Cambridge: Cambridge University Press, 2010), which has opened up a new stage of debate on Augustine's theology of the Trinity.

13. Michael Schmaus, *Die psychologische Trinitätslehre des hl. Augstinus* (Münster: Aschendorf, 1927).

14. Anselm offers this paradoxical formula in the concluding section 79 of the *Monologion.* See Anselm of Canterbury, *The Major Works*, ed. Brian Davies and G. R. Evans (Oxford: Oxford University Press, 1998), 79–80.

15. One of the best guides to these medieval debates is the collection of essays in *Trinitarian Theology in the Medieval West*, Schriften der Luther-Agricola-Gesellschaft 61 (Helsinki: Luther-Agricola-Society, 2007).

16. Cf. Karl Rahner, *The Trinity* (London: Burns & Oatts, 1970).

17. For Thomas's Trinitarian theology, see the magisterial work by Gilles Emery, OP, *The Trinitarian Theology of St. Thomas Aquinas* (New York: Oxford University Press, 2007). See also Anselm K. Min, *Paths to the Triune God: An Encounter between Aquinas and Recent Theologies* (Notre Dame: Notre Dame University Press, 2005). A brief overview is offered in Christoph Schwöbel, "Trinitätslehre," in *Thomas-Handbuch*, ed. Volker Leppin (Tübingen: Mohr Siebeck, 2016), 307–21.

18. Cf. Christoph Schwöbel, "The Triune God of Grace: The Doctrine of the Trinity in the Theology of the Reformers," in *The Christian Understanding of God Today*, ed. J. M. Byrne (Dublin: Columba Press, 1993), 49–64. Compare to the more extensive treatment in the article "Trinität III. Reformationszeit," in *Theologische Realenzyklopädie* 34 (Berlin: de Gruyter, 2002), 105–10. See also *Oxford Research Encyclopedia on Religion*, s.v. "Martin Luther and the Trinity," by Christoph Schwöbel, published online March 2017, https://doi.org/10.1093/acrefore/9780199340378.013.326.

19. I have tried to develop this insight systematically in the essay "God as Conversation: Reflections on a Theological Ontology of Communicative Relations," in *Theology of Conversation: Towards a Relational Theology*, ed. J. Haers (Leuven: Peeters, 2003), 43–67.

20. See Andreas Pečar and Damien Tricoir, *Falsche Freunde: War die Aufklärung wirklich die Geburtsstunde der Moderne?* (Frankurt: Campus, 2015).

21. On the history and systematic interpretation of "monotheism," see my article "Monotheismus V. Systematisch-theologisch," in *Theologische Realenzyklopädie* 23 (Berlin: de Gruyter, 1993), 256–62.

22. More of the narrative can be found in my article "Trinität IV. Systematisch-theologisch (mit Berücksichtigung der Kirchengeschichte seit 1577)," in *Theologische Realenzyklopädie* 34 (Berlin: de Gruyter, 2002), 110–21.

23. See for a concise summary of Hegel's and Schelling's Trinitarian philosophies, Cyril O'Regan, "The Trinity in Kant, Hegel, and Schelling," in *The Oxford Handbook on the Trinity*, ed. Gilles Emery and Matthew Levering (Oxford: Oxford University Press, 2011), 254–66.

24. The most recent example of this systematic connection is Veli-Matti Kärkkäinen, *Trinity and Revelation*, vol. 2 of his *A Constructive Christian Theology for the Pluralistic World* (Grand Rapids, MI: Eerdmans, 2014).

25. For an assessment of the development of Trinitarian theology in the last twenty years, compare my introduction to the volume *Trinitarian Theology Today* (1995), "The Renaissance of Trinitarian Theology: Reasons, Problems and Tasks," 1–30, with the article "Where Do We Stand in Trinitarian Theology? Resources, Revisions, and Reappraisals," in *Recent Developments in Trinitarian Theology: An International Symposium*, ed. C. Chalamet and M. Vial (Minneapolis: Fortress, 2014), 9–71.

26. See Veli-Matti Kärkkäinen, *Trinity and Religious Pluralism: The Trinity in Christian Theology of Religion* (London: Routledge, 2004).

27. This was systematically developed in Wolfhart Pannenberg, *Systematic Theology*, reprint ed. (Grand Rapids, MI: Eerdmans, 2001), vol. 1.

28. Cf. Sarah Coakley, *God, Sexuality, and the Self: An Essay "On the Trinity"* (Cambridge: Cambridge University Press, 2013).

29. Cf. Michael C. Rea, ed., *Oxford Readings in Philosophical Theology*, vol. 1: *Trinity, Incarnation, Atonement* (Oxford: Oxford University Press, 2009).

30. Alvin Plantinga, *Does God Have a Nature?* (Milwaukee: Marquette University Press, 1980).

31. From the recent debates on divine simplicity, see Stephen R. Holmes, Paul D. Molnar, Thomas H. McCall, and Paul S. Fiddes, *Two Views on the Doctrine of the Trinity* (Grand Rapids, MI: Zondervan, 2014). A passionate philosophical defense of a "social Trinity" is William Hasker, *Metaphysics and the Tri-personal God* (Oxford: Oxford University Press, 2013). A philosophical critique of social doctrines of the Trinity that nevertheless argues for divine complexity is Keith Ward, *Christ and the Cosmos: A Reformulation of Trinitarian Doctrine* (Cambridge: Cambridge University Press, 2015).

32. An important attempt has been proposed by David Burrell, *Towards a Jewish-Christian-Muslim Theology* (Oxford: Wiley-Blackwell, 2011).

33. Jürgen Moltmann, *Trinität und Reich Gottes*, 3rd ed. (Munich: Christian Kaiser, 1994), 147.

34. H. Richard Niebuhr, *Radical Monotheism and Western Culture: With Supplementary Essays* (London: Faber, 1950).

35. Christoph Schwöbel, "Radical Monotheism and the Trinity," *Neue Zeitschrift für Systematische Theologie und Religionsphilosophie* 43 (2001): 54–74.

Of Storytellers and Storytelling

A Muslim Response to Christoph Schwöbel

MARTIN NGUYEN

Christoph Schwöbel has provided an incredibly rich and intricate overview of the historical development of Trinitarian theology that directed my thinking in sometimes interesting and unexpected ways. When he discusses the second-century Trinitarian account articulated by Irenaeus of Lyon (ca. 135–ca. 202), he describes "the person and work of Jesus" as the central "plot" to the larger narrative of the divine economy, a "quasi-horizontal historical construction of the activity and being of God."[1] The invocation of "narrative" here, as well as the general nature of the historical discourse, has prompted me to step back and assess the larger currents under way, or in other words, to focus on the forest rather than the trees. I leave the "tree work," so to speak, to historical theologians and period historians. What I make of the forest, by which I mean the ongoing Trinitarian discourse, is that it is very much akin to storytelling, with all its movements and intricacies. I think the connection is apt, given the many ways in which the "story" of the Trinity was and is constantly being revisited, revised, and retold.

The story continually being retold is a single narrative—ostensibly the *same* story being told each time. Core elements are carried over in every retelling. The same three persons and seemingly the same fundamental activities, setting, plot, and narrative arc appear again and again. And yet, as Schwöbel has related, there have been numerous refinements, clarifications, and inflections made in later successive narrations of the story. These changes are neither cosmetic nor aesthetic. As subtle as each change seems, each change is stressed emphatically.

Remarkably, the retellings do not make the story any easier to tell. The elements of the story grow more complex and, I would venture, unwieldy. Part of the challenge is that each storyteller faces a new audience living in different circumstances, and each community engenders perspectives and frameworks different from those that came before. It also matters *how* the story is told. Is this story that is so central to Christianity told in Latin or Greek? How must the story change when told in German, English, or Arabic? Ought it be told with a philosophical bent? How is it told differently through liturgy than through councils and creeds?

While reception clearly plays an important role in how the story is told, more is at play than shifting contexts. The story to be told is itself demanding. The story has something to say. It does not afford error and wants to be conveyed correctly. Each storyteller, as a teacher and theologian, struggles to tell the story truly. How will each person be cast and described? How is each person related to the other? What does each person do, and in which scene does the action unfold? Whether theologians are debating *ex patre filioque* or *essentia* versus *substantia*, it is clear that the words must be right and the phrasing must be precise—lest the story be belied or betrayed. It is as if the unity of the triune God is a moving target, and we are constantly recalibrating our trajectories so as to hit the mark. This image is not quite right, because God's unity is not that which is at issue. It is not that which is "moving." Rather it is we humans, in our finitude, that waver and struggle to see what is precisely happening in the Godhead. It is difficult for us to make out and then to talk about. Nevertheless, the story that is passed down to us tells us something about what is going on therein.

Many of the debates and tensions that Schwöbel discussed were circumscribed largely "within" the Christian tradition. What are Christians saying or shouting at each other? Yet Schwöbel also points to what might be learned "between" our faith traditions. His reference to Thomas Aquinas's Baghdadian "intellectual paradigm" prompted yet another analytical maneuver in reading the historical Trinitarian discourse. What does all this Christian storytelling look like from the perspective of Muslim storytellers? How would Muslim narrative devices, strategies, and techniques fare if put to the Christian task?

This Muslim storyteller, at least, has come to appreciate the complexity involved by trying to think this out. It becomes apparent that the persons of the Trinity cannot be equated with, nor are they congruent with, the attributes or actions of God—what Muslim theologians traditionally call *ṣifāt* and *afʿāl*, respectively. Nor can Father, Son, and Spirit be thought of as simply names (*asmāʾ*) of God—proper names like Adonai, Elohim, or El Shaddai. The Trinity cannot be exegetically decoupled completely from the anchor terms of Father, Son, and Spirit via metaphorical, symbolic, or figurative interpretations. The immediate signification, what some Muslim theologians deem the *ẓāhir* (apparent) or *ḥaqīqa* (real) meaning, must somehow be maintained. Father is Father, Son is Son, and Spirit is Spirit. Nor can judgment of the matter be suspended or deferred for a future eschatological realization as the doctrine of *irjāʾ* (deferment or suspension) would dictate. The Trinity is not a matter for God to sort out but has been revealed to humanity. Indeed, the entire Christian soteriological enterprise seems to rest on the proper construal of God the Father, God the Son, and God the Spirit. Nor is it enough to accept on faith that God is Father, Son, and Spirit but then set aside any attempt to understand the "what" and "how" of it all (*tafwīḍ al-maʿnā* and *tafwīḍ al-kayfiyya*). Indeed, the pronouncement *bi-lā kayf*, meaning "without asking how"—a form of "epistemological self-restriction" that some Muslim theologians deploy in response to particular complexities with respect to the divinity—does not suffice here.[2] The divine essence may be ineffable, but the Trinity therein has been made known—such that Trinitarian theology is the very endeavor to understand the how-ness of the triune God that has been revealed through word and experience, scripture and history.

Nor can Father, Son, and Spirit be neatly and evenly distinguished across the theological complementarity of God's transcendence (*tanzīh*) and immanence (*tashbīh*). While the eternal Father lends itself to the apophatic discourse of transcendence, the Son and Spirit seem to vie for the same cataphatic space of immanence as they move in time and alongside humanity. Of course, that the Trinity seems more confluent with conceptions of divine immanence, however, seems appropriate. After all, the "plot" of this narrative hinges critically on the activity and person of Jesus, God the Son incarnate, which is understood not as a problem but as a fact and fulfillment.

What I appreciate most in Schwöbel's essay, however, is that, after extensive treatment of his topic, he concludes with a forest analysis—namely, that according to the notion of radical monotheism posited by H. Richard Niebuhr, the entire historical Christian enterprise of telling and retelling the Trinitarian story is fundamentally the story of monotheism as well. In other words, this entire historical pageant of Trinitarian storytelling also marks the work of the divine in history to disclose or precipitate a more robust, vigorous, or perhaps fuller understanding of God's unity.

In Schwöbel's discussion of the functions of Trinitarian discourse, I find another thought-provoking line. He writes, "Trinitarian speech not only frames Christian worship according to the rhythm of gathering and sending; it also punctuates the liturgy at various places."[3] And so we find that this story, which is painstakingly being told and retold over and over in theological writings, is also being told and retold through the form of Christian worship. The theological discourse encompasses the communal liturgical life of the community. Later creeds, like *Quicumque vult* (ascribed to Athanasius), are not just careful expressions of doctrinal arguments but are professions that are recited, performed, and witnessed by faithful congregants in the pews of the church. No humanly determined creed or *ʿaqīda* in Islam has ever played such a performative or binding role in Muslim devotional life.[4] Moreover, Muslim theological discussions of *tawḥīd* or divine unity in general seem to rarely if ever bring into consideration the form and place of worship. The Islamic scholastic tradition does not seem as attentive to this point.[5] Or to look at it another way, the ritual acts performed by the everyday faithful, like the form of prayer or the rhythm of fasting, hardly seem to shape the monotheistic discourses of Muslim theologians, at least not to the same extent as they shape our Christian counterparts. At best the scholastic theologians speak of prescriptions.

It is intriguing, then, to imagine how the Muslim discourse on *tawḥīd* might be enriched or granted greater clarity and precision if the many dimensions of worship and performed devotion were to be brought more explicitly into the orbit of our theological ruminations. What aspects of God's immanence and transcendence might come into sharper relief if we allow our theological discourse to be informed by not just what we believe but *how* we believe it and *how* we embody it. Indeed, to ask the question "how" has proved itself to be an incredibly generative pursuit across both these traditions of theological storytelling.

Notes

1. See p. 67 in this volume.
2. Frank Griffel, "Al-Ġazālī's Concept of Prophecy: Introduction of Avicennan Psychology into Ašʿarite Theology," *Arabic Sciences and Philosophy* 14 (2004): 139.
3. Schwöbel, p. 64 in this volume.
4. My emphasis here is on "humanly determined" since formulas derived from the Qurʾān and traditions of the Prophet Muḥammad, both of which are understood as revelatory and hence divinely determined, do have a strongly performative and binding role in Muslim devotional life.
5. Notably, other discourses, like the Sufi tradition, are more attentive to theologizing devotional practices.

Texts from the Christian Tradition

The following texts are offered as a basis for discussion of how, over the centuries, Christians have grappled with the unity question in the elaboration of Christian doctrine.

Irenaeus, *Against Heresies*, selections

One of the earliest of the church fathers, Irenaeus (c. 120–c. 202), Bishop of Lyons, had a profound influence on the early development of Christian scripture, theology, institutional development, and exegetical method. His best-known work is his Against Heresies *(ca. 180 CE), a multivolume rebuttal of Gnosticism.*[1]

1.22.1. The rule of truth, which we hold, is that there is one God Almighty, who made all things by His Word, and fashioned and formed, out of that which had no existence, all things which exist. . . . There is no exception or deduction stated; but the Father made all things by Him, whether visible or invisible, objects of sense or of intelligence, temporal, on account of a certain character given to them, or eternal; and these eternal things He did not make by angels or by any power separated from His Ennœa [the name given to Sophia in the gnostic system of Simon Magus; God's power of thought, a feminine figure since the descent from the first principle is "sexed"]. For God needs none of all these things, but is He who, By His Word and His Spirit, makes, and disposes and governs all things, and commands all things into existence,—He who formed the world (for the world is of all)—He who fashioned man, He [who] is the God of Abraham, and the God of Isaac, and the God of Jacob, above whom there is no other God, nor initial principle, nor power nor Pleroma—He is the Father of our Lord Jesus Christ . . .

4.20.1. It was not angels, therefore, who made us. . . . For God did not stand in need of these [beings], in order to the accomplishing of what He had Himself determined with Himself beforehand should be done, as if He did not possess His own hands. For with Him were always present the Word and Wisdom, the Son and the Spirit, by whom and in whom, freely and spontaneously He made all things, To whom also He speaks, saying, "Let Us Make man after Our image and likeness"; He taking from Himself the substance of the creatures [formed], and the pattern of things made, and the type of all the adornments in the world.

4.20.3. I have also largely demonstrated, that the Word, namely the Son, was always with the Father; and that Wisdom also, which is the Spirit, was present with Him, anterior to all creation. . . .

4.20.4. There is therefore one God, who by the Word and Wisdom created and arranged all things; but this is the Creator who has granted this world to the human race, and who, as regards His greatness, is indeed unknown to all who have been made by Him (for no man has searched out His height, either among the ancients who gone to their rest, or any of those who are now alive); but as regards His love, He is always known through Him by whose means He ordained all things. Now this is His Word, our Lord Jesus Christ, who in the last times was made man among men, that He might join the end to the beginning, that is man to God. Wherefore the prophets, receiving the prophetic gift from the same Word, announced His advent according to the flesh, by which the blending and communion of God and man took place according to the good pleasure of the Father, the Word of God foretelling from the beginning that God should be seen by men, and hold converse with them upon earth, should confer with them upon earth, and should be present with His own creation, saving it, and becoming capable of being perceived by it, freeing us from the hands of all that hate us, that is from every spirit of wickedness; and causing us to serve Him in holiness and righteousness all our days, in order that man having embraced the Spirit of God, might pass into the glory of the Father. . . .

4.20.5. . . . For man does not see God by his own powers; but when He pleases He is seen by men, by whom He wills, and when He wills, and as He wills. For God is powerful in all things, having been seen all that time indeed, prophetically through the Spirit, and seen, too, adoptively through the Son; and He shall also be seen paternally in the kingdom of heaven, the Spirit truly preparing man in the Son of God, and the Son leading him to the Father, while the Father, too confers [on him] incorruption for eternal life which comes to every one from the fact of his seeing God. For as those who see the light are within the light, and partake of the brilliancy; even so, those who see God are in God, and receive his splendor. But [His] splendor vivifies them; those therefore, who see God, do receive eternal life.

Basil the Great of Caesarea, *On the Holy Spirit* 18.44–45, 47

An early Christian monastic with a classical education, Basil of Caesarea (337–79 CE)—with his brother Gregory of Nyssa and friend Gregory of Nazianzus—is known as one of the "Great Cappadocian Fathers," a reference to their location in Asia Minor. The writings of these theologians were pivotal in the development and articulation of the doctrine of the Trinity. This excerpt from Basil's On the Holy Spirit *provides an example of their thought.*[2]

44. In delivering the formula of the Father, the Son, and the Holy Ghost, our Lord did not connect the gift with number. He did not say "into First, Second, and Third," nor yet "into one, two, and three," but He gave us the boon of the knowledge of the faith which leads to salvation, by means of holy names. So that what saves us is our faith. Number has been devised as a symbol indicative of the quantity of objects. But these men [heretics of a radical Arian persuasion], who bring ruin on themselves from every possible source, have turned even the capacity for counting against the faith. Nothing else undergoes any change in consequence of the addition of number, and yet these men in the case of the divine nature pay reverence to number, lest they should exceed the limits of the honour due to the Paraclete. But, O wisest sirs, let the unapproachable be altogether above and beyond number, as the ancient reverence of the Hebrews wrote the unutterable name of God in peculiar characters, thus endeavouring to set forth its infinite excellence. Count, if you must; but you must not by counting do damage to the faith. Either let the ineffable be honoured by silence; or let holy things be counted consistently with true religion. There is one God and Father, one Only Begotten, and one Holy Ghost. We proclaim each of the hypostases singly; and, when count we must, we do not let an ignorant arithmetic carry us away to the idea of a plurality of Gods.

45. For we do not count by way of addition, gradually making increase from unity to multitude, and saying one, two, and three,—nor yet first, second, and third. For "I," God, "am the first, and I am the last." And hitherto we have never, even at the present time, heard of a second God. Worshipping as we do God of God, we both confess the distinction of the Persons, and at the same time abide by the Monarchy. We do not fritter away the theology in a divided plurality, because one Form, so to say, united in the invariableness of the Godhead, is beheld in God the Father, and in God the Only Begotten. For the Son is in the Father and the Father in the Son; since such as is the latter, such is the former, and such as is the former, such is the latter; and herein is the Unity. So that according to the distinction of Persons, both are one and one, and according to the community of Nature, one.

47. And when, by means of the power that enlightens us, we fix our eyes on the beauty of the image of the invisible God, and through the image are led up to the

supreme beauty of the spectacle of the archetype, then, I ween [suppose], is with us inseparably the Spirit of knowledge, in Himself bestowing on them that love the vision of the truth the power of beholding the Image, not making the exhibition from without, but in Himself leading on to the full knowledge. "No man knoweth the Father save the Son." And so "no man can say that Jesus is the Lord but by the Holy Ghost." For it is not said through the Spirit, but by the Spirit, and "God is a spirit, and they that worship Him must worship Him in spirit and in truth," as it is written "in thy light shall we see light," namely by the illumination of the Spirit, "the true light which lighteth every man that cometh into the world." It results that in Himself He shows the glory of the Only Begotten, and on true worshippers He in Himself bestows the knowledge of God. Thus the way of the knowledge of God lies from One Spirit through the One Son to the One Father, and conversely the natural Goodness and the inherent Holiness and the royal Dignity extend from the Father through the Only-begotten to the Spirit. Thus there is both acknowledgment of the hypostases and the true dogma of the Monarchy is not lost. They on the other hand who support their sub-numeration by talking of first and second and third ought to be informed that into the undefiled theology of Christians they are importing the polytheism of heathen error. No other result can be achieved by the fell device of sub-numeration than the confession of a first, a second, and a third God. For us is sufficient the order prescribed by the Lord. He who confuses this order will be no less guilty of transgressing the law than are the impious heathen.

Gregory of Nazianzus, *Third Theological Oration* 29.2

As did his friends Basil of Caesarea and Gregory of Nyssa, Gregory of Nazianzus (ca. 329–390 CE)—who served for a time as archbishop of Constantinople—brought his extensive training in classical rhetoric and philosophy to bear on his theological writings. As noted earlier, these "Great Cappadocian Fathers" played a major role in the search for resolution of controversy regarding articulation of the Christian doctrine of the Trinity.[3]

2. The three most ancient opinions concerning God are Anarchia, Polyarchia, and Monarchia. The first two are the sport of the children of Hellas, and may they continue to be so. For Anarchy is a thing without order; and the Rule of Many is factious, and thus anarchical, and thus disorderly. For both these tend to the same thing, namely disorder; and this to dissolution, for disorder is the first step to dissolution.

But Monarchy is that which we hold in honour. It is, however, a Monarchy that is not limited to one Person, for it is possible for Unity if at variance with itself to come into a condition of plurality; but one which is made of an equality of Nature and a Union of mind, and an identity of motion, and a convergence of its elements to unity—a thing which is impossible to the created nature—so that though numerically distinct there is no severance of Essence. Therefore Unity having from all eternity arrived by motion at Duality, found its rest in Trinity. This is what we mean by Father and Son and Holy Ghost. The Father is the Begetter and the Emitter; without passion of course, and without reference to time, and not in a corporeal manner. The Son is the Begotten, and the Holy Ghost the Emission; for I know not how this could be expressed in terms altogether excluding visible things. For we shall not venture to speak of "an overflow of goodness," as one of the Greek Philosophers dared to say, as if it were a bowl overflowing, and this in plain words in his Discourse on the First and Second Causes. Let us not ever look on this Generation as involuntary, like some natural overflow, hard to be retained, and by no means befitting our conception of Deity. Therefore let us confine ourselves within our limits, and speak of the Unbegotten and the Begotten and That which proceeds from the Father, as somewhere God the Word Himself saith.

Gregory of Nyssa, *On "Not Three Gods" to Ablabius*

The younger brother of Basil of Caesarea, Gregory of Nyssa (c. 335–c. 394)—another of the "Great Cappadocian Fathers" of early Christianity—brought particular command of the ideas of Plato and Origen to the work of clarifying the Christian doctrine of the Trinity.[4]

As we have to a certain extent shown by our statement that the word "Godhead" is not significant of nature but of operation, perhaps one might reasonably allege as a cause why, in the case of men, those who share with one another in the same pursuits are enumerated and spoken of in the plural, while on the other hand the Deity is spoken of in the singular as one God and one Godhead, even though the Three Persons are not separated from the significance expressed by the term "Godhead,"—one might allege, I say, the fact that men, even if several are engaged in the same form of action, work separately each by himself at the task he has undertaken, having no participation in his individual action with others who are engaged in the same occupation. For instance, supposing the case of several rhetoricians, their pursuit, being one, has the same name in the numerous cases: but each of those who follow it works by himself, this one pleading on his own account, and that on his own account. Thus, since among men the action of each in the same pursuits is discriminated, they are properly called many, since each of them is separated from the others within his own environment, according to the special character of his operation. But in the case of the Divine nature we do not similarly learn that the Father does anything by Himself in which the Son does not work conjointly, or again that the Son has any special operation apart from the Holy Spirit; but every operation which extends from God to the Creation, and is named according to our variable conceptions of it, has its origin from the Father, and proceeds through the Son, and is perfected in the Holy Spirit. For this reason the name derived from the operation is not divided with regard to the number of those who fulfil it, because the action of each concerning anything is not separate and peculiar, but whatever comes to pass, in reference either to the acts of His providence for us, or to the government and constitution of the universe, comes to pass by the action of the Three, yet what does come to pass is not three things. We may understand the meaning of this from one single instance. From Him, I say, Who is the chief source of gifts, all things which have shared in this grace have obtained their life. When we inquire, then, whence this good gift came to us, we find by the guidance of the Scriptures that it was from the Father, Son, and Holy Spirit. Yet although we set forth Three Persons and three names, we do not consider that we have had bestowed upon us three lives, one from each Person separately; but the same life is wrought in us by the Father, and prepared by the Son, and depends on the will of the Holy Spirit. Since then the Holy Trinity fulfils every operation in a manner similar to that of which I have spoken, not by separate action according to the number of the Persons, but so that there is one motion and disposition of the good will which is communicated from the Father through the Son to the Spirit (for as we do not call those whose operation gives one life three Givers of life, neither do we call those who are contemplated in one goodness three Good beings, nor speak of them in the plural by any of their other attributes); so neither can we call those who exercise this Divine and superintending power and operation towards ourselves and all creation, conjointly and inseparably, by their mutual action, three Gods. For as when we learn concerning the God of the universe, from the words of Scripture, that He judges all the earth, we say that He is the Judge of all things through the Son: and again, when we hear that the Father judgeth no man, we do not think that the Scripture is at variance with itself,—(for He Who judges all the earth does this by His Son to Whom He has committed all judgment; and everything which is done by the Only-begotten has its reference to the Father, so that He Himself is at once the Judge of all things and judges no man, by reason of His having, as we said, committed all judgment to the Son, while all the judgment of the Son is conformable to the will of the Father; and one could not properly say either that They are two judges, or that one of Them is excluded from the authority and power implied in judgment);—so also in the case of the word "Godhead," Christ is the power of God and the wisdom of God, and that very power of superintendence and beholding which we call Godhead, the Father exercises through the Only-begotten, while the Son perfects every power by the Holy Spirit, judging, as Isaiah says, by the Spirit of judgment and the Spirit of burning, and acting by Him also, according to the saying in the Gospel which was spoken to the Jews. For He says, "If I by the Spirit of God cast out devils"; where He includes every form of doing good in a partial description, by reason of the unity of action: for the name derived from operation cannot be divided among many where the result of their mutual operation is one.

Augustine, *On the Trinity* 15.28–29

A philosopher and theologian of the early church, Augustine (ca. 354–430), Bishop of Hippo, had an unparalleled impact on the development of Western Christian thought.[5]

28. "God," then, "is love"; but the question is, whether the Father, or the Son, or the Holy Spirit, or the Trinity itself: because the Trinity is not three Gods, but one God. But I have already argued above in this book, that the Trinity, which is God, is not so to be understood from those three things which have been set forth in the trinity of our mind, as that the Father should be the memory of all three, and the Son the understanding of all three, and the Holy Spirit the love of all three; as though the Father should neither understand nor love for Himself, but the Son should understand for Him, and the Holy Spirit love for Him, but He Himself should remember only both for Himself and for them; nor the Son remember nor love for Himself, but the Father should remember for Him, and the Holy Spirit love for Him, but He Himself understand only both for Himself and them; nor likewise that the Holy Spirit should neither remember nor understand for Himself, but the Father should remember for Him, and the Son understand for Him, while He Himself should love only both for Himself and for them; but rather in this way, that both all and each have all three each in His own nature. Nor that these things should differ in them, as in us memory is one thing, understanding another, love or charity another, but should be some one thing that is equivalent to all, as wisdom itself; and should be so contained in the nature of each, as that He who has it is that which He has, as being an unchangeable and simple substance. If all this, then, has been understood, and so far as is granted to us to see or conjecture in things so great, has been made patently true, I know not why both the Father and the Son and the Holy Spirit should not be called Love, and all together one love, just as both the Father and the Son and the Holy Spirit is called Wisdom, and all together not three, but one wisdom. For so also both the Father is God, and the Son God, and the Holy Ghost God, and all three together one God.

29. And yet it is not to no purpose that in this Trinity the Son and none other is called the Word of God, and the Holy Spirit and none other the Gift of God, and God the Father alone is He from whom the Word is born, and from whom the Holy Spirit principally proceeds. And therefore I have added the word principally, because we find that the Holy Spirit proceeds from the Son also. But the Father gave Him this too, not as to one already existing, and not yet having it; but whatever He gave to the only-begotten Word, He gave by begetting Him. Therefore He so begot Him as that the common Gift should proceed from Him also, and the Holy Spirit should be the Spirit of both. This distinction, then, of the inseparable Trinity is not to be merely accepted in passing, but to be carefully

considered; for hence it was that the Word of God was specially called also the Wisdom of God, although both Father and Holy Spirit are wisdom. If, then, any one of the three is to be specially called Love, what more fitting than that it should be the Holy Spirit?—namely, that in that simple and highest nature, substance should not be one thing and love another, but that substance itself should be love, and love itself should be substance, whether in the Father, or in the Son, or in the Holy Spirit; and yet that the Holy Spirit should be specially called Love.

Nicene Creed

The Nicene (or Niceno-Constantinopolitan) Creed is the most ecumenical of any Christian statement of faith, in that Orthodox, Roman Catholic, and Anglican branches, as well as many Protestant denominations, accord it authority as a summary of doctrine and use it liturgically.[6]

First Council of Nicaea (325)

We believe in one God, the Father Almighty, Maker of all things visible and invisible. And in one Lord Jesus Christ, the Son of God, begotten of the Father the only-begotten; that is, of the essence of the Father, God of God, Light of Light, very God of very God, begotten, not made, being of one substance with the Father; by whom all things were made both in heaven and on earth; Who for us men, and for our salvation, came down and was incarnate and was made man; and suffered, and rose again on the third day, and ascended into heaven; from thence he shall come to judge the quick and dead, And in the Holy Spirit. But those who say: "There was a time when he was not;" and "He was not before he was made;" and "He was made out of nothing," or "He is of another substance" or "essence," or "The Son of God is created," or "changeable," or "alterable"—they are condemned by the holy catholic and apostolic Church.

Council of Constantinople (381)

We believe in one God, the Father Almighty, Maker of heaven and earth, and of all things visible and invisible. And in one Lord Jesus Christ, the only-begotten Son of God, begotten of the Father before all worlds, Light of Light, very God of very God, begotten, not made, being of one substance with the Father; by whom all things were made; who for us men, and for our salvation, came down from heaven, and was incarnate by the Holy Spirit of the Virgin Mary, and was made man; he was crucified for us under Pontius Pilate, and suffered, and was buried, and the third day he rose again, according to the Scriptures, and ascended into heaven, and sitteth on the right hand of the Father; from thence he shall come again, with glory, to judge the quick and the dead; whose kingdom shall have no end. And in the Holy Spirit, the Lord and Giver of life, who proceedeth from the Father, who with the Father and the Son together is worshiped and glorified, who spake by the prophets. In one holy catholic and apostolic Church; we acknowledge one baptism for the remission of sins; we look for the resurrection of the dead, and the life of the world to come. Amen.

Athanasian Creed, excerpt

A Western Christian assertion of Trinitarian and Christological doctrine, most likely composed in Latin in the fifth century and meant as a rebuttal of the heresy of Arianism. Despite the title by which it is typically known, scholars have long affirmed that Athanasius was not the author of this formula.[7]

Whosoever will be saved, before all things it is necessary that he hold the Catholic Faith. Which Faith except everyone do keep whole and undefiled, without doubt he shall perish everlastingly. And the Catholic Faith is this: That we worship one God in Trinity, and Trinity in Unity, neither confounding the Persons, nor dividing the Substance. For there is one Person of the Father, another of the Son, and another of the Holy Spirit. But the Godhead of the Father, of the Son, and of the Holy Spirit, is all one, the Glory equal, the Majesty co-eternal. Such as the Father is, such is the Son, and such is the Holy Spirit. The Father uncreate, the Son uncreate, and the Holy Spirit uncreate.

The Father incomprehensible, the Son incomprehensible, and the Holy Spirit incomprehensible.

The Father eternal, the Son eternal, and the Holy Spirit eternal. And yet they are not three eternals, but one eternal. As also there are not three incomprehensibles, nor three uncreated, but one uncreated, and one incomprehensible. So likewise the Father is Almighty, the Son Almighty, and the Holy Spirit Almighty. And yet they are not three Almighties, but one Almighty. So the Father is God, the Son is God, and the Holy Spirit is God. And yet they are not three Gods, but one God.

So likewise the Father is Lord, the Son Lord, and the Holy Spirit Lord. And yet not three Lords, but one Lord. For like as we are compelled by the Christian verity to acknowledge every Person by himself to be both God and Lord, So are we forbidden by the Catholic Religion, to say, There be three Gods, or three Lords. The Father is made of none, neither created, nor begotten. The Son is of the Father alone, not made, nor created, but begotten. The Holy Spirit is of the Father and of the Son, neither made, nor created, nor begotten, but proceeding. So there is one Father, not three Fathers; one Son, not three Sons; one Holy Spirit, not three Holy Spirits. And in this Trinity none is afore, or after other; none is greater, or less than another; But the whole three Persons are co-eternal together and co-equal. So that in all things, as is aforesaid, the Unity in Trinity and the

Trinity in Unity is to be worshipped. He therefore that will be saved must think thus of the Trinity.

Thomas Aquinas, *Summa Theologiae*, Prima Pars, Question 29, Article 4

Thomas Aquinas (ca. 1225–74) was the most influential of the medieval Scholastics. His Summa Theologiae *is a massive yet incomplete exercise in the reconciliation of faith and reason.*[8]

Article 4. Whether this word "person" signifies relation?

Objection 1. It would seem that this word "person," as applied to God, does not signify relation, but substance. For Augustine says (*On the Trinity* 7.6): "When we speak of the person of the Father, we mean nothing else but the substance of the Father, for person is said in regard to Himself, and not in regard to the Son."

Objection 2. Further, the interrogation "What?" refers to essence. But, as Augustine says: "When we say there are three who bear witness in heaven, the Father, the Word, and the Holy Ghost, and it is asked, Three what? the answer is, Three persons." Therefore person signifies essence.

Objection 3. According to the Philosopher (*Metaphysics* 4), the meaning of a word is its definition.[9] But the definition of "person" is this: "The individual substance of the rational nature," as above stated. Therefore "person" signifies substance.

Objection 4. Further, person in men and angels does not signify relation, but something absolute. Therefore, if in God it signified relation, it would bear an equivocal meaning in God, in man, and in angels.

On the contrary, Boethius says (*On the Trinity*) that "every word that refers to the persons signifies relation." But no word belongs to person more strictly than the very word "person" itself. Therefore this word "person" signifies relation.

I answer that, A difficulty arises concerning the meaning of this word "person" in God, from the fact that it is predicated plurally of the Three in contrast to the nature of the names belonging to the essence; nor does it in itself refer to another, as do the words which express relation.

Hence some have thought that this word "person" of itself expresses absolutely the divine essence; as this name "God" and this word "Wise"; but that to meet heretical attack, it was ordained by conciliar decree that it was to be taken in a relative sense, and especially in the plural, or with the addition of a distinguishing adjective; as when we say, "Three persons," or, "one is the person of the Father, another of the Son," etc. Used, however, in the singular, it may be either absolute or relative. But this does not seem to be a satisfactory explanation; for, if this word "person," by force of its own signification, expresses the divine essence only, it follows that forasmuch as we speak of "three persons," so far from the heretics being silenced, they had still more reason to argue. Seeing this, others maintained that this word "person" in God signifies both the essence and the relation.

Some of these said that it signifies directly the essence, and relation indirectly, forasmuch as "person" means as it were "by itself one" [*per se una*]; and unity belongs to the essence. And what is "by itself" implies relation indirectly; for the Father is understood to exist "by Himself," as relatively distinct from the Son. Others, however, said, on the contrary, that it signifies relation directly; and essence indirectly; forasmuch as in the definition of "person" the term nature is mentioned indirectly; and these come nearer to the truth.

To determine the question, we must consider that something may be included in the meaning of a less common term, which is not included in the more common term; as "rational" is included in the meaning of "man," and not in the meaning of "animal." So that it is one thing to ask the meaning of the word animal, and another to ask its meaning when the animal in question is man. Also, it is one thing to ask the meaning of this word "person" in general; and another to ask the meaning of "person" as applied to God. For "person" in general signifies the individual substance of a rational figure. The individual in itself is undivided, but is distinct from others. Therefore "person" in any nature signifies what is distinct in that nature: thus in human nature it signifies this flesh, these bones, and this soul, which are the individuating principles of a man, and which, though not belonging to "person" in general, nevertheless do belong to the meaning of a particular human person.

Now distinction in God is only by relation of origin, as stated above [in Prima Pars, Question 28, Article 2], while relation in God is not as an accident in a subject, but is the divine essence itself; and so it is subsistent, for the divine essence subsists. Therefore, as the Godhead is God so the divine paternity is God the Father, Who is a divine person. Therefore a divine person signifies a relation as subsisting. And this is to signify relation by way of substance, and such a relation is a hypostasis subsisting in the divine nature, although in truth that which subsists in the divine nature is the divine nature itself. Thus it is true to say that the name "person" signifies relation directly, and the essence indirectly; not, however, the relation as such, but as expressed by way of a hypostasis. So likewise it signifies directly the essence, and indirectly the relation, inasmuch as the essence is the same as the hypostasis: while in God the hypostasis is expressed as distinct by the relation: and thus relation, as such, enters into the notion of the person indirectly. Thus we can say that this signification of the word "person" was not clearly perceived before it was attacked by heretics. Hence, this word "person" was used just as any other absolute term. But afterwards it was applied to express relation, as it lent itself to that signification, so that this word "person" means relation not only by use and custom, according to the first opinion, but also by force of its own proper signification.

Reply to Objection 1. This word "person" is said in respect to itself, not to another; forasmuch as it signifies relation not as such, but by way of a substance—which is a hypostasis. In that sense Augustine says that it signifies the essence, inasmuch as in God essence is the same as the hypostasis, because in God what He is, and whereby He is are the same.

Reply to Objection 2. The term "what" refers sometimes to the nature expressed by the definition, as when we ask; What is man? and we answer: A mortal rational animal. Sometimes it refers to the "suppositum," as when we ask, What swims in the sea? and answer, A fish. So to those who ask, Three what? we answer, Three persons.

Reply to Objection 3. In God the individual—i.e. distinct and incommunicable substance—includes the idea of relation, as above explained.

Reply to Objection 4. The different sense of the less common term does not produce equivocation in the more common. Although a horse and an ass have their own proper definitions, nevertheless they agree univocally in animal, because the common definition of animal applies to both. So it does not follow that, although relation is contained in the signification of divine person, but not in that of an angelic or of a human person, the word "person" is used in an equivocal sense. Though neither is it applied univocally, since nothing can be said univocally of God and creatures.[10]

Martin Luther, *Confession Concerning Christ's Supper*, selections

Martin Luther (1483–1546) was the leader of the first and arguably most influential Christian reform movement of the sixteenth century. A fine scholar, skilled debater, and critic of Scholasticism, Luther was a prolific author—in both Latin and German—in a wide range of theological, exegetical, ecclesial, and liturgical genres. The treatise excerpted here, written in 1528, is a presentation of Luther's understanding of the Real Presence of Christ in the Eucharist.[11]

First, I believe with my whole heart the sublime article of the majesty of God, that the Father, Son, and Holy Spirit, three distinct persons, are by nature one true and genuine God, the Maker of heaven and earth; in complete opposition to the Arians, Macedonians, Sabellians, and similar heretics, . . .

These are the three persons and one God, who has given himself to us all wholly and completely, with all that he is and has. The Father gives himself to us, with heaven and earth and all the creatures, in order that they may serve us and benefit us. But this gift has become obscured and useless through Adam's fall. Therefore the Son himself subsequently gave himself and bestowed all his works, sufferings, wisdom, and righteousness, and reconciled us to the Father, in order that restored to life and righteousness, we might also know and have the Father and his gifts.

But because this grace would benefit no one if it remained so profoundly hidden and could not come to us, the Holy Spirit comes and gives himself to us also, wholly and completely. He teaches us to understand this deed of Christ which has been manifested to us, helps us receive and preserve it, use it to our advantage and impart it to others, increase and extend it. He does this both inwardly and outwardly—inwardly by means of faith and other spiritual gifts, outwardly through the gospel, baptism, and the sacrament of the altar, through which as through three means or methods he comes to us and inculcates the sufferings of Christ for the benefit of our salvation.

Martin Luther, The Large Catechism, excerpt (1529)

Published in 1529, Luther's Large Catechism *was a resource manual for clergy for the teaching of the Christian faith, with sections devoted to the Ten Commandments, the Apostles' Creed, the Lord's Prayer, Baptism, and the Eucharist.*[12]

Behold, here you have the entire divine essence, will, and work depicted most exquisitely in quite short and yet rich words wherein consists all our wisdom, which surpasses and exceeds the wisdom, mind, and reason of all men. For although the whole world with all diligence has endeavored to ascertain what God is, what He has in mind and does, yet has she never been able to attain to [the knowledge and understanding of] any of these things. But here we have everything in richest measure; for here in all three articles He has Himself revealed and opened the deepest abyss of his paternal heart and of His pure unutterable love. For He has created us for this very object, that He might redeem and sanctify us; and in addition to giving and imparting to us everything in heaven and upon earth, He has given to us even His Son and the Holy Spirit, by whom to bring us to Himself. For (as explained above) we could never attain to the knowledge of the grace and favor of the Father except through the Lord Christ, who is a mirror of the paternal heart, outside of whom we see nothing but an angry and terrible Judge. But of Christ we could know nothing either, unless it had been revealed by the Holy Spirit.

John Calvin, *Institutes of the Christian Religion* 13.1–2, 17

John Calvin (1509–64 CE), another of the major Christian reformers of the sixteenth century, first published his Institutes of the Christian Religion in 1536. His intent being to go beyond the scope of Luther's Large Catechism *by addressing "all" Christian doctrines, he revised and expanded this work several times. This excerpt is from Calvin's final edition (1559).*[13]

1. The doctrine of Scripture concerning the immensity and the spirituality of the essence of God, should have the effect not only of dissipating the wild dreams of the vulgar, but also of refuting the subtleties of a profane philosophy. One of the ancients thought he spake shrewdly when he said that everything we see and everything we do not see is God (Seneca, preface to *Natural Questions* 1). In this way he fancied that the Divinity was transfused into every separate portion of the world. But although God, in order to keep us within the bounds of soberness, treats sparingly of his essence, still, by the two attributes which I have mentioned, he at once suppresses all gross imaginations, and checks the audacity of the human mind. His immensity surely ought to deter us from measuring him by our sense, while his spiritual nature forbids us to indulge in carnal or earthly speculation concerning him. With the same view he frequently represents heaven as his dwelling-place. It is true, indeed, that as he is incomprehensible, he fills the earth also, but knowing that our minds are heavy and grovel on the earth, he raises us above the worlds that he may shake off our sluggishness and inactivity. And here we have a refutation of the error of the Manichees, who, by adopting two first principles, made the devil almost the equal of God. This, assuredly, was both to destroy his unity and restrict his immensity. Their attempt to pervert certain passages of Scripture proved their shameful ignorance, as the very nature of the error did their monstrous infatuation. The Anthropomorphites also, who dreamed of a corporeal God, because mouth, ears, eyes, hands, and feet, are often ascribed to him in Scripture, are easily refuted. For who is so devoid of intellect as not to understand that God, in so speaking, lisps with us as nurses are wont to do with little children? Such modes of expression, therefore, do not so much express what kind of a being God is, as accommodate the knowledge of him to our feebleness. In doing so, he must, of course, stoop far below his proper height.

2. But there is another special mark by which he designates himself, for the purpose of giving a more intimate knowledge of his nature. While he proclaims his unity, he distinctly sets it before us as existing in three persons. These we must hold, unless the bare and empty name of Deity merely is to flutter in our brain without any genuine knowledge. Moreover, lest any one should dream of a threefold God, or think that the simple essence is divided by the three Persons, we must here seek a brief and easy definition which may effectually guard us from error. But as some strongly inveigh against the term Person as being merely of human inventions let us first consider how far they have any ground for doing so. When the Apostle calls the Son of God "the express image of his person," (Heb 1:3), he undoubtedly does assign to the Father some subsistence in which he differs from the Son. For to hold with some interpreters that the term is equivalent

to essence (as if Christ represented the substance of the Father like the impression of a seal upon wax), were not only harsh but absurd. For the essence of God being simple and undivided, and contained in himself entire, in full perfection, without partition or diminution, it is improper, nay, ridiculous, to call it his express image (*charaktes*). But because the Father, though distinguished by his own peculiar properties, has expressed himself wholly in the Son, he is said with perfect reason to have rendered his person (*hypostasis*) manifest in him. And this aptly accords with what is immediately added—viz. that he is "the brightness of his glory." The fair inference from the Apostle's words is, that there is a proper subsistence (*hypostasis*) of the Father, which shines refulgent in the Son. From this, again it is easy to infer that there is a subsistence (*hypostasis*) of the Son which distinguishes him from the Father. The same holds in the case of the Holy Spirit; for we will immediately prove both that he is God, and that he has a separate subsistence from the Father. This, moreover, is not a distinction of essence, which it were impious to multiply. If credit, then, is given to the Apostle's testimony, it follows that there are three persons (hypostases) in God. The Latins having used the word Persona to express the same thing as the Greek *hypostatis* it betrays excessive fastidiousness and even perverseness to quarrel with the term. The most literal translation would be subsistence. Many have used substance in the same sense. Nor, indeed, was the use of the term Person confined to the Latin Church. For the Greek Church in like manner, perhaps, for the purpose of testifying their consent, have taught that there are three *prosopa* in God. All these, however, whether Greeks or Latins, though differing as to the word, are perfectly agreed in substance. . . .

17. On the other hand, the Scriptures demonstrate that there is some distinction between the Father and the Word, the Word and the Spirit; but the magnitude of the mystery reminds us of the great reverence and soberness which ought to be employed in discussing it. It seems to me, that nothing can be more admirable than the words of Gregory Nazianzus: "I cannot think of the unity without being irradiated by the Trinity: I cannot distinguish between the Trinity without being carried up to the unity" (Greg. Naz. in *Serm. de Sacro Baptis.)*.[14] Therefore, let us beware of imagining such a Trinity of persons as will distract our thoughts, instead of bringing them instantly back to the unity. The words Father, Son, and Holy Spirit, certainly indicate a real distinction, not allowing us to suppose that they are merely epithets by which God is variously designated from his works. Still they indicate distinction only, not division. The passages we have already quoted show that the Son has a distinct subsistence from the Father, because the Word could not have been with God unless he were distinct from the Father; nor but for this could he have had his glory with the Father. In like manner, Christ distinguishes the Father from himself when he says that there is another who bears witness of him (John 5:32, 8:16). To the same effect is it elsewhere said, that the Father made all things by the Word. This could not be, if he were not in some respect distinct from him. Besides, it was not the Father that descended to the

earth, but he who came forth from the Father; nor was it the Father that died and rose again, but he whom the Father had sent. This distinction did not take its beginning at the incarnation: for it is clear that the only begotten Son previously existed in the bosom of the Father (John 1:18). For who will dare to affirm that the Son entered his Father's bosom for the first time, when he came down from heaven to assume human nature? Therefore, he was previously in the bosom of the Father, and had his glory with the Father. Christ intimates the distinction between the Holy Spirit and the Father, when he says that the Spirit proceedeth from the Father, and between the Holy Spirit and himself, when he speaks of him as another as he does when he declares that he will send another Comforter; and in many other passages besides (John 14:6, 15:26, 14:16).

Daniel L. Migliore, *Faith Seeking Understanding: An Introduction to Christian Theology*, 3rd edition

Migliore (b. 1935), a Presbyterian, is Charles Hodge Professor Emeritus of Systematic Theology, Princeton Theological Seminary (Princeton, New Jersey). First published in 1991, with a third edition released in 2014, this textbook has been celebrated for its presentation of doctrines from a Reformed perspective in conversation with other Christian points of view, in a manner that is readily understandable by today's students of theology.

As theologians and local congregations explore new images of God, it is utterly crucial, as many feminist theologians agree, that we not lose the trinitarian depth grammar. I have defined this depth grammar of trinitarian faith as the grammar of wondrous divine love that freely gives of itself to others and creates community, mutuality, and shared life. In God's work of creation, reconciliation, and redemption, God is true to Godself; God does not act "out of character." On the contrary, loving in freedom is the way God is eternally God. I want to expand this thesis by offering three additional interpretative statements about the doctrine of the Trinity.

1. To confess that God is triune is to affirm that the life of the one and only God is incomparably rich and uniquely personal. The Bible describes God as "the living God" (Matt 16:16). Unlike the dead idols, the living God speaks and acts. As personal rather than impersonal reality; the God of the biblical witness freely enters into relationships with creatures as their creator, redeemer, and transformer. Moreover, according to trinitarian faith, the living God does not first come to life, begin to love, and attain to personhood by relating to the world. In all eternity God lives and loves as Father, Son, and Holy Spirit. In God's own eternal being there is movement, life, personal relationship, and the giving and receiving of love.

God is one, but the unity of the living God is not the abstract unity of absolute oneness. God's unity is an incomparably rich and dynamic unity, a unity of plenitude that includes difference and relationship. If the New Testament witness reliably describes the one God as the faithful Father, the servant Son, and the enlivening Spirit, then according to the doctrine of the Trinity, these distinct ways of God's being present in the world and acting for our salvation are rooted in the eternal being of God. Not just any idea of unity defines God, but God—the triune God—defines God's true and rich unity. The unity of the triune God is essentially a unity of "persons" in the bond of love.

Some twentieth-century theologians, preeminently Karl Barth and Karl Rahner, are understandably reluctant to speak of three "persons" in God because of the modern philosophical conceptions of "person" as constituted by autonomous existence and separate self-consciousness. Their recommendation is to speak instead of "three modes of the one being of God," or of God's "three distinct ways of subsisting": Other theologians, however, are hesitant to simply relinquish the concept of person in reference to Father, Son, and Holy Spirit.

They contend that trinitarian theology has the responsibility not only to clarify the special meaning of "persons" as used of the three of the Trinity but also to challenge regnant understandings of the meaning of human personhood. In other words, while the trinitarian "persons" are not to be understood as separate and autonomous selves or as independent centers of self-consciousness, the positive point is that Father, Son, and Spirit have their personal identity only in relationship with each other. "Persons" in God are not self-enclosed subjects whose personal identity is defined in separation from others. Instead, sharing a common essence, Father, Son, and Holy Spirit are differentiated by their relationships with each other, existing in the mutual giving and receiving of love. Their "mutual indwelling" (*perichoresis*) is an intimacy far beyond any relationship known to creatures. Yet without denying the radical difference between divine and human persons, a trinitarian understanding of personhood in God must surely question the adequacy of individualistic views of human persons that equate personal life with absolute autonomy and that lack all reference to relationship with others as constitutive of personhood. In the fecundity and dynamism of the eternal triune life there is differentiation and otherness rather than mere mathematical oneness. A unity lacking differentiation could not be a unity of love. In contrast to sinful human attitudes and practices that rest on fear or hatred of the other and seek to remove or conquer the other, the triune God generates and includes otherness in the inner dynamism of the divine life. That God's own being is a being in personal differentiation and relationship is expressed outwardly in the creation of a world filled with an extravagance of different creatures. So much of the spirit of conquest that manifests itself in our relationships with the natural world and with people of other nations, cultures, races, and gender stems from a fear of the other that ultimately betrays a monarchical rather than a trinitarian conception of God.

2. To confess that God is triune is to affirm that God exists in communion far deeper than the relationships and partnerships we know in our human experience.

We cannot fully understand or adequately describe the triune life in its richness and self-differentiation and as the source and power of reconciled and inclusive community among creatures. Since human beings are created in the image of God (Gen 1:27), theologians have looked for "vestiges" or analogies of the triune being of God in the creation and especially in human life. In particular, two types of analogy have been prominent in trinitarian theology. One is the so-called psychological analogy that is based on a view of personhood as constituted by differentiated but inseparable activities of the self. To be a person is to be a self-conscious subject possessing the intertwined faculties of memory, understanding, and will. The other type of trinitarian analogy is the so-called social analogy that takes the human experience of life-in-relationship as the best clue to an understanding of the triune life of God (a favorite triad being lover, beloved, and their mutual love). Traditional Western trinitarian theology has given primary emphasis to the psychological analogy, while a number of contemporary theologians favor the social analogy and contend that the Eastern theological tradition offers considerable support for the use of this analogy.

Both the psychological and social analogies have their strengths and weaknesses. Certainly neither can claim to comprehend fully the mystery of God. When the psychological analogy is stretched too far, there is the danger of reducing God to a solitary individual and of neglecting the reality of personal relationship in God (the heresy of modalism). When the social analogy is pressed beyond proper limits, there is the danger of thinking of God as three separate individuals who decide to work in concert with each other or who are related in a hierarchical order (the heresy of tritheism). Fortunately, we do not have to choose between the psychological and social analogies. The church has never declared one of them right and the other wrong, although it has rejected the dangers to which either may lead if pushed to an extreme. There is no reason why the two analogies should not serve, when their limitations are recognized, to complement and correct each other. Every trinitarian theology does well to remember the wise comment of Gregory of Nazianzus: "I cannot think of the one without being quickly encircled by the splendor of the three; nor can I discern the three without being immediately led back to the one" (*Orations* 50.41).

In the judgment of many contemporary theologians, much can be learned from fresh reflection on the social analogy. Trinitarian faith attests the "sociality" of God. The God of the Bible establishes and maintains life in communion. God is no supreme monad existing in eternal solitude; God is the covenantal God. That God wills life in relationship with and among the creatures is the faithful expression of God's own eternal life, which is essentially life in communion. According to classical trinitarian theology, the three persons of the Trinity have their distinctive identity only in deep and inseparable relationship with each other. Since John of Dasmascus, a revered Eastern Orthodox theologian, this ineffable communion of the triune life has been expressed by the Greek word *perichoresis*, "mutual indwelling" or "being-in-one-another." The three of the

Trinity "indwell" and pervade each other; they "encircle" each other, being united, as it were, in an exquisite divine dance; or to use still another metaphor, they "make room" for each other, are incomparably hospitable to each other.

That God's life can be described in the light of the gospel with the beautiful metaphors of trinitarian hospitality and the dance of trinitarian love has far reaching implications. It points to experiences of friendship, caring family relationships, and an inclusive community of free and equal persons as faint hints or intimations of the eternal life of God and of the reign of God that Jesus proclaimed. That God is a trinity of love means that concern for new community in which there is a just sharing of the resources of the earth and in which relationships of domination are replaced by relationships of honor and respect among equals has a basis in the divine way of life. . . . The Christian understanding of human life and Christian social ethics are thus grounded in the person and work of Jesus Christ and in the corresponding trinitarian understanding of God. This does not mean that the doctrine of the Trinity provides us with an elaborate blueprint for theological anthropology or a detailed program for the renovation of human society. We must never forget that God is God and we are creatures. It would be a mistake either to project our own ideas of ideal community onto God or to demand that our human communities perfectly reflect our vision of the triune life. The mystery and otherness of God must always be respected. Christian faith and theology must ever resist all idols, whether made with our hands, imaginations, or words. Nevertheless, even if God's being in depth of communion is beyond our comprehension, it is in line with the scriptural witness and church doctrine that human life created in the image of God finds its fulfillment only in loving relationship with God and our neighbors. The Christian hope for peace with justice and freedom in community among peoples of diverse cultures, races, and gender corresponds to the trinitarian logic of God. Confession of the triune God, properly understood, radically calls into question all totalitarianisms that deny the freedom and dignity of all people, and resists all idolatrous individualisms that subvert the common welfare. The doctrine of the Trinity seeks to describe God's "being in love," God's "ecstatic," outreaching, ingathering love as the source of all genuine community, beyond all sexism, racism, and classism. Trinitarian theology, when it rightly understands its own depth grammar, offers a profoundly personal and relational view both of God and of life created and redeemed by God.

3. To confess that God is triune is to affirm that the life of God is essentially self-giving love whose strength embraces vulnerability. The triune God is the living God, and the life of God is a singular act of love. God's eternal act of self-giving love is communicated to the world in "the grace of the Lord Jesus Christ, the love of God, and the communion of the Holy Spirit" (2 Cor 13:13). However scandalous the idea may be, the gospel narrative identifies God as the power of compassionate love that is stronger than sin and death. To have compassion means

to suffer with another. According to the biblical witness, God suffers with and for creatures out of love for them. Above all in Jesus Christ, God goes the way of suffering, alienation, and death for the salvation of the world. It is this compassionate journey of God into the far country of human brokenness and misery that prompts a revolution in the understanding of God that is articulated—although never fully comprehended—in the doctrine of the Trinity. God loves in freedom not only in relation to us but in God's own eternal being. God is faithful to Godself in entering into vulnerable interaction with the world, even to the depths of temporality, deprivation, suffering, and death, because as Father, Son, and Holy Spirit God is essentially an inexhaustible history of mutual self-surrendering love. This boundless love of the triune God is decisively revealed in the cross of Christ and is the eternal source and energy of human friendship, compassion, sacrificial love, and inclusive community.

A trinitarian understanding of God thus coheres with the witness of the Old and New Testaments, with the suffering love of the God declared by the prophets (see Hos 11:8–9), and with all aspects of the gospel story: the compassion of Jesus for the sick, his solidarity with the poor, his parables of the Good Samaritan and the Prodigal Child, and above all his sacrificial passion and glorious resurrection. Moreover, a trinitarian faith redefines the meaning of salvation. If the triune God is self-giving love that liberates life and creates new and inclusive community, then there is no salvation for the creature apart from sharing in God's agapic way of life in solidarity and hope for the whole creation (cf. Rom 8:18–39). Thus a trinitarian understanding of God and of salvation gives new depth and direction to our awakening but still fragile sense of the interdependence of life and our still half-hearted commitment to struggles for justice and freedom for all people.

If the life of the triune God is the mutual self-giving love of Father, Son, and Spirit, and if the triune God is active in history out of love for the creation, it follows that we must not, as has often happened in the theological tradition, think of the Trinity only in retrospect, looking backward from God's dealings with the world to the Trinity before creation. We must think of the Trinity first of all as the life of God with and for us here and now, which we receive by faith, and in which we participate by worship and service as we hear and respond to God's Word and Spirit. Then, too, we must think of the Trinity prospectively, looking ahead to the glorious completion of the purpose for which God created and reconciled the world. The history of the triune God encompasses past, present, and future. It includes suffering and death but also new life and resurrection, and it moves forward to the consummation symbolized as the reign or commonwealth of God. The glory of the triune God will be complete only when the creation is set free from all bondage and God is praised as "all in all" (1 Cor 15:28). Trinitarian faith is thus expressed not only with our lips but also in our daily practice of Christian life, and it finds its completion not primarily in doctrinal definitions but in doxology, praise, adoration, and service.[15]

Notes

1. Irenaeus, *Against Heresies*, ed. and trans. Alexander Roberts and William Rambaut, Ante-Nicene Fathers 1 (Buffalo, NY: Christian Literature Publishing, 1885), 347, 487–89.

2. Basil of Caesarea, *On the Holy Spirit* (Migne, *PG* 32), trans. Blomfield Jackson, Nicene and Post-Nicene Fathers, Second Series 8 (Buffalo, NY: Christian Literature Publishing, 1895), 28–30.

3. Gregory of Nazianzus, *Third Theological Oration* (Migne, *PG* 36), trans. Charles Gordon Browne and James Edward Swallow, Nicene and Post-Nicene Fathers, Second Series 7 (Buffalo, NY: Christian Literature Publishing, 1894), 301–2.

4. Gregory of Nyssa, *On "Not Three Gods" to Ablabius* (Migne, *PG* 45), trans. H. A. Wilson, Nicene and Post-Nicene Fathers, Second Series 5 (Buffalo, NY: Christian Literature Publishing, 1893), 333–35.

5. Augustine, *On the Trinity* (Migne, *PL* 42; *CCSL* 50), trans. Arthur West Haddan, Nicene and Post-Nicene Fathers 3 (Buffalo, NY: Christian Literature Publishing, 1887), 215–16, 224–25.

6. The texts of the Nicene and Constantinopolitan Creeds provided here are according to Philip Schaff's translation from the Greek in his *The Creeds of Christendom, With a History and Critical Notes, Vol. 1: The History of the Creeds*, 6th ed., revised and enlarged (New York: Harper & Brothers, 1877), 29. We have replaced Schaff's use of "Holy Ghost" with "Holy Spirit."

7. Also known by the Latin title, *Quicumque vult* (Whosoever wishes). The text given here is the English translation from the Latin as found in the Book of Common Prayer, 1549.

8. The text provided here is excerpted from Fathers of the English Dominican Province, ed., *The Summa Theologica of St. Thomas Aquinas*, 2nd ed. (London: Burns Oates and Washbourne, 1920), 30–34.

9. "Philosopher" is Thomas's moniker for Aristotle.

10. For his further thoughts on this matter, Thomas directs his readers to Summa I, Question 13, Article 5.

11. Martin Luther, *Confession Concerning Christ's Supper*, ed. and trans. Robert H. Fischer, in *Word and Sacrament III*, Luther's Works 37, ed. Jaroslav Pelikan (Minneapolis: Fortress Press, 1970), 361, 366.

12. Martin Luther, "The Large Catechism," in *Triglot Concordia: The Symbolical Books of the Evangelical Lutheran Church*, trans. F. Bente and W. H. T. Dau (St. Louis: Concordia Publishing House, 1921), 773. Published online by Project Wittenberg: http://www.iclnet.org/pub/resources/text/wittenberg/luther/catechism/web/cat-10.html. Last accessed January 18, 2018. We have replaced the translator's use of "Holy Ghost" with "Holy Spirit."

13. John Calvin, *Institutes of the Christian Religion*, trans. Henry Beveridge (Edinburgh: T&T Clark, 1863), 1:109–11, 125–26.

14. Gregory of Nazianzus, *The Oration on Holy Baptism* (Constantinople, January 6, 381), para. 41. The original renders Gregory's surname "Nanzianzen," but the spelling we've used, "Nazianzus," is more common.

15. Daniel L. Migliore, *Faith Seeking Understanding: An Introduction to Christian Theology*, 3rd ed. (Grand Rapids, MI: Eerdmans, 2014), 78–85.

PART IV

Safeguarding *Tawḥīd* in the Elaboration of the Islamic Tradition

God Is One but Unlike Any Other

Theological Argumentation on Tawḥīd *in Islam*

SAJJAD RIZVI

Theology insofar as it constitutes an account or rationale for a deity expresses a certain standing apart from or before the divine, an attempt to bracket oneself and one's position and consider what is beyond in some trepidation; indeed, the Qur'ān itself states the virtue of such a stance before God in trepidation—"As for one who stands before his Lord in trepidation, there are two gardens" (al-Raḥmān [55]:46). Such a stance is in humility, in abasement, but also very precisely an act, not a thought. But this does not point once again to the superficiality of the contention that the God of Islam is desirous of our acts and not our beliefs and thoughts. It is merely an exercise in a mindful theology predicated on an act of humility. We can never truly know God in her absolute essence, but theology attempts to make sense of what it might mean for God to be and, more important, perhaps, what that disclosure entails for us creatures.[1] For the believer does not need to articulate and think through the arguments—for her, it suffices that God is, and the very mention of the divine makes her heart joyful and ecstatic; as the Qur'ān says, "Truly the believers are those whose hearts rejoice in ecstasy when God is mentioned, and when his signs are narrated to them, they grow in their faith and they trust in their Lord" (al-Anfāl [8]:2). Ecstasy and trepidation are the lot of the believer—and the role of argumentation then becomes a form of *askesis* that complements and bolsters that already existing faith and practice of adhering to God.

Of course, in their humility before God, Muslim theologians were nevertheless not lacking in the audacity to utter how they understood their Lord and how to explain him to others, sometimes in concert but often in conflict with others. To state that Islam is a religious tradition wherein the primary belief affirms the existence of one true God is rather banal. The critique of idolatry and the embrace of monotheism were not ideas that Islam invented.[2] There is plenty of evidence, not only of the prevalence of the belief in one supreme deity in the ancient Near

East and Egypt whether pointing directly to monotheism or henotheism (or whether to what Jan Assmann calls "revolutionary" versus "evolutionary" monotheism), but also of its resonances in the Islamic traditions as they developed intellectually in conversation with the faiths of their context.[3] While it sounds like a commonality with those other traditions that we describe nowadays as "Abrahamic faiths" (a concept that is arguably deeply Islamic but is also a commonality that has arisen from interfaith dialogue[4]), monotheism also divides us because the simple question arises: what does it mean to say God is one? Even if we affirm that the singular cause and principle of all that exists is identical, the same God, the same ultimate reality, we can still differ fundamentally on what that means across religious traditions and, most important, within religious traditions. Perhaps my One True God is not identical with nor even conceptualized in the same way as your One True God. Similarly, there has been a strong tendency to see monotheism in terms of exclusivity: the truth claims of monotheists are considered to be intolerant of others—one God, one Truth, one Path to salvation.[5] The God of the Bible as a paramount deity was considered to be a jealous god whose postulations and communications lived in conversation with other forms of theism and even atheisms in the ancient world.[6] The Qur'ān itself in numerous places recognizes the fundamental nature of humans to incline toward the truth of monotheism as the "nature upon which God created people. There is no change in God's creation. That is the established religion [*al-dīn al-qayyim*], but most people know not" (al-Rūm [30]:30).[7] However, diversity even in the understanding of monotheism is a natural state of affairs—if God had mandated, all would possess the same faith (cf. al-Baqara [2]:213; al-Mā'ida [5]:48, inter alia), but then the variety of life would be sorely missing. At the same time, the presence of forms of materialism, perhaps even atheism, is similarly recognized, as in Sūrat al-Jāthiyah (45):24: "And they say: 'What is there but our life in this world? We shall die and we live, and nothing but time can destroy us.' But of that they have no knowledge: they merely conjecture."[8] Monotheisms and their discontents abound.

But in particular, we want not only to affirm one God but also a God who is a creator and sustainer, a transcendent being who establishes norms and a path from her and to her, but also one who is immanent in this cosmos and who has qualities and names that scripture uses to communicate and describe her reality in immanentist and anthropomorphic terms. God creates with her hands; he sits on his throne; he speaks in human language; she is merciful, loving, and wrathful. The former transcendental element is reflected in the central and early chapter of the Qur'ān that addresses the unity of the divine—namely, Sūra 112, the chapter of "sincere faith" (*ikhlāṣ*) or *tawḥīd* (making one):

> Say: He is God, One [*aḥad*]
> God, the Self-sufficient Besought of all [*al-ṣamad*],
> He neither begot nor was begotten,
> Nor is there anyone equal to Him.[9]

Fakhr al-Dīn al-Rāzī (d. 1209) notes that the name of the chapter, "sincere faith," denotes that qualities are negated of God in these verses, and thus the chapter constitutes an apophatic approach to affirming God's oneness, including a denial of the "numerical sense" of one.[10] Another exegete, al-Ṭabrisī (d. 1154), links this negation to a denial of the idols of the Meccan polytheists as well as to those who relate God in familial terms with others (including Christians by implication).[11] Thus, the thrust of the apophatic element of the verses concerns the need for monotheistic belief to eschew associationism (*shirk*) that may arise in henotheism and "compromised" forms of monotheism. Going a step further, Hawting asserts that the Qur'ānic associationists (*mushrikūn*) are usually those considered to be imperfect monotheists.[12]

Nevertheless, another famous verse of the Qur'ān, in its affirmation of divine transcendence, opens the way for God's immanence: "[He is the] Originator of the heavens and the earth. He has made for you mates, and for the beasts mates as well. There is nothing that is a similitude to Him, but He is the seeing, the hearing" (al-Shūrā [42]:11). Here the transcendence and the immanence of God are balanced in the same verse; the majesty of creation and the sustaining of the cosmos are balanced with her direct intervention in human and animal life, as well as the insistence that while God is unlike anything, she communicates to us in linguistic forms including those of her names that are comprehensible because they denote human qualities. Modern exegete ʿAllāma Ṭabāṭabā'ī (d. 1981) argues that the verse and what follows demonstrates the majesty of God as the sole reality and giver of existence whose agency can be comprehensible to us only through the use of the language of the nurturer who guides and provides sustenance and one who possesses the "keys to heavens" (*maqālid al-samāwāt*) that expresses his dominion over the cosmos but also her ability to decide the fate of her creatures.[13] Transcendent and immanent is he. This paradoxical nature of the divine is expressed succinctly in a text that is much cited in the Islamic intellectual traditions, a sermon of ʿAlī bin Abī Ṭālib, the cousin and son-in-law of the Prophet:

> Praise is God's whom speakers cannot eulogise, and whose bounties cannot be enumerated by those counting, nor can one give Him His due despite the attempts of those striving; the heights of intellectual endeavour cannot perceive Him, nor can the depths of understanding fathom Him. No limit can be established to describe Him, nor praise, neither in space and time that encompasses Him. He originated creatures with His power, dispersed the winds with His mercy, and fixed His trembling earth with rocks.
>
> The beginning of the faith is acknowledging Him (*ma'rifatuhu*), the perfection of acknowledging Him is bearing witness to Him (*taṣdīquhu*), the perfection of bearing witness to Him is believing and making Him One (*tawḥīduhu*), perfection of making Him One is sincere faith in Him (*ikhlāṣ lahu*), the perfection of sincere faith in Him is negating attributes of Him

> (*nafī al-ṣifāt ʿanhu*) because every attribute is recognisably different from what is described and what is described is recognisably different from every attribute. Whoever describes God ascribes a like to Him, and whoever ascribes a like to Him makes Him two, and whoever makes him two divides Him into parts. Whoever divides Him into parts is ignorant of Him (*jahilahu*), and whoever is ignorant of Him has pointed to Him, and whoever has pointed to Him has limited Him. Whoever has limited Him has numbered Him. Whoever asks: "In what is He?," has contained Him, and whoever says: "Above what is He?" has missed Him.
>
> A being but not after becoming (*kāʾin lā ʿan ḥadath*), an existent but not after not existing (*mawjūd lā ʿan ʿadam*), with everything without being like them (*maʿ kulli shayʾ lā bi-muqārina*), unlike everything but not distinct from them (*ghayr kulli shayʾ lā bi-muzāyila*), acting without movement or instrument, seeing even though there is nothing in creation that looks towards Him, absolutely One such that there is none that keeps Him company nor anyone whom He may miss in his absence.[14]

This text testifies to a fairly early occurrence of dialectical and argumentative language that places the paradox of God's hiddenness and manifestation, his transcendence and immanence within the paradigm—and further paradox—of recognizing and yet not being able to know God.[15] The Shiʿi Sufi Kāshānī (d. 1336 CE) in his exegesis of the chapter on sincere faith explicitly cites this sermon in a more monistic vein, making the distinction between the Unique (*al-aḥad*) and the One (*al-wāḥid*).[16]

In this passage, Kāshānī draws on the distinction in the school of Ibn ʿArabī between two levels of considering God to be one: at the level of uniqueness, which is worship and recognition of God in his pure essence devoid of any limitation (including the limitation of being "undelimited"), and at the level of oneness, which is God in all his glory and names. He also draws on the Shiʿi tradition and its preference for a more apophatic approach of denying the reality of the attributes as distinct to the divine essence. At the same time as God *an sich* is described apophatically, there is a cataphatic affirmation of the *deus revelatus* in the person of the Imam that characterizes this tradition.

Of course, plunging into the ocean without a shore that is the Islamic intellectual traditions and their engagement on this pivotal issue of divine uniqueness is quite a task. The way that I propose to examine it in this essay is through the paradigm of the paradox of the transcendent and immanent One, first considering arguments from philosophical theology and philosophy and then turning to more mystical and Shiʿi arguments on the latter.

Tawḥīd as Transcendence

Whether one begins with the rational imperative or the scripturalist approach to the unity of God, what is clear is that these involve both kataphatic and apophatic elements. An example of a traditionalist approach to this lies in the creed (*ʿaqīda*) of al-Ṭaḥāwī (d. 935 CE):

> We assert the unity of God, believing by God's succour that God is one. He has no partner, nothing is like Him; nothing resembles him. Nothing renders Him impotent. There is no deity except Him. He is existent from eternity, without beginning; He is enduring to eternity without end. He does not become non-existent nor cease to exist. Nothing exists except what He wills. Imagination does not reach Him, and understanding does not comprehend Him. He is living; He does not die, upstanding. He does not sleep; creator, without any need; giver of sustenance, without receiving any provision; giver of death, without any fear of retaliation; restorer to life without any difficulty. With His attributes He existed always from eternity before His creation; by their coming into existence he did not increase in any point that was not previously included among His attributes. As He was with His attributes from eternity, so He will be always with them to eternity.[17]

The Muʿtazila—and those influenced by them, such as the Zaydī Imam al-Qāsim ibn Ibrāhīm (d. 860)—were more epistemologically optimistic, demonstrating a similar approach to a dual form of theology with a distinct preference for the apophatic: "The knowledge of God is rational. It is divided into two aspects: affirmation and negation. Affirmation means certain knowledge of God (*al-yaqīn bi'llāh*) and acknowledgement of Him, and negation means negation of his anthropomorphism (*tashbīh*), which in turn is a declaration of his unity (*tawḥīd*)."[18] The arguments for the transcendence of the one are directly related to both types of cosmological and teleological arguments for the existence of God, ones that arise from the contemplating of the signs on the "horizons" and those that emerge from the reflection on the human self or the "selves" as expressed in the famous verse: "We will show them our signs on the horizons, and in their own souls, until it becomes manifest to them that this is the Truth. Is it not enough that your Lord does witness all things?" (al-Shūrā [42]:53). This verse constitutes the basis of what Avicenna described as the proof or the judgment of God's existence that was of the "veracious ones" (*ḥukm al-ṣiddīqīn*).[19]

The *kalām* cosmological argument and similar arguments that move from establishing the existence of God on the basis of observation of the existence of the cosmos and its design to the need for that principle and creator to be one and only one predated Avicenna and then underwent an "ontological" turn with his famous argument.[20] In essence, they were trying to develop the intuition of God's singularity that was expressed in scripture and affirmed in the traditionalist creeds of the early period. In one sense, the shift from the early stark God who lay outside the cosmos as both a remote creator and the goal of one's petitions and desire—as described in Ian Netton's famous phrase "the Qurʾānic creator paradigm"—to a God that was ordered and assimilated as the transcendent one in monistic and illuminationist accounts constitutes the very stuff of Islamic intellectual history.[21] For Netton, the Qur'ānic creator paradigm constitutes four features that arise from scripture: that God creates all things as he wishes, that God creates ex nihilo in historical time, that God's creative agency is clear and comprehensible (expressing a wise purpose?), and that God's creation allows him to be knowable *indirectly* through the data of scripture.[22] One can see the beginnings of expressions of God's unity as creator and sustainer in early philosophy such as the work of al-Kindī (d. ca. 870 CE) and theologians such as al-Ash'arī (d. 923 CE). Al-Kindī reconciles in himself a number of tendencies: a scripturalist reference to the words of the Prophet to demonstrate God's unity, the recourse to the Aristotelian etiology of the four causes to show that God's creative agency lies in him being the efficient and final cause of the cosmos, and a Mu'tazilī approach to an apophatic emphasis on God's uniqueness. On the latter, he wrote in his major work *On First Philosophy* (*Fī-l-falsafa al-ūlā*):

> It is clear that the True One is not an intelligible thing, nor matter, nor genus nor a species nor an individual nor a differentia or a property nor a general accident nor a movement nor a soul nor an intellect. It is neither a whole nor a part, nor can it be described by the terms "all" or "some." It is not characterized as One because of its relations to something else. No! It is absolutely One and does not accept multiplication.[23]

Already in this passage, we see the author drawing on and apophatically separating God from the categories of Aristotelian philosophy and the classification system of the Porphyrian tree. Among the proofs from the selves is the reflection on the design of the human and on the unity and diversity of humanity as such pointing toward the need for a fashioner to have mandated this fact. Arguments from contingency and particularization brought them together in indicating God's design; as Fakhr al-Dīn al-Rāzī stated in his *Transcendental Questions* (*al-Maṭālib al-'āliya*): "Whoever contemplates the various parts of the higher and lower worlds will find that this world is constructed in the most advantageous and best manner, and the most superlative and perfect order. The mind unambiguously testifies that this state of affairs cannot be except by the governance of a wise and knowledgeable being."[24] The language of the "best of all possible worlds" and theodicy is not accidentally linked to divine unity and constitutes Rāzī's approach to the proofs on the horizons and in ourselves.

But the most important early argument—and we shall see its influence on al-Ghazālī—was Avicenna's that followed from his proof for the existence of God as the necessary being. The key account is in part 4 of his *Remarks and Admonitions* (*al-Ishārāt wa-l-tanbīhāt*), which begins with the vital metaphysical insight that what exists is not reducible to the sensible (*maḥsūs*) and then moves on to the importance of the "category" of being and its divisions, ending up with the proof that God is the only being that necessarily is and necessarily must be one. This is summed up in the following manner:

> That whose existence is necessary is something specific. If its specificity is due to the fact that it is that whose existence is necessary, then there is nothing else whose existence is necessary. If, on the other hand, its specificity is not due to this but to something else, then it is caused. This is because (1) if the existence of that whose existence is necessary necessarily attaches to its specificity, then existence necessarily attaches to the quiddity or to an attribute of something other than it. But this is impossible. (2) If the existence of that whose existence is necessary is an accident to its specificity, then it is more appropriate that this existence be due to an external cause. (3) If that which specifies that whose existence is necessary is an accident of its specificity, then that which specifies is also due to a cause. If its specificity and that by means of which it is specified are one quiddity, then the cause is a cause of the singularity of that whose existence is necessary by essence. But this is impossible. (4) Finally, if its occurrence as an accident is posterior to the specificity of a prior first thing, then our discourse is about that prior thing and the remaining divisions are impossible.[25]

This amounts to three elements of an argument: if necessity were a quidditative property of a class of necessary beings, then God would have multiplicity within him and hence would be contingent; if God had parts, then those parts would be contingent and depend on another to be—the necessary must be indivisible and simple—and third, if necessity were shared, then it would be a genus and dependent on its instances. Al-Ghazālī (d. 1111 CE) developed this argument on whether there could be more than one necessary being (which in later parlance became known in a specific form as the doubt of Ibn Kammūna) in his *al-Iqtiṣād*, based on three possible options that either the two necessary beings were equal or one or the other was higher or lower in rank to its counterpart:

> The reason for the impossibility of its being similar to Him in all respects is that every two things must be different. If there were no difference at all, duality would be inconceivable. For we do not conceive of two blacks except in two loci, or in one locus but at two timers, so that one of them would be separate, dissimilar, and different from the other either in locus or time. Two things must differ in their definitions and true natures, just as motion and colour differ, since they are two things even if they coexist in one locus at the same time. For one of them is different from the other in its true nature. If two things are equal in their true nature and definition, such as black, the difference between them would be either in locus or in time. . . . Thus if there were a counterpart to God that was identical to Him in its true nature and attributes, its existence would be impossible. For it could

> not be distinguished from Him by place, since there is no place, nor in time since there is no time, because they would both be eternal; therefore, there would be no differentiation. If every difference is removed, multiplicity is necessarily removed, and hence unity is necessitated.
>
> It is also impossible to say that it differs from Him by being superior to Him, because the one who is superior is god. The god is the most sublime and supreme of existents. The posited other is deficient; hence not the god. We reject the multiplicity of gods. The god is the one who is described in superlative terms: He is the most supreme and the most sublime of all existents.
>
> On the other hand, if it were inferior to Him, that, too, would be impossible because it would then be deficient. We designate by "god" the most sublime of all existents. The most sublime, then, must be one, and that is the god. It is inconceivable that there are two who are equal in all qualities of majesty, for differentiation would be removed, and there could be no multiplicity as mentioned previously.[26]

Within the context of oneness, there were three critical issues raised by theologians and philosophers. The first revolved around the relationship of the divine essences to the names and attributes. Were the latter real and distinct from the former, and what did that mean in terms of affirming or possibly violating strict monotheism? The traditionalists and even the Sunnī Ashāʿira opted for a position known as the *balkafa*, that one asserted what scripture said without asking how—although there was a spectrum of understanding from those who denied all allegorical usage of language to those who insisted that the usage was figurative but the mode was unknown to us as humans. The traditionalist Abū Zurʿa (d. 878) put it in these terms: "God is on His Throne and is separated from his creation as he described himself in his book and through his messenger 'without modality' (*bilā kayfa*). God knows everything thoroughly: 'There is none like Him and He is the all-hearing and the all-seeing'" (al-Shūrā [42]:11).[27] However, this could lead to various contentious positions: the traditionalists and the Ashāʿira—just like their opponents—drew on scripture to argue that God could be seen in the afterlife. Again, Abū Zurʿa: "God will be seen in the world to come. The people of paradise will see him with their eyes and will hear his speech in the manner that he wills and as he wills."[28] Al-Ṭaḥāwī tempers this by insisting that this does not entail God having a body since that would require constitution and parts and violate divine simplicity, while insisting on the "knowing without modality or comprehension" formula.[29] For the Muʿtazila, this would entail a constraint on God, regardless of whether it fit the contradiction of using human standards to critique lack of sufficient transcendence.

The second issue specifically concerned the nature of the Qurʾān as the word of God and whether it was "created" or uncreated and, if the latter, identical with the eternal knowledge of God that was described as an essential attribute of the divine. The third examined God's knowledge and her agency in human history.[30] All of these questions lie on the spectrum between unity and multiplicity and identity and alterity. The Qur'ān directly mentioned not only divine names that proximate human characteristics and even anthropomorphisms. The Ash'āira and other types of Sunni traditionalists insisted that one needed to affirm the truth of the literal language: their realist position insisted that the names, while referring to the essence of the divine, had to be distinct entities and meanings. For the Mu'tazila and their later successors among the Zaydī and Twelver Shī'a, such an attempt at saving the appearance of the text potentially compromised monotheism: nothing could be coeval with God, not even attributes of his agency. Of course, it could be countered that the Mu'tazilī position was internally incoherent: they criticized the Ash'arī position that insisted on the human understanding of these terms, and yet their own rejection of the reality of the attributes was based on the reduction of their meaning to the historical contingencies of human language. The philosophers similarly insisted that God's essence had to be identical to his existence; attributes could not be real, as they would imply multiplicity within the necessary existent. Even the possibility that God might know all things in their particularity would entail a multiplicity, and therefore, it was insisted that God knew particulars in a merely universal sense—God's knowledge had to conform to the model presented in Aristotle's *Metaphysics* lambda.[31]

As we can see in the theological texts that have proliferated, many of these specific questions have disappeared sometimes in favor of the notion that monotheism is a "basic" belief. What has survived is the critique of Christian beliefs as a violation of monotheism—interestingly, even by those realists who affirm the meaningful distinction of the attributes from the divine essence—while at times affirming the importance of saints and intercessors who reveal the hidden God.[32] A good example of this is the contemporary Shi'i theologian Shaykh Ja'far Subḥānī in his *Doctrines of Shi'i Islam*. While reiterating the unity and exclusivity of God as creator and sustainer, the unity of his attributes and acts and totality of his agency, he leaves space for the work of saints and their veneration as true piety, even true *tawḥīd*:

> Now we must focus on the element that distinguishes worship from veneration, and ask the question: How can a given act in certain circumstances—such as the prostration of the angels before Adam—be at one with *tawḥīḍ* while the same act in different circumstances—such as prostration before idols—be an expression of *shirk* and idol-worship? The type of worship which is directed to what is other than God, and which is therefore rejected and forbidden, is that whereby the person humbles himself before a relative, engendered being, in the belief that this being possesses independent

> power to change the destiny of man and the universe, wholly or in part; in other words in the belief that such a being is the lord or master of the world and of men.
>
> On the other hand, if humility is manifested before a person who is himself a righteous slave of God, one who is blessed with virtue and nobility, and is, moreover, a model of piety and righteousness for mankind, then such humility is an aspect of proper respect and reverence for that person and not worship of him.[33]

This already opens up the way to the question of how does the One True God manifests herself in this cosmos and the roles of her friends.

Tawḥīd as Immanence

Immanence-centered approaches to *tawḥīd* attempt to avoid the problem of *taʿṭīl*—or what one might term "agnosticism," or maybe even a denial of realism. They also assume that transcendentist arguments against dualism—that characterize much of the classical debates—have been won.[34] As we just saw, on the one hand, they take the form of the veneration of saints and the friends of God as possessing the spiritual currency and hem of the Lord by way of which God may be understood indirectly. As the famous Sufi saying, often in the guise of a divine utterance (*ḥadīth qudsī*), has it, God said, "I was a hidden treasure and I loved to be known, therefore I created a creation whereby I might be known." The beloved creation of God through which she is manifest is her friends, the *awliyāʾ* of the Sufi tradition and the Imams of the Shiʿi traditions.

Shiʿi Islam is a religious tradition in which it is precisely the presence of the divine through the Imam as both vicegerent of God and of the Prophet (cf. al-Baqara [2]:30; al-Fāṭir [35]:39) and as *deus revelatus*, intervening in and defining human history, the immanence of God in the cosmos, that provides not only the foundations for authority and sovereignty in human communities of belief but also the path to salvation. The everlasting and indeed ever-revealing countenance of the divine mentioned in the Qurʾān (al-Qaṣaṣ [28]:88, inter alia) is glossed in the tradition as the person of the Imam. The Imam is not the defender of the law; he is the law—he is not the exegete of scripture; he is revelation itself. One recognizes the Imams through their manifestation of divine attributes in their totality, not least in the particular privileging of their knowledge of the unseen, of the true nature of scripture and revelation, of the metaphysical, of what comes to pass and what will be. This "gnostic" and sophiological aspect of the mode in which God presents himself to humans is critical. Through the person of the Imam, that transcendent God, the origin and the true king, is manifest, and through devotion and what the believers owe the Imam, the path to salvation is traversed—in fact, the theme of allegiance, association, and dissociation (*walāʾ/barāʾ*) directly linking one's communal personality in this world of trials with one's afterlife seems to have been an early development in Islam. The Imams are witnesses of God over his creation and aware of both those loyal to them and those who reject them. It is because they are witnesses who teach the art of living that encompasses the governance of the self that they must also be martyrs teaching the art of dying. What believers owe to the Imams encompasses a set of practices from recognition (including processes of anagnorisis as well as visitation and devotion in *ziyāra* [pilgrimage] to their persons and thresholds that are in the form of their shrines) all the way through to walking along their path to perfection. The way of imitation of the divine Imam indicates the centrality of *theosis*, of becoming godlike (*al-tashabbuh bi-l-bāri'*) as the art of living and dying in the Shī'i tradition.

Such immanence of the divine suggests an almost Christian approach to the revelation of the One True God. However, it is also an expression of a form of monism in which not only is there nothing in existence save God—a particular reading of the Muslim affirmation of faith in its denial of idols and other deities and its singular embrace of the One—but that deity constitutes the very meaning and essence of all that is and pervades it. Only God truly is. As the famous Sufi Ibn 'Arabī (d. 1240) put it in his *Meccan Illuminations*:

> There is nothing in *wujūd* but He, and *wujūd* is acquired only from Him. No entity of any existent thing becomes manifest except through His self-disclosure. So the mirror is the presence of possibility, the Real is the one who looks within it, and the form is you in keeping with the mode of your possibility. You may be an angel, a celestial sphere, a human being, a horse. Like the form in the mirror, you follow the guise of the mirror's own essence in terms of height, breadth, circularity, and diverse shapes, even though it is a mirror in every case.
>
> In the same way, the possible things are like shapes in possibility. The divine self-disclosure imparts *wujūd* to the possible things. The mirror imparts shapes to them. Then angel, substance, body, and accident become manifest, but possibility remains itself. It does not leave its own reality.[35]

The truth lay in the recognition that nothing could claim to exist save God. *Tawḥīd* therefore came to be understood hierarchically in the ability to understand true oneness that tended toward monism. The Shi'i student of the school of Ibn 'Arabī, Muḥsin Fayḍ Kāshānī (d. 1680 CE), understood this in his expression of the layers and levels in his *Hidden Words*:

> The first level of *tawḥīd* is that a person says on his tongue, "there is no god but God" but his heart is negligent of it or denying of it like the *tawḥīd* of the hypocrite. The second is that he realizes the meaning of the utterance in his heart just as the generality of Muslims affirm as their faith. The third is that he witnesses it by the eye of his heart through the mediation of the

> light of the Truth and that is the rank of those brought close such that he sees many things but he sees them as issuing from the One the Compeller. The fourth is that he does not see in being except the One; that is the witnessing of the veracious ones and the people of gnosis call this annihilation (*al-fanāʾ*) in *tawḥīd* because insofar as he sees save the One he even does not see himself, and if he does not see himself he is submerged in the One, annihilating himself in His *tawḥīd.*
>
> As for the first, he is merely a monotheist in name that saves him from punishment in this world.
>
> As for the second, he is a monotheist who has faith in his heart that is free from falsehood that might run against what is in his heart; however, he has no opening or inner revelation. This protects its possessor from the punishment in the afterlife if he dies and he is not too encumbered by disobedience that loosens his tie. . . .
>
> As for the third, he is a monotheist in the sense that he only witnesses a sole actor as the Truth has revealed to him the reality of things but this does not require his heart to have faith in the meaning of the utterance since that is the rank of the generality and the theologians. . . .
>
> As for the fourth, he is a monotheist in the sense that in his witnessing only the One is present; he does not see everything in the sense of multiplicity but insofar as it is One and that is the desired goal of *tawḥīd.*
>
> The first is like the outer husk of the nut, the second is like the inner husk of the nut, the third is like the kernel and the fourth is like the oil that is extracted from the kernel. There is no good in the outer husk and it is bitter in taste. . . . If you were to take it as fuel and burn it, it would produce much smoke and if you were to use it as building material it would weaken your house. . . . This is the parable of *tawḥīd* purely on the tongue, lacking in vitality, full of harm and to be condemned both outwardly and inwardly. However, it can be useful to dwell a while with the inner husk that is like the receptacle of the body. . . . The outer husk protects the kernel from contamination. The inner revelation takes the person beyond his reason that he may have his heart opened through the illumination of the light of the Truth in it. . . . The kernel is noble in itself with respect to the husk and is what is desired from [the removal of] the husk. But in comparison to the oil that is extracted it is still contaminated. That oil is the *tawḥīd* of act that is the higher desire of the wayfarers. Even that may be contaminated by paying attention to the other and turning to multiplicity in addition to the one who only witnesses the True One.[36]

These few examples should suffice to demonstrate some of the riches of the Islamic intellectual traditions on the arguments for God's oneness. *Tawḥīd,* while a denial of all else including one's own agency, does also bear within it the kernel of a thoroughgoing monism in which all that exists is reduced to an illusory self-reflection of the divine. What these few ideas should indicate is that *tawḥīd* is both the source of commonality and divergence both within Islam and between Islam and other faiths. But it remains a powerful notion—at its simplest, a focus on the divine that entails both a humility before the divine and before others (since it is not for us to judge) but, at its most extensive and mystically inclined, an allusion to a monistic vision of the cosmos in which the contemplation of the divine means that one sees none other.

Notes

1. In this essay, as one effort toward acknowledging monotheism's complexity, when referring to God, the gender of the pronoun will alternate between feminine and masculine.

2. Gerald Hawting, *The Idea of Idolatry and the Emergence of Islam* (Cambridge: Cambridge University Press, 1999); and Moshe Halbertal and Avishai Margalit, *Idolatry* (Cambridge, MA: Harvard University Press, 1998).

3. Michael Frede and Polymnia Athanassiadi, eds., *Pagan Monotheism in Late Antiquity* (Oxford: Clarendon Press, 1999), among others. Cf. Guy Stroumsa, *The End of Sacrifice: Religious Transformations of Late Antiquity* (Chicago: University of Chicago Press, 2009), 95–107.

4. For contrasting views, see Aaron Hughes, *Abrahamic Religions: On the Uses and Abuses of History* (Oxford: Oxford University Press, 2012); and Guy Stroumsa, *The Making of Abrahamic Religions in Late Antiquity* (Oxford: Oxford University Press, 2015).

5. See, among others, Jan Assmann, *The Price of Monotheism*, trans. R. Savage (Stanford, CA: Stanford University Press, 2009).

6. Keith Hopkins, *A World Full of Gods: Pagans, Jews, and Christians in the Roman World* (London: Weidenfeld and Nicholson, 1999); David Sedley, *Creationism and Its Critics in Late Antiquity* (Berkeley: University of California Press, 2009); F. Stavrakopoulou and J. Burton, eds., *Religious Diversity in Ancient Israel and Judah* (Edinburgh: T&T Clark, 2010); and Tim Whitmarsh, *Battling the Gods: Atheism in the Ancient World* (London: Faber & Faber, 2015).

7. Aziz al-Azmeh suggests that Arab monolatry was often conflated with the imperfect monotheism of Jews and Christians in the Ḥijāz in the early Islamic period to provide a monotheistic provenance for the new faith. See his *The Emergence of Islam in Late Antiquity: Allah and His People* (Cambridge: Cambridge University Press, 2014), 248–63.

8. On the presence of materialism and atheism in the world of early Islam, see ʿAbd al-Raḥmān al-Badawī, *Min taʾrīkh al-ilḥād fī-l-islām* (Beirut: al-Muʾassasa al-ʿarabīya, 1980); Melhem Chokr, *Zanādiqa et zindīqs en islam en 2e siècle d'hegire* (Damascus: Institut français, 1993); and Aziz al-Azmeh, *The Emergence of Islam in Late Antiquity* (Cambridge: Cambridge University Press, 2014).

9. Qurʾān translations in this chapter are the author's. For further discussion of this passage, see Feras Hamza and Sajjad Rizvi, *An Anthology of Qurʾanic Commentaries*, vol. 1, *On the Nature of the Divine* (Oxford: Oxford University Press, 2008), 491 passim.

10. Ibid., 535.

11. Ibid., 525–32.

12. This is precisely Hawting's main point in his *Idea of Idolatry*.

13. Al-ʿAllāma al-Ṭabāṭabāʾī, *al-Mīzān fī tafsīr al-Qurʾān* (Beirut: Muʾassasat al-Aʿlamī, 1998), 18.25–26.

14. Sermon collated and cited in al-Sharīf al-Raḍī, *Nahj al-balāgha*, ed. Sayyid Hāshim al-Milānī et al. (Najaf: al-ʿAtaba al-ʿalawīya al-muqaddasa, 2015), 39–40. Translation mine.

15. For a brief link of this sermon and others to the development of a philosophical understanding of *tawḥīd*, see ʿAbdullāh Jawādī Āmulī, *al-Ḥikma al-naẓarīya wa-l-ʿamalīya fī Nahj al-balāgha* (Qum: Dhawī l-qurbā, 1384 Sh/2005), 32–42.

16. For the text, see Hamza and Rizvi, *Anthology*, 550–51.

17. Trans. William Montgomery Watt in his *Islamic Creeds* (Edinburgh: Edinburgh University Press, 1994), 48.

18. Al-Qāsim ibn Ibrāhīm, *Kitāb uṣūl al-ʿadl wa-l-tawḥīd*, in *Islamic Theology*, trans. Binyamin Abrahamov (Edinburgh: Edinburgh University Press, 1998), 64.

19. Ibn Sīnā, *al-Ishārāt wa-l-tanbīhāt*, ed. Mujtabā Zāriʿī (Qum: Bustān-i kitāb, 1392 Sh/2013), 276. For a discussion of this particular proof, see Toby Mayer, "Ibn Sīnā's Burhān al-ṣiddīqīn," *Journal of Islamic Studies*, 12, no. 1 (2001): 18–39.

20. On this argument, see William Lane Craig, *The Kalām Cosmological Argument* (London: Macmillan, 1979).

21. See Ian Netton, *Allah Transcendent: Studies in the Structure and Semiotics of Islamic Philosophy, Theology and Cosmology* (London: Routledge, 1989).

22. Ibid., 23–25.

23. Author's translation of Al-Kindī, *Rasāʾil*, ed. M. Abū Rīda (Cairo: Dār al-fikr al-ʿarabī, 1950), 1:160; see also Netton, *Allah Transcendent*, 57–58.

24. Fakhr al-Dīn al-Rāzī, *al-Maṭālib al-ʿaliya*, ed. A. al-Saqqā (Beirut: Dār al-kitāb al-ʿarabī, 1987), 1:233; Ayman Shihadeh, trans., "The Existence of God," in *The Cambridge Companion to Classical Islamic Theology*, ed. Tim Winter (Cambridge: Cambridge University Press, 2008), 202. See Eric Ormsby, *Theodicy in Islamic Thought: al-Ghazālī on the Best of All Possible Worlds* (Princeton, NJ: Princeton University Press, 1984).

25. Ibn Sīnā, *al-Ishārāt wa-l-tanbīhāt*, *namat* IV, *faṣl* 18, in *Remarks and Admonitions: Physics and Metaphysics*, trans. Shams Inati (New York: Columbia University Press, 2014), 125–26.

26. Al-Ghazālī, *al-Iqtiṣād fī-l-iʿtiqād*, in *Moderation in Belief*, trans. Aladdin Yaqub (Chicago: University of Chicago Press, 2013), 73–74.

27. Abū Zurʿa, *ʿAqīda*, in Abrahamov, *Islamic Theology*, 56.

28. Ibid., 57.

29. Ṭaḥāwī, *ʿAqīda*, in Watt, *Islamic Creeds*, 54.

30. On these issues, see Nader el-Bizri, "God: Essence and Attributes," in Winter, *Cambridge Companion*, 121–40.

31. For a discussion on this point, see Peter Adamson, "On Knowledge of Particulars," in *Proceedings of the Aristotelian Society* (2005): 273–94.

32. It is worth remembering that the very notion and language of *tawḥīd* arises in a sectarian milieu of debate with different types of Christians (the word itself is not Qurʾānic); see Olga Lizzini, "What Does *Tawḥīd* Mean? Yaḥyā ibn ʿAdī's *Treatise on the Affirmation of the Unity of God* between Philosophy and Theology," in *Ideas in Motion in Baghdad and Beyond: Philosophical and Theological Exchanges between Christians and Muslims*, ed. Damien Janos (Leiden: Brill, 2016), 253–80.

33. Subḥānī, *Manshūr-i ʿaqāʾid-i imāmīya*, in *The Doctrines of Shiʿi Islam*, trans. Reza Shah Kazemi (London: I. B. Tauris, 2001), 31–32. By permission of the Institute of Ismaili Studies.

34. For a study that demonstrates the importance of early discourses on *tawḥīd* as responses to dualisms, see Ghazoan Ali, "Substance and Things: Dualism and Unity in the Early Islamic Field" (PhD dissertation, University of Exeter, 2012).

35. Ibn ʿArabi, *al-Futūḥāt al-Makkīya*, III, 80, in *The Self-Disclosure of God*, trans. William Chittick (Albany: State University of New York Press, 1998), 15–16.

36. Fayḍ Kāshānī, *Kalimāt-i maknūna*, ed. ʿAlī-Riḍā Aṣgharī (Tehran: Sipahsālār, 1387 Sh/2008), 252–53. Translation mine.

Christianity, Trinity, and the One God

A Response to Sajjad Rizvi

JANET SOSKICE

By introducing us to texts from different historical periods, countries, and contexts, Sajjad Rizvi has reminded us that there is no single story of monotheism in Islam. Muslim scholars and sages have addressed themselves to the foundational belief in the existence of the One True God for many reasons and in many theological genres—apologetic, analytic, spiritual, and pedagogical.

Rizvi reminds us at the outset that it is not enough to say that "God is One." We need to ask, "What kind of monotheism does a text want to affirm, and what kind of question does the text address?" Certainly, as in Christianity, the oneness of God is not, in Islam, the oneness of the first of a series of cardinal numbers. It is not an assertion that, as it happens, there is only one God, but there might have been six. God alone is One in this privileged sense. Islam also wants to avoid various types of "compromised monotheism," and undoubtedly the Trinitarian God of Christianity may appear to be one such. I shall try to suggest it is not. But initially we need to remember that Islam, in its insistence on monotheism, was not challenging Christianity, or certainly not Christianity alone. As important in the history of Islam, or even more important at some periods, has been the rejection of Aristotelian monotheism—a variant of monotheism also rejected by Jews and Christians.

We need to remember that most sophisticated philosophical schemes of antiquity were monotheistic. Aristotle taught there was one God, and this God was the cause of motion (though not of being). What Aristotle and for that matter Plato lacked was the doctrine of *creatio ex nihilo*. This teaching, and with it the monotheism of radical transcendence, is not a product of the philosophical schools but enters the bloodstream of Western metaphysics through the teachings of the Jews, and then the Christians and Muslims.[1]

Creatio ex nihilo can be briefly defined as the belief that God creates "all that is," including space and time, from nothing (not even a vacuum) and does so freely and from no compulsion. This teaching, I suggest, emerged in Second Temple Judaism and passed into early Christianity, where, after bedding down, it became a foundational orthodoxy by the fourth century. It is not, to my mind, stated straight out in scripture, nor is it a gratuitous add-on from Greek philosophy. On the contrary, *creatio ex nihilo* is not a teaching of Hellenistic philosophy at all—if by that we mean the classical philosophical sources. On the contrary, as David Sedley points out in his *Creationism and Its Critics in Antiquity*, "That even a divine creator would, like any craftsman, have to use pre-existing materials is an assumption that the ancient Greeks apparently never questioned."[2] While Greek philosophers had "creationisms" in abundance, they did not have the radically transcendent deity of Jewish, Christian, and Muslim orthodoxy. I do not want to get bogged down in intellectual genealogy, but even if there were pagan precedents for this radical divine transcendence, it was certainly the language of scripture that was the driver for Jews, Christians, and Muslims. Moses Maimonides (d. 1204 CE) thought this was the only teaching that all three of these faith traditions shared. "Compromised monotheism" for Maimonides would be the monotheism of Aristotle—a philosopher for whom he otherwise had great admiration. Aristotle (and arguably Plato) were both philosophical monotheists, but neither had a creator God. Plato's demiurge molds a preexistent matter. Aristotle's God (or perhaps we should say "god") is the cause of motion but not being itself. Aristotle's god is like the DNA of the universe. In Aristotle's scheme, one could not have the world without god, nor could one have god without the world. The two imply one another and are both, in his terms, eternal.

Aristotle's god has no knowledge of particulars; it is not provident; it is not "capable" of self-disclosure. "Revelation" would be far too anthropomorphic for Aristotle's scheme. Indeed, it is often said that theology of Aristotle is more a branch of his natural science than it is of what we would think of as religion. His is a monotheism that underscores the validity and self-positing of the existent order, with no possibility of divine in-breaking or ultimate origin. Although Aristotle understood the idea of *creatio ex nihilo*, he thought it absurd. If there was ever "entirely nothing," not even space and time, he not unreasonably argued, there would be nothing now. Not so the religions of radical monotheism.

Creatio ex nihilo emerges not from philosophy but from reflection on scripture. For the first-century Jewish writer Philo of Alexandria, and the early Christian theologians who followed him, this is not primarily the creation narratives of Genesis, but the language of the Psalms and the Prophets: "Our help is in the Name of the LORD, who made heaven and earth";[3] and (YHWH speaks):

> 12b I, and none else, am the first,
> I am also the last.
> 13 My hand laid the foundation of the earth
> And my right hand spread out the heavens. (Isa. 48:12b–13 NJB)

God alone creates. God, Philo insists, cannot be ranked among creatures. God cannot be assigned to genus or species. Strictly speaking, God is unnameable, for all our language, all our predication, is devised for creatures, and the same terms cannot be simply predicated of God.

Philo is very interested in naming, and in naming God. Philosophers like Plato had a certain interest in naming, in the roots of language, and even in naming God, but in Philo, this interest is acute. For a Jew, to pray is "to call upon the name of the LORD." How can we call on the name of the unnameable one? Philo understands the disclosure of the divine name to Moses in Exodus 3:15 (where the holy name, YHWH, is both given and glossed as "I Am the One Who Is") as suggesting that God is the source of all that is but that his "nature" cannot be known. Philo expresses relief that, after God says to Moses, "I AM He who IS," God continues saying, "I am the God of Abraham, and of Isaac and of Jacob." Philo believes that human understanding can never grasp what God is (Augustine and Aquinas will say the same in later centuries). What we humans can know is who God is for us—the God who has disclosed himself to us through his mighty acts and preeminently as recorded in scripture.

Scripture is invoked here not as an alternative to reason but as its necessary complement. Before the unknowability of the One who creates all that is, reason falls short and must be crowned with revelation. Here in Philo, we find the fundamental dynamics of transcendence and immanence that are the major structuring poles of Rizvi's paper. God is wholly other yet intimately present to us. Careful speaking of God requires the strategic practices of negation (for God is not a creature) and affirmation, for God is the sole source of all creaturely reality. Here we may look to a portion of Zaydī Imām al-Qāsim b. Ibrāhīm al-Rassī's *The Principles of Justice and Unity*, which is included in this volume.[4]

Given the requirement to be extremely cautious—and pious—of grammar *in divinis*, we might ask ourselves what theology or philosophy of religion in these traditions is *for*. Among other things, this religious philosophy (for Muslims, Jews, and Christians) is a type of spiritual exercise. We meditate on the ultimacy of God, stripping away anthropomorphisms, to gain some awareness of God's intimacy. Another creature can come only so close to me. God, as Augustine said, is closer to me than my own hands and feet. We need, when doing theology, to constantly remind ourselves of the holiness of God. This, in fact, is the way in which Thomas Aquinas begins his *Summa Theologiae*, by reminding his readers of the need for holy teaching. God's revelation is necessary for our *salus*—literally our "health," but here "well-being" or "salvation." While reason has its esteemed place, and is indeed God's gift, reason alone will never grasp or comprehend the divine reality, a perspective echoed in the creed composed by Muslim scholar al-Ṭaḥāwī (d. 935): "He who does not guard against denial of God's attributes and assimilation of them to human attributes is mistaken and has not attained purity of conception."[5] Thus, Aquinas's famous—and famously short—"Five Ways," which demonstrate the existence of God, serve to open his first expansion of the doctrine of God.[6] Indeed, to focus solely on their efficacy as proofs (always somewhat unaccountable, in light of their brevity) and to fail to see that they serve to open his discussion of knowing and naming God is to get the argument of the *Summa* wrong from the outset. Aquinas and his intended audience did not doubt the existence of God, but there is real therapy (spiritual exercise) needed by way of reminding us how it is that we can know God or, more accurately, first know "what manner of being he is not" (Aquinas, *Summa Theologiae* Prologue to Questions 3–11). It is under this chaste rubric that he will now discuss divine simplicity, perfection, limitlessness, and so on—all ways in which the Creator is not like the creature.

Again following Christian consensus, Aquinas believes that God cannot accurately be "named" by us but that we have names, disclosed by God in revelation, that we can use to call on God (for how else should we pray?). Aquinas privileges "He Who Is," a name given to Moses in Exodus 3.[7] Aquinas notes that God is, strictly speaking, incommunicable but also that we may "signify" God by various names, all with degrees of inadequacy.[8] Aquinas—following Maimonides—says that the incommunicable name, YHWH, is probably most appropriate, but in terms of names that for us signify the divine nature, he prefers "He Who Is." He gives us three reasons for this preference: because of its meaning (as not signifying any particular form—but rather, existence itself), by virtue of its universality or indeterminacy (for, citing John Damascene, "In this life our minds cannot grasp what God is in himself"), and because of its tense "for it signifies being in the present and this is especially appropriate to God whose being knows neither past nor future, as Augustine says" (Aquinas, *Summa Theologiae* Prima Pars, q. 13, a. 11; citing Augustine, *de Trinitate* 5.2).

Thomas is here faithful to Maimonides, who, expanding in the *Guide to the Perplexed* (I.65) on the "I Am Who I Am," explains that this name (YHWH, also known as the Tetragrammaton after its four letters) is given so that the Israelites might acquire "a true notion of the existence of God." This name, Maimonides explains, is derived from the Hebrew "to be" (*hayah*). The scriptures, he believes, make it clear that "he is existent not through existence. . . . That there is a necessarily existent thing that has never been, or ever will be, non-existent."[9] This absolute existence, Maimonides says, implies that he shall always be. This is the eternal nature of the God of Moses—not a bald metaphysical token but "the one who was and is and shall always be" who meets Moses at Sinai.

To understand Christian monotheism, we should also note that Augustine and Aquinas and the broad stretch of premodern theology identified this "I Am Who Disclosed Himself to Moses" with Christ. This is because the Christian scriptures themselves identify Jesus as the Word through whom all things came into being. The first chapter of the Gospel of John, echoing Genesis 1, makes this identification, as do a number of startling "I Am" sayings in the same gospel. In these, Jesus appears to identify himself with *the One Who Is who spoke to Moses* (e.g., "before Abraham was I Am"; John 8:58). These "I Am" sayings on the lips of Jesus in John's gospel take us back to Exodus but also to the "I Am" sayings of Deutero-Isaiah. There, in a striking sequence of divine self-designations, YHWH declares that he alone is God:

For thus says YHWH,
who created the heavens
  (he is God!),
who formed the earth and made it
  (he established it;
he did not create it a chaos,
  he formed it to be inhabited!):
"I AM YHWH, and there is no other." (Isa. 45:18)[10]

Elsewhere in the New Testament, the Pauline literature frequently alludes to Christ's role in creation, identifying him with the Word or Wisdom. Although this might suggest two gods (and thus imperfect monotheism), the received understanding is that there is only one Lord who creates all that is and is to be worshipped, but that this Lord became incarnate and dwelled among us in Christ—thus, Trinitarian monotheism.

Thus, the fulcrum of piety. The God we worship, in both Islam and Christianity, is a self-revealing God—revealed to us as ultimacy and intimacy. God is at once "unnameable" yet gives us names and attributes by which we may call on the Lord. God is wholly other yet can disclose Godself to us. Here I intend to pick up Sajjad Rizvi's remarks about Shiʿi Islam as a tradition of transcendence and immanence—a self-revealing God disclosing a path to salvation. Here I see parallels in Christianity—where Jesus is, nonetheless, not just the teacher of Truth, but Truth; not just a person, but the Way. As Augustine says, it is through him we travel to him (*per ipsum ad ipsum*; Augustine, *City of God* 13.24).

Spiritual life is to be *in via*, "on the way," and this, in both our traditions, is a path of knowledge and wisdom. All things come from God and return to God. This is the structuring principle of Aquinas's *Summa*, but with resonances to the Qurʾānic "Verily we are for God, and verily unto Him are we returning."[11] Whether this leaves us with a "thoroughgoing monism," as Rizvi suggests at the end of his essay, is a question for another day—and one of the richly interesting questions that both of our traditions have debated during their long histories and that now we can debate together.

Notes

1. On this, and for Jewish, Christian, and Muslim contributions, see Carlo Cogliati, David Burrell, Janet Soskice, and William Stoeger, eds., *Creation and the God of Abraham* (Cambridge: Cambridge University Press, 2010).

2. Sedley mentions *creatio ex nihilo* in order to distinguish it from the topic he is addressing in his book, creationism, which was prevalent and contested among ancient philosophers and which he defines as "the thesis that the world's structure and contents can be adequately explained only by postulating at least one intelligent designer, a creator god." David Sedley, *Creationism and Its Critics in Antiquity* (Berkeley: University of California Press, 2009), xvii. Paul Blowers's excellent *Drama of the Divine Economy* (New York: Oxford University Press, 2012) makes good use of Sedley and provides an extremely helpful guide to early creation theology.

3. Psalm 123:8, according to the Vulgate numbering of the psalms; Psalm 124:8, according to the Hebrew numbering of the Psalms used in the NRSV, REB, and NAB.

4. *Kitāb uṣūl al-ʿadl wa-l-tawḥīd.* For this text, see p. 143.

5. For more of al-Ṭaḥāwī's text, see p. 144 in this volume.

6. Or rather in Aquinas's more cautious formulation, of that "to which everyone gives the name 'God.'" *Summa Theologiae* Ia.2. Aquinas does not believe he has proved the God of the Bible, but variously a first cause, unmoved mover, and so on, which all "call" God.

7. As he explains in Ia.13.11, the question here is, Is "He Who Is" the most appropriate name for God? I have written about this name and its controversial relation to the name YHWH in a number of places. See, for instance, my article "Creatio ex Nihilo: Its Jewish and Christian Foundations," in Cogliati et al., *Creation and the God of Abraham.*

8. Aquinas does, following Maimonides, say that the incommunicable name, YHWH, is probably even more appropriate.

9. Moses Maimonides, *The Guide of the Perplexed,* trans. Shlomo Pines (Chicago: University of Chicago Press, 1963), 1:154–55.

10. NRSV, adapted slightly.

11. I am grateful to Building Bridges Seminar 2016 participant Waleed El-Ansary for this insight.

Texts from the Islamic Tradition

The following texts are offered as a basis for discussion of how *tawḥīd* has been safeguarded in the elaboration of the Islamic tradition.

Abū Zurʿa al-Rāzī (d. 264/878), ʿAqīda [Creed]

From Rayy, in northern Iran, al-Rāzī was deemed among the most esteemed ḥadīth scholars of his time. A disciple of Ḥanbal and a great opponent of dialectical theology, his contribution to the development of Sunni theology was significant.[1]

1. Belief is action and saying, it increases and decreases.

2. The Qurʾān is God's uncreated speech in all its aspects. . . .

6. God is on His Throne and is separated from his creation as he described himself in his book and through his messenger "without modality" (*bilā kayfa*). God knows everything thoroughly: "There is none like Him and He is the all-hearing and the all-seeing" (al-Shūrā [42]:11).

7. God will be seen in the world to come. The people of paradise will see him with their eyes and will hear his speech in the manner that he wills and as he wills.[2]

Al-Qāsim b. Ibrāhīm al-Rassī (d. 246/860), attributed, *The Principles of Justice and Unity* (*Kitāb uṣūl al-ʿadl wa'l-tawḥīd*)

A scholar of the Zaydī sect of Shīʿi Islam, Imam al-Rassī wrote epistles that carried great authority for centuries. His position on human free will and God's absolute otherness were informed, not by Muʿtazilī thought, but rather by his dialogical engagements on theology with Christians in Egypt.[3]

The knowledge of God is rational. It is divided into two aspects: affirmation and negation. Affirmation means certain knowledge of God (*al-yaqīn bi'llāh*) and acknowledgement of Him, and negation means negation of his anthropomorphism (*tashbīh*), which in turn is a declaration of his unity (*tawḥīd*).[4]

Abū Jaʿfar al-Ṭaḥāwī (d. 323/935), *ʿAqīda*

Al-Ṭaḥāwī was an Egyptian Ḥanafī jurist and muḥāddith *(scholar and collector of ḥadīth). His creed is an "enduringly popular" presentation of Sunni doctrine.*[5]

1. We assert the unity of God, believing by God's succour that God is one. He has no partner, nothing is like Him; nothing resembles him. Nothing renders Him impotent. There is no deity except Him. He is existent from eternity, without beginning; He is enduring to eternity without end. He does not become non-existent nor cease to exist. Nothing exists except what He wills. Imagination does not reach Him, and understanding does not comprehend Him. He is living; He does not die, upstanding. He does not sleep; creator, without any need; giver of sustenance, without receiving any provision; giver of death, without any fear of retaliation; restorer to life without any difficulty. With His attributes He existed always from eternity before His creation; by their coming into existence he did not increase in any point that was not previously included among His attributes. As He was with His attributes from eternity, so He will be always with them to eternity.

2. It is not merely since the creating of creatures that He obtained the name of Creator; it is not by His originating of the created world that he obtained the name of world-maker. He has the character of Lordship where there is nothing lorded over, and the character of Creator where there is no created thing. . . . He has power over all things and all things are in need of Him. All affairs are easy for Him and He requires nothing. "There is nothing like Him, and He is the hearing the seeing one" (al-Shūrā [42]:11).

3. He created the creatures by His knowledge, and measured to them their measures. He fixed for them appointed terms of life. Even before His creating of them, nothing of their acts was hidden from Him; He knew what they would do before He created them. . . . None opposes His decree; none disputes His judgement; none prevails in His affairs. We believe in all that and we are certain that all is from Him. . . .

4. We assert that the Qur'ān is the speech of God; it proceeded from Him amodally as words; he sent it down upon His servant by revelation; the believers truly counted it true. . . . It is not created like the speech of the creature. Whoever hears it and considers it human speech is an unbeliever. . . .

5. Whoever attributes to God any of the characteristics belonging to humanity is an unbeliever. . . .

6. The vision of God is a reality for the people of Paradise, without comprehension or modality. . . .

7. He who does not guard against denial of God's attributes and assimilation of them to human attributes is mistaken and has not attained purity of conception. . . .

8. We do not engage in discussion about God and we do not argue violently about religion. We do not dispute about the Qur'ān.[6]

Abū ʿAlī al-Ḥusayn ibn ʿAbd Allāh Ibn Sīnā (d. 428/1037), *Remarks and Admonitions* (*Al-Ishārāt wa-tanbīhāt*)

Recognized as a leading physician by the age of twenty-one, Persian polymath Ibn Sīnā (often, Avicenna) penned two encyclopedic treatises on medicine that were later translated into Latin. He also formulated a system of Islamic philosophy synthesized with ancient Greek thought. Late in his life, he wrote the philosophical treatise excerpted here.

Fourth Class, Chapters 18–29

18. Remark: Proof for the unity of the necessary in existence

That whose existence is necessary is something specific. If its specificity is due to the fact that it is that whose existence is necessary, then there is nothing else whose existence is necessary. If, on the other hand, its specificity is not due to this but to something else, then it is caused. This is because (1) if the existence of that whose existence is necessary necessarily attaches to its specificity, then existence necessarily attaches to the quiddity or to an attribute of something other than it. But this is impossible. (2) If the existence of that whose existence is necessary is an accident to its specificity, then it is more appropriate that this existence be due to an external cause. (3) If that which specifies that whose existence is necessary is an accident of its specificity, then that which specifies is also due to a cause. If its specificity and that by means of which it is specified are one quiddity, then the cause is a cause of the singularity of that whose existence is necessary by essence. But this is impossible. (4) Finally, if its occurrence as an accident is posterior to the specificity of a prior first thing, then our discourse is about that prior thing and the remaining divisions are impossible.

19. A Benefit: Concerning the difference among things with the same specific definition

One learns from this that things having the same specific definition differ only by causes other than their specific nature. If one of these things is not accompanied by the capacity for receiving the influence of such causes—this capacity being the matter—this thing will not be specified except if it belongs to a nature whose species requires the existence of one individual. If, on the other hand, it were possible for the nature of its species to be predicable of many, then the specification of every one is due to a cause, for there are no two blacks nor two whites in the same thing, if they do not differ in place and the like.

20. A Follow-up: The necessary in existence is neither a species nor a genus

The conclusion of this is that that whose existence is necessary is one in accordance with the specification of its essence and in no way can it be stated of many.

21. Remark: That whose essence is necessary is simple and indivisible

If the essence of that whose existence is composed of two or more things that unite, it becomes necessary by them. One of these things or every one of them will be prior to it and a constituent of it. Therefore that whose existence is necessary is indivisible, whether in concept or in quantity.

22. Remark: A thing whose concept of essence does not include existence derives its existence from something other than its essence

Everything, the comprehension of whose essence does not include existence, according to our earlier consideration, such that existence is not a constituent of its quiddity. Further, it is not permissible that existence be a concomitant of its essence, as has been made clear. It remains, therefore, that existence is due to something other than its essence.

23. Admonition: That which is necessary in itself is neither a body nor dependent on a body

Everything whose existence is dependent on a sensible body is necessitated by that body and not by its essence. Every sensible body multiplies into matter and form by quantitative division and by conceptual division. Again, for every sensible body, you find another body of its species or of another species, if considered in relation to its corporeality. Thus every sensible body and everything dependent on it is caused.

24. Remark: That which is necessary in itself has no genus or species

That whose existence is necessary does not share in the quiddity of anything; for any quiddity belonging to anything other than to that whose existence is necessary requires the possibility of existence. As for existence, it is not a quiddity of something nor a part of the quiddity of something. I mean that things having quiddities do not include existence in the comprehension of their quiddities. Rather, existence is something that occurs to these quiddities.

That whose existence is necessary does not share a generic or a specific idea with anything. Therefore, it does not need to be distinguished from anything by a differential or an accidental idea. Rather, it is distinguished by its essence. Hence its essence has no definition, since this essence has neither a genus nor a differentia.

25. Delusion and Admonition: Refutation of the view that that which is necessary in itself falls under the genus of substance

One may think that the idea of the existent that does not inhere in a subject is common to the First and to other things, in the manner that a genus is common. Thus the First falls under the genus of substance.

But this is an error. For the existent that does not inhere in a subject—this being like a description for substance—does not signify that which exists in actuality, such that its existence lies outside a subject; so that he who knows that Zayd in himself is a substance also knows from this that Zayd primarily exists in actuality, let alone the manner of that existence.

Rather, the idea of that which is predicable of substance, such as its description, is something in which specific substances participate when they are in potentiality, as they participate in a genus. It is a quiddity or an essential reality that exists only outside a subject. This predication is applicable to Zayd and to Amr due to their essences and not to an external cause. Regarding its being in actual existence, which is a part of its being in actual existence outside a subject, this may belong to it due to an external cause. What about, then, that which is composed of it and of an additional idea?

Therefore, that which is predicable of Zayd as a genus cannot be in any way predicable of that whose existence is necessary, because that whose existence is necessary does not have a quiddity that is necessarily accompanied by such a judgment. Rather, necessary existence belongs to it as a quiddity belongs to other things.

You must know that since that which exists in actuality is not stated of the well-known predicables as a genus, it does not become a genus of anything by the addition of a negative idea. Since existence is not one of the constituents of the quiddity, but one of its concomitants, it cannot fall outside of a subject as a part of a constituent would, for then it will become a constituent. If this is not so, then, by the addition of an affirmative idea to it, it becomes a genus for the accidents that exist in a subject.

26. Remark: That which is necessary in itself has no contrary

The multitude use contrary in the sense of an opposite equal force. Everything other than the First is caused but that which is caused is not equal to the necessary Principle. Therefore, there is no contrary to the First in this sense.

The elite on the other hand uses contrary in the sense of that which shares in a subject consecutively and not simultaneously—if it is naturally at the extreme end. But the essence of the First does not depend on anything, let alone a subject. Therefore, in no way does the First have a contrary.

27. Admonition: That which is necessary in itself has no definition

The First has no alike, no contrary, no genus, and no difference. Thus it has no definition and cannot be indicated except by pure intellectual knowledge.

28. Remark: That which is necessary in itself is an intelligence that knows itself and is known by itself

The essence of the First is intelligible and independent. Thus the First is self-subsistent, free from attachments, defects, matter, and other things that make the essence in a state additional to itself. It has been learned that that of which this statement is true intellects its essence and is intellected by its essence.

29. Admonition: Proof for the existence of that which is necessary in itself by means of reflection on existence itself

Reflect on how our demonstration of the First's existence, oneness and detachment from accidental qualities does not require reflection on anything other than existence itself, nor does it require consideration of its creation or its acts, even though such things give evidence of it. But the former way of demonstration is more solid and nobler. That is, if we consider the state of existence, existence attests to the First inasmuch as it is existence. After that, the First attests to all things that follow it in existence. Something like this is pointed out in the Divine Book: "we will show them our signs in the horizons and in themselves so that it becomes clear to them that He is the Truth" (Fuṣṣilat [41]:53). I say that this is the rule for a group of people. The Book continues: "is it not sufficient that your Lord attests to everything?" I say that this is a rule for truthful people who draw testimony from Him for other things and not from other things for Him.[7]

Al-Ḥaramayn al-Juwaynī (d. 478/1085), *A Guide to Conclusive Proofs for the Principles of Beliefs* (*Kitāb al-irshād ilā qawāṭiʿ al-adilla fī uṣūl al-iʿtiqād*)

*Persian theologian and Shāfiʿī jurist Imam al-Juwaynī was a pioneer in the theory of jurisprudence (*uṣūl al-fiqh*) and a teacher of theologian and mystic al-Ghazālī.*

Section on Attributes, Chapter Proving the Impossibility That the Exalted Lord Is a Substance

In the idiom of the theologians, substance is what is spatially extended and we have already adduced a proof of the impossibility that the Creator is spatially extended. Substance is also often stipulated as that which receives accidents. We have also already established the impossibility of the Creator—hallowed and exalted is He!—being susceptible to temporal contingencies. To whomever qualifies the Exalted Creator as being a substance, the following dichotomy should be posed in rebuttal: If you intend, in speaking of Him as a substance, to characterize Him by the specific properties of substances, the proof of the impossibilities of that was given previously. Alternatively, you might intend the appellation not to carry with it the characterization that fits its property and particularity. However, either kind of appellation derives solely from tradition because reason provides no indication of them and there is no evidence for this sort of naming in traditional sources. It is, moreover, not permitted in any religion to make rules for the naming of the Creator arbitrarily.

The Christians teach that the Creator—hallowed and exalted is He beyond their claims—is a substance and He is the third of a trinity. In His being a substance, they mean that he is the basis for the hypostases. The hypostases according to them are three: existence, life and knowledge. Further they call existence the father, knowledge the word (also called the son) and life the holy spirit. The word does not mean speech in this instance because in their doctrine speech is created.

Thus these hypostases are, according to them, substance pure and simple without anything added. Substance is one and the hypostases are three. The hypostases in their view are not existent beings in and of themselves but rather they are possessions of substance that confirm to modal states like the ones affirmed by those in Islam who accept the modes. The modal state is, for example, spatial extension in the case of substance; it is a mode that is additional to the substance's existence. The modal state is characterized thus neither by non-existence nor by existence but is instead an attribute of existence. The hypostases in Christian doctrine are conditions of the substrate to which these modal states apply.

Following this, they claim that the word is one with the Messiah and is clothed in his humanity. Various schools among them have different opinions about this incarnation of the divine in the human. Some insist that it means that the word resides in the physical body of the Messiah in the same way an accident resides in its substrate. The Byzantines hold the doctrine that the word amalgamates with the body of the Messiah and mixes with it as thoroughly as might wine with milk.

These then are the basic principles of their doctrine and, in answer, we say to them: There is no sense in your restricting the hypostases in the manner you mention. What keeps you from claiming that the hypostases are four among which one is power? There is no better reason to exclude power from the list of hypostases than knowledge. Likewise, if it is permitted to argue that existence is a hypostasis, what prevents considering perpetuity a hypostasis? And, in accord with the preceding line of reasoning, such a consequence applies as well to hearing and seeing.

At this point we would say: If you insist that the word becomes incarnate in the Messiah and you explain it as an indwelling, one must respond to you as follows. Is the knowledge which is called the word separable from substance or not? If now they claim that it is separable, they must necessarily admit that substance cannot have a hypostasis of knowledge, since knowledge is not merged with the Messiah, but this they refuse to accept.

In contrast, if they insist that the hypostasis of knowledge is inseparable from substance, accordingly, it would be impossible for it to dwell in the physical body of Jesus, on whom be peace, due to its particularization in the first substance. It is impossible for an accident to become incarnate in a certain body while that accident adheres to another body. If that is impossible with respect to the accident, even more so is that impossible with respect to the particularity conferred by the situation of the attributes of the self. Were it allowed that the word unites with the Messiah, it is also allowed that substance unites with the humanity. The latter is not a different case. None the less, they reject union of the substance with the humanity.

It might be said to them as well: Since the word unites with the Messiah, why does it not unite with the holy spirit, which is the hypostasis of life? One of the characteristics of knowledge is that it is inseparable from life. All this clearly demonstrates the confusion of the Christians.

The refutation of the Byzantines is essentially the same as the refutation of those who uphold incarnation. They would specify that once amalgamated it bears the attributes solely of animals and inanimate bodies. What possible means is there to argue that the hypostasis is a particular property?

Among some other difficult considerations against them, we ask: How do you deny the claim of someone who maintains that the word was united with Moses—may the blessings of God be with him—and, for that reason, he could change the rod into a veritable serpent, split the sea into two, each side like a towering mountain, and do other miraculous things?

That in which they believe, however, and on account of which their faith is corrupted is what was done by Jesus—God bless him and protect him—such as curing the blind and the leper, and reviving the dead with the consent of God. When they are presented with the miracles of the other prophets—on whom be peace—their doctrine becomes confused and yields no firm result, since their basic principle rests on the notion of union only in the case of the Messiah—peace be upon him.

As for their doctrine that the hypostases are divine, all Christians, regardless of their sectarian differences, agree on the trinity. We say to them: While each hypostasis in your view does not have the attribute of existence in and of itself, how can what does not bear the attribute of existence have the attribute of divinity?

Nevertheless, the Christians are in agreement that the Messiah is a god and moreover they all confess that he is the son and concur that he is of both divine and human nature. This is self-contradictory: to ascribe the name god denotes exclusively a judgement of divinity, whereas the Messiah is not purely divine. Beyond that, they agree that the Messiah was crucified. When confronted, however, they insist that what was crucified was the humanity alone and that the humanity in and of itself was not the Messiah.

Section on the Knowledge of God's Absolute Oneness

The Creator—hallowed and exalted is He—is one. One, in the idiom of the metaphysicians is the thing that is indivisible. If one says that the one is the thing, this should be a sufficient stipulation. The Lord—hallowed and exalted is He—is a unique existent, transcending all possibility of division and difference. Speaking of Him as one means that He has no like or peer. A clear consequence of the reality of the doctrine of the absolute oneness is the proof that God is not a composition, because, if that were the case—exalted is He and glorified above that—each separate portion of Him would subsist as knowing, living, and powerful in and of itself. And that is an admission of belief in two gods.[8]

Abū Ḥāmid Muḥammad ibn Muḥammad al-Ghazālī (d. 505/1111), *Moderation in Belief (al-Iqtiṣād fī-l-iʿtiqād)*

The scope of al-Ghazālī's contributions to Islamic theology, philosophy, and mysticism cause him to be ranked as one of the foremost Islamic thinkers of all time. Revival of the Religious Sciences, *his most well-known work, marks an effort to synthesize diverse arenas of study. Toward the later part of his life, al-Ghazālī spent several years withdrawn from the world, only reluctantly returning to university life when he was summoned by authorities.*

Treatise 1, Proposition 10 on God Is One

We claim that God (Exalted is He) is one. His being one is based on affirming the existence of His essence and denying the existence of other such essences. Since [the matter of God's oneness] is not a theoretical reflection on an attribute that is additional to His essence, this issue should be discussed in this treatise.

We say that "being one" might be used to indicate that the thing is indivisible, that is, it has not quantity, part, or magnitude. The Creator is one in the sense that a quantity, which brings divisibility, is negated of Him. He is indivisible, for divisibility applies to that which has quantity. To divide a thing is to act on its quantity through separation and diminution. If a thing has no quantity, its division is inconceivable.

"Being one" might also be used to indicate that the thing has no analogue of its kind, as we say that the sun is one. The Creator is also one in this sense. There is no counterpart to Him.

As for His having no alternate, this is obvious. By "alternate" is understood that which alternates with the thing in one locus, and never combines with it. Whatever has no locus has no alternate. The Creator has no locus; hence he has no alternate.

Regarding our saying that there is no counterpart to Him, we mean by it that He, and no other, is the creator of everything other than Himself. The proof for this claim is that if a partner for Him were posited, it would be either similar to Him in all respects, higher than Him in rank, or lower than Him in rank. Since each of these is impossible, what leads to them is also impossible.

The reason for the impossibility of its being similar to Him in all respects is that every two things must be different. If there were no difference at all, duality would be inconceivable. For we do not conceive of two blacks except in two loci, or in one locus but at two times, so that one of them would be separate, dissimilar, and different from the other either in locus or time. Two things must differ in their definitions and true natures, just as motion and colour differ, since they are two things even if they coexist in one locus at the same time. For one of them is different from the other in its true nature. If two things are equal in their true nature and definition, such as black, the difference between them would be either in locus or in time. . . . Thus if there were a counterpart to God that was identical to Him in its true nature and attributes, its existence would be impossible. For it could not be distinguished from Him by place, since there is no place, nor in time since there is no time, because they would both be eternal; therefore, there would be no differentiation. If every difference is removed, multiplicity is necessarily removed, and hence unity is necessitated.

It is also impossible to say that it differs from Him by being superior to Him, because the one who is superior is god. The god is the most sublime and supreme of existents. The posited other is deficient; hence not the god. We reject the multiplicity of gods. The god is the one who is described in superlative terms: He is the most supreme and the most sublime of all existents.

On the other hand, if it were inferior to Him, that, too, would be impossible because it would then be deficient. We designate by "god" the most sublime of all existents. The most sublime, then, must be one, and that is the god. It is inconceivable that there are two who are equal in all qualities of majesty, for differentiation would be removed, and there could be no multiplicity as mentioned previously.

It might be said: What objection do you have against the one who does not dispute with you concerning the existence of what is designated by the name "god" inasmuch as the god is identified with the most sublime of all existents, but he says: "The world as a whole is not the creation of one creator; rather it is the creation of two creators; for instance, one of them is the creator of the heavens and the other is the creator of the earth, or one of them is the creator of inanimate objects and the other is the creator of the animals and plant?" What is impossible about this? If there is no proof for the impossibility of this, of what use is your statement that none of those can be called by the name "god"? Such a speaker designates by "god" a creator. He might even say that one of them is the creator of good and the other the creator of evil, or that one of them is the creator of substances and the other the creator of modes. So there must be a proof for the impossibility of this.

We say: The impossibility of this is proved by showing, that, according to this questioner, the distribution of the created things among the creators is inescapably of two kinds. Either it requires dividing bodies and modes together, so that one of them creates some of the bodies and modes, but not others, or it is said that all the bodies are created by one and all the modes by the other.

It is false to claim that some of the bodies, such as the heavens but not the earth are created by one. We would ask whether the creator of the heavens is capable of creating the earth or not. If he is capable, just as the other is, then neither one can be differentiated from the other in terms of power. And so, neither one can be differentiated by what is within his power. The object of power would be within the domain of both creators, so that attributing it to one of them would be no more fitting than attributing it to the other. The impossibility here arises from what we already mentioned with respect to positing a multiplicity of similar things without there being a difference between them. . . . It becomes necessary, therefore, to deny that there is a limit to what is within his power; all substances whose existence is possible are within his power.

The second case is to say that one of them is capable of creating substances and the other modes so they are different; for having power over one kind of thing does not entail having power over another kind. This is impossible, because modes cannot dispense with substance and substance cannot dispense with mode. Thus the act of each one of them would be dependent on the other. . . .

It might be said: "Whenever one of them wants to create a substance, the other cooperates with him by creating a mode and conversely." We say: "Is this cooperation necessary, such that the intellect cannot conceive of its absence, or not?" If you claim that it is necessary, your claim is arbitrary; moreover it nullifies power. For it is as if the creation of substance by one of them would make it incumbent upon the other to create a mode, and conversely. Hence he would have no power to abstain. Under this condition, power cannot be established.

In summation, if it were possible to abstain from cooperation, then the act of creation might not be carried out and the meaning of power would be nullified. If cooperation is necessary, then the one who has to cooperate would be compelled to act and would have no power.

If it is said that one of them is the creator of evil and the other is the creator of benevolence, then we say: "This is madness, for evil is not evil due to its essence rather in essence it is equivalent to benevolence and similar to it." To have power over something is to have power over things that are like it. The burning by fire of the body of a Muslim is evil but the burning of the body of an infidel is benevolent and is a repelling of evil. The burning of the same person, if he utters the declaration of Islam, would transform into an evil act. . . . Thus all kinds of burning are equivalent. Power, therefore, must attach to all of them. . . .

In general, however that matter is supposed to be, disarray and corruption result from it. This is what God intends by His saying: had there been deities apart from God both [the heavens and the earth] would have been corrupted (al-Anbiyāʾ [21]:22). Nothing can be added to the explanation of the Qurʾān.[9]

ʿAbū ʿAbdullāh Muḥammad ibn ʿAlī ibn Muḥammad ibn ʿArabī (d. 1240), *Al-Futūḥāt al-Makkīya* (*The Meccan Illuminations*), selections

A brilliant and controversial scholar of philosophy and mysticism, Ibn ʿArabī was born in Islamic Spain and spent most of his life there, apart from a three-year period spent living at Mecca. His most well-known work, The Meccan Illuminations, *is a 560-chapter compendium of thought on Islamic issues from psychology to law.*[10]

All the cosmos is a word that has come with a meaning, and its meaning is God, so that He may make His properties manifest within it, since he is not a locus in Himself for the manifestation of His properties. Hence, the meaning always remains intertied with the word, and God remains always with the cosmos. He says, "And He is with you wherever you are" (al-Ḥadīd [57]:4). . . .[11]

There is nothing in *wujūd* but God. In the same way, if you were to say, "there is nothing in the mirror except the one who is disclosing himself to it," you would be speaking the truth. Nevertheless, you know that there is nothing at all "in the mirror," nor is there anything of the mirror in the viewer. But within the very form of the mirror, the display of variations and traces is perceived. At the same time, the viewer is as he was, and he displays no traces. So glory be to Him who strikes likenesses and makes the entities appear so as to signify that nothing is similar to Him, and He is similar to nothing! There is nothing in *wujūd* but He, and *wujūd* is acquired only from Him. No entity of any existent thing becomes manifest except through His self-disclosure. So the mirror is the presence of possibility, the Real is the one who looks within it, and the form is you in keeping with the mode of your possibility. You may be an angel, a celestial sphere, a human being, a horse. Like the form in the mirror, you follow the guise of the mirror's own essence in terms of height, breadth, circularity, and diverse shapes, even though it is a mirror in every case.

In the same way, the possible things are like shapes in possibility. The divine self-disclosure imparts *wujūd* to the possible things. The mirror imparts shapes to them. Then angel, substance, body, and accident become manifest, but possibility remains itself. It does not leave its own reality. . . .

In Himself, God's knowledge of the cosmos brings together His knowledge of Himself, so the cosmos emerges in His form. This is why we say the Real is identical with *wujūd*. . . .

Although the possible thing exists, it has the property of the nonexistent thing. The truest verse spoken by the Arabs is the words of Labīd, "Is not everything other than God unreal?" and the unreal is nonexistence.[12]

Nasafī Creed and Its Commentary (Sharḥ ʿalā l-ʿAqāʾid al-Nasafīya)

Persian Ḥanafī jurist Najm ad-Dīn Abū Ḥafṣ ʿUmar ibn Muḥammad al-Nasafī (1067–1142) was a prolific author, writing theology, scriptural exegesis, and history—in addition to jurisprudence. His creed attempts to encapsulate the essentials of Islam, doing so from a Māturīdī perspective. It is best known through Taftazānī's commentary, which in turn attracted other commentaries from medieval times until the present.[13]

Divine Attributes and Speech

Nasafī:

He has attributes; they are eternal and subsist in His essence. They are not He, nor are they other than He. They are knowledge, power, life, strength, hearing, seeing, will, desire, doing, creating, sustaining and speech (*kalām*). He speaks by means of a *kalām*, which is an attribute of His, an eternal attribute which is not of the genus of letters and sounds. It is an attribute opposed to silence and defect. Through it God speaks, ordering, prohibiting and informing. The Qurʾān, the speech of God, is uncreated. It is written in our volumes, recited by our tongues, heard by our ears, but it is not incarnate (*ḥāll*) in them.

Taftazānī:

1. *Speech*: this is an eternal attribute to which [God] has given expression, by that ordered speech which is called the Qur'ān and is composed of letters. Everyone who commands or prohibits or informs finds an idea (*maʿnā*) in his soul (*nafs*), and then indicates it by expression, or by writing, or by gesture. This attribute is not knowledge; for a man may give information concerning things of which he has no knowledge, or of which he knows the

contrary. Nor is it will; for a man may order what he does not will, such as a man who orders his slave, intending thereby to demonstrate his disobedience and recalcitrance. This [speech found in the soul] is called the speech of the soul. . . .

2. The evidence for the establishment of the attribute of speech is the *ijmāʿ* of the community and the *tawātur* transmission from the prophets both of which confirm that God speaks, granted also the certain knowledge of the impossibility of speaking without the attribute of speech.

3. It is established then that God has eight attributes: knowledge, power, life, hearing, seeing, will, creativity and speech. Since there is on the last three a great deal of dispute and obscurity, al-Nasafī in his creed repeated the affirmation of their being established, and presented them in some detail.

4. *He:* that is, God; *speaks by means of a* kalām *which is an attribute of His,* because it is necessarily impossible to establish a derivative in a thing without establishing also the source of the derivative in that thing [i.e., if God speaks (derivative), He must possess speech (source)]. This constitutes a refutation of the Muʿtazila who claim that He speaks, by means of a *kalām* which subsists in something other than Him and is not an attribute of His. *An eternal attribute*: because it is necessarily impossible that originated things should subsist in His essence. *Which is not of the genus of letters and sounds*, because these are necessarily accidents subject to origination, the origination of some of them being conditional upon the completion of others. The impossibility of pronouncing the second letter of a word without finishing the first letter is evident. This constitutes a refutation of the Ḥanābila and the Karrāmiyya who claim that God's *kalām* is an accident of the genus of sounds and letters, and yet, in spite of this, is eternal.

5. *It*, that is, speech, *is an attribute*, that is, an idea existing in the essence; opposed to silence: which is not speaking yet having the power to speak; and defect. . . . *Through it God speaks, ordering, prohibiting and informing.* This means that it is one attribute [implying simple, undivided] which becomes many in the form of commands, prohibitions and propositions, through a variety of connections. So also with knowledge, power and the other attributes; each one of them is a single eternal attribute. Multiplicity and origination take place through connections and relationships. This is more fitting to the perfection of God's oneness; and also there is no evidence for multiplicity [division] within each attribute. Someone may object, saying that these [i.e., multiplicity and originations and so forth] are divisions of speech; the existence of speech without them is inconceivable. We reply that it is not so. Rather, any one of these divisions only comes into existence

as a result of connections. That of course relates only to things that are ongoing. In eternity there is no division whatsoever. . . .

6. When al-Nasafī spoke of the eternity of God's speech, he tried also to show that the term "the Qur'ān" is applied to the eternal speech of the soul just as it is applied to the ordered speech which is recited and originated. And so he said, *the Qur'ān, the speech of God, is uncreated.* He followed the term, "the Qur'ān," with the words, "the speech of God," because of what the early shaykhs said, namely, that it is acceptable to say that the Qur'ān, the speech of God, is uncreated; but it is not acceptable to say that the Qur'ān is uncreated. This is so that it should not occur to the mind that the thing composed of sounds and letters is eternal. This, however, is the position taken up by the Ḥanābila, out of ignorance and obstinacy. . . . The evidence for our position is what has been already stated, namely, that it is established by *ijmā'* and by *tawātur*, from the prophets, that God speaks; and there can be no meaning to this statement except that He has the attribute of speech. And since the subsistence of verbal, originated speech in His essence is impossible, it is sure that His speech is of the soul and eternal. . . .

7. The Mu'tazila, since they were unable to deny that God speaks, claimed that He speaks only in the sense of bringing into existence sounds and letters in their places; or He speaks in the sense of bringing into existence the forms of writing on the preserved tablet, though they are not read there. There is some dispute amongst them on the last point. But you are aware that the concept "one who moves" refers to one in whom movement subsists and does not mean one who brings movement into existence. If the Mu'tazilī argument were correct, it would be correct to attribute to God all the accidents created by Him. May He be exalted above such an idea.

8. That is among the strongest arguments of the Mu'tazila. You are agreed that the Qur'ān is a name given to what is transmitted to us between the covers of the volumes, by *tawātur*. This belief requires that it be written in the volumes, recited on the tongues, heard by the ears; and all of these things are necessarily signs of origination. So, al-Nasafī indicated the answer by saying, *It*, that is, the Qur'ān, the *kalām* of God; *is written in our volumes*, that is, by the forms of writing and the shapes of letters, which signify it; *preserved in our hearts*, that is, by verbal expressions which are imagined; *recited on our tongues*, with sounds uttered and heard; *heard by our ears*, in the same manner; *not incarnate in them*, this means that, in spite of all this, the eternal *kalām* of God is not incarnate in the volumes, nor in the hearts, tongues or ears. For it is an eternal idea subsisting in God's essence. This idea is uttered and heard by means of ordered speech

which signifies the eternal speech. It is preserved [i.e., in memory] by means of ordered speech which is imagined. And it is written by signs, forms and characters which represent sounds indicating it [i.e., signifying the eternal speech].

9. It is like this. Fire is a burning substance which is mentioned by means of an utterance, and written by means of a pen. But it does not follow from this that the reality of fire is a sound and a letter. The truth is that a given thing has an existence in substances, and an existence in expressions, and an existence in writing. The writing signifies the expression, and the expression signifies what is in the mind, and this signifies what is instantiated in substances. So, wherever the Qur'ān is described as necessarily linked to the eternal, as in our saying that the Qur'ān is uncreated, the meaning is its true nature, existent outside the world of created things. But when it is described as necessarily linked to created and originated things, then it is the words which are uttered or heard that are meant, as when we say, "I have recited half the Qur'ān." Or it is the imagined words of the Qur'ān that are meant as when we say, "I have memorized the Qur'ān." Or it is the written letters that are meant, as when we say, "It is forbidden for a person in a state of ritual impurity to touch the Qur'ān." Since the guide to the legal judgments is the verbal form and not the eternal idea, the *imāms* in the field of theological truths have defined it as written in the volumes and transmitted by *tawātur*. They made it a name both for the ordered speech ī(*naẓm*) and for the eternal idea. That is, it refers to the ordered speech in so far as it signifies the eternal idea; it is not applied solely to the eternal idea.

Ṣadrā al-Dīn al-Shīrāzī (d. 1045/1636), *Wisdom of the Throne* (*al-Ḥikma al-'Arshiyya*)

A highly creative and influential Shi'i philosopher and a key figure of the "Iranian renaissance" of the seventeenth century, Mullā Ṣadrā was influenced by Ibn Sīnā, Ibn 'Arabī, Iṣfahānian Illuminationism, and Ismā'īlī thought.[14]

Principle Concerning His Speech

[God's] Speech is not, as the Ash'arites have said, an "attribute of [His] soul" and the eternal meanings subsisting in His Essence that they called the "speech of the soul." For His speech is something other than a [pure] intelligible, or it would be Knowledge and not Speech.

But neither is His Speech [as the Mu'tazilites have argued] [merely] an expression for the creation of sounds and words signifying meanings since in that case all speech would be God's Speech. Nor does it help [as some Mu'tazilites have attempted] to restrict God's Speech to [that which is spoken] "in the intention of informing another on the part of God" or "with the intention of their presentation on His behalf" since everything is from Him. And if [by these restrictions] they were intending a speech without any human intermediary, this would also be impossible since in such a case there would be no sounds or words at all.

No, God's "Speech" is an expression for His establishment of Perfect Words and the "sending down of definite Signs—They are the Mother of the Book—and others that are similitudes" (Āl ʿImrān [3]:7), in the clothing of words and expressions. Hence His Speech is "Qurʾān" (that is, "joining" or the noetic unity of Being) from one point of view and "Furqān" (that is, "separate," manifest reality) from another point of view.

[As Qurʾān or the inner noetic reality of being and the "Mother of the Book"] God's Speech is different from the "Book," because the "Book" belongs to the world of [manifest] Creation: "You [Muḥammad] did not recite any book before this, nor did you write one with your right hand for else those who would oppose [you] might have doubted [your purely divine inspiration]" (al-ʿAnkabūt [29]:48).

For His Speech belongs to the World of the Command [i.e., the noetic modality of being], and Its dwelling is the hearts and breasts [of humankind] as in His saying: "The Faithful Spirit brought down upon your heart, with God's permission" (conflating al-Shuʿarāʾ [26]:193–94 and al-Qadr [97]:4), and His saying: "Verily It is clear signs in the breasts of those who have been given knowledge" (al-ʿAnkabūt [29]:49). The "Book" [of manifest, contingent beings] can be perceived by everyone: "And We wrote down for him [Moses] upon the tablets the counsel to be drawn from every thing" (al-Aʿrāf [7]:145). But God's Speech [i.e., noetic being] is "a hidden Book that can only be touched by those purified" (cf. Wāqiʿah [56]:78–79) from the pollution of the world of man's mortal [animal] nature.

The Qurʾān was [God's] creation of the Prophet [perhaps as the noetic pleroma or "Adam," the "Complete Human Being"] before the "Book" [of contingent being]. The difference between the Qurʾān and the "Book" is like that between Adam and Jesus. [Both were alike to the extent that] "the likeness of Jesus is with God as is the likeness of Adam: He created him from dust; then he said to him, 'Be!' and he comes to be" (Āl ʿImrān [3]:59). But Adam is the Book of God, "written with the two Hands" (Ṣād [38]:75) of His Power.

You (O Adam) are the "Clear Book" (al-Māʾida [5]:15, etc.)
Through Whose letters what was hidden appears.

Jesus [on the other hand] was His Saying, resulting from His Command [Kun! "Be!"] and "His Word that He conveyed to Mary, and a spirit from Him" (al-Nisāʾ [4]:171). That which was created by God's "two Hands" is not to be likened in nobility in rank to that which came to exist through two letters [*k—n*, of the divine command "Be!"]. So whoever maintains the opposite of this is mistaken.

Principle [Deriving from] the Source of Illumination [concerning the Union of God and His Speech in All Beings: The "Breath of the Merciful"]

The speaker is he through whom speech subsists. The writer is he who causes speech—that is, the book—to exist. And each of these has several levels. Every book is speech in some respect, since every speaker is a writer in some way, and every writer is in some way also a speaker.

A visible image of that is the following: when you witness a man speaking, the form of letters and the shapes of speech arise from his breath in his chest, throat, and the other places that produce the sounds and letters; and his breath is from the one who causes the speech to be. So he "writes" with the "pen" of his power on the "tablet" of his breath, and ultimately on the places that produce the various sounds. He is the same individual through whom the speech subsists, so he becomes the speaker.

Now take this analogy for What is above it [i.e., the eternal creative self-manifestation or the "Breath of the Merciful"] and be among "those who speak wisely" (al-Qaṣaṣ [28]:20) and do good, not among "those who quarrel among themselves" (Qaf [50]:28).[15]

Fayḍ Kāshānī (d. 1091/1680), *Hidden Words* (*Kalimāt maḍnūna*)

Shi'i mystic Mullā Muḥammad b. Murtaḍā b. Maḥmūd al-Kāshānī was a scholar of Qur'ān exegesis, Ḥadīth, fiqh (of the Akbari School), and philosophy—heavily influenced by Platonism.

Know that *tawḥīd* is a deep ocean without a shore, and has four levels that are the kernel, the kernel of the kernel, the husk and the husk of the husk. We use the similitude of the nut to explain this to weak minds. . . .

The first level of *tawḥīd* is that a person says on his tongue, "there is no god but God" but his heart is negligent of it or denying of it like the *tawḥīd* of the hypocrite. The second is that he realizes the meaning of the utterance in his heart just as the generality of Muslims affirm as their faith. The third is that he witnesses it by the eye of his heart through the mediation of the light of the Truth and that is the rank of those brought close such that he sees many things but he sees them as issuing from the One the Compeller. The fourth is that he does not see in being except the One; that is the witnessing of the veracious ones and the people of gnosis call this annihilation (*al-fanā'*) in *tawḥīd* because insofar as he sees save the One he even does not see himself, and if he does not see himself he is submerged in the One, annihilating himself in His *tawḥīd*.

As for the first, he is merely a monotheist in name that saves him from punishment in this world.

As for the second, he is a monotheist who has faith in his heart that is free from falsehood that might run against what is in his heart; however, he has no opening or inner revelation. This protects its possessor from the punishment in the afterlife if he dies and he is not too encumbered by disobedience that loosens his tie. . . .

As for the third, he is a monotheist in the sense that he only witnesses a sole actor as the Truth has revealed to him the reality of things but this does not require his heart to have faith in the meaning of the utterance since that is the rank of the generality and the theologians. . . .

As for the fourth, he is a monotheist in the sense that in his witnessing only the One is present; he does not see everything in the sense of multiplicity but insofar as it is One and that is the desired goal of *tawḥīd.*

The first is like the outer husk of the nut, the second is like the inner husk of the nut, the third is like the kernel and the fourth is like the oil that is extracted from the kernel. There is no good in the outer husk and it is bitter in taste. . . . If you were to take it as fuel and burn it, it would produce much smoke and if you were to use it as building material it would weaken your house. . . . This is the parable of *tawḥīd* purely on the tongue, lacking in vitality, full of harm and to be condemned both outwardly and inwardly. However, it can be useful to dwell a while with the inner husk that is like the receptacle of the body. . . . The outer husk protects the kernel from contamination. The inner revelation takes the person beyond his reason that he may have his heart opened through the illumination of the light of the Truth in it. . . . The kernel is noble in itself with respect to the husk and is what is desired from [the removal of] the husk. But in comparison to the oil that is extracted it is still contaminated. That oil is the *tawḥīd* of act that is the higher desire of the wayfarers. Even that may be contaminated by paying attention to the other and turning to multiplicity in addition to the one who only witnesses the True One.[16]

Sir Sayyid Aḥmad Khān (d. 1898), *ʿAqīda*

A nineteenth-century Indian philosopher who published on a wide range of topics, Khān was a Muslim reformer who worked for the British colonial administration. He advocated for political modernism and an embrace of Western science and education. Though often accused of heterodoxy, he is still seen as a founding father of Pakistan. The following excerpt from his writings provides an example of a modern Sunni creedal formulation.

The Doctrine of waḥdat al-wujūd and of waḥdat ash-shuhūd

On this matter the opinion of the great men of Islam has remained divided. Most of them say that in this imperishable existence there are two potencies, the *potentia activa* and the *potentia passiva*, the latter being understood as the potency to "receive" accidents. For this reason these people hold the theory of unity of Being (*waḥdat al-wujūd*) and speak thus:

> He Himself is the earthen pot. He Himself is the potter. He Himself is the clay of the pot. He Himself came to the market as customer. He broke it into pieces and went off.

And some say that the cause of this *potentia passiva* is another existence and for this reason they hold the theory of the unity of appearance (*waḥdat ash-shuhūd*). But basically the following is true:

> Oh you who are higher than thought and analogy, than imagination and guess, who are higher than all we have been told and we have heard and read of.

In any case, whichever of the two propositions is true, it does not in any way affect the Islamic doctrine that there is One Creator of all beings.

People have considered the doctrine of Unity of Appearance to be unbelief. They have fallen into the error of holding this imperishable existence, for which we have to postulate a second being as the cause for its [functioning as] *potentia passiva*, as being equally eternal, without beginning and end, which is outright associationism (*shirk*). Or their religion is to hold God and matter to be two separate eternal entities, without beginning and end, and some express the same reality by [the terms] light and darkness. But this is a mistake in the understanding of these people because the existence of an effect, by necessity, is linked with the existence of a cause and since the effect exists because of the existence of the cause then where is there any trace of *shirk*? The effect of an eternal cause without beginning and end is itself, also, eternal without beginning and end. If you are eternal without beginning and end, then we too are eternal without beginning and end.

> We became creatures and walked with the Creator. Where God was there we were, too.

So from the existence of the existing things alone we come to the firm belief in a Creator.[17]

Ayatollah Jafar Sobhani (b. 1930), *Doctrines of Shiʿi Islam*

A contemporary Iranian Shiʿi scholar commended for his advanced expertise in the Islamic sciences, Sobhani is well known for his ongoing, multivolume Qurʾān commentaries (one each in Arabic and Persian) and his major biographies of the Prophet Muḥammad and Imam ʿAlī.[18]

Article 27

Belief in the reality of God is a principle held in common by all heavenly religions; herein lies the decisive distinction between a religious person and a materialist.

The Holy Qur'ān asserts that the reality of God is a self-evident fact, one that does not stand in need of proof; doubt and obscurity on this question should not, as a rule, enter into this axiomatic principle. As the Qur'ān says: "Can there be doubt concerning God, the Creator of the heavens and the earth?" (Ibrāhīm [14]:10). This dazzling self-evidence of divine reality notwithstanding, the Qur'ān also opens up ways of removing contingent doubts from the minds of those who seek to arrive at belief in God by means of rational reflection and argument. To begin with, the individual normally has the sense of being connected to, and dependent upon, some entity that transcends the domain revealed by his particular consciousness; this sense is as an echo of that call from the primordial human nature. . . . The Qur'ān says: "So set thy purpose for religion as a man by nature upright—the nature of God in which he hath created man" (al-Rūm [30]:30). . . . Man is continuously invited to study the natural world and meditate upon its marvels. . . .

Article 28

All divinely revealed religions are based on *tawḥīd*, that is, the Oneness of God, and on the worship of this one and only God. . . .

The first degree of *tawḥīd* pertains to the essence of God . . . that the essence of God is absolutely one and peerless; nothing analogous or similar to Him is conceivable. God's nature is absolutely simple, non-compound, without any plurality.

Imam 'Alī states: "He is one and there is nothing similar to Him among existent things and He—glorified and exalted be He—is one in meaning. He is not divided into parts by outward existence, by the imagination or by the intellect."

The *sūra* of *Tawḥīd* [al-Ikhlāṣ (112)], the veritable cornerstone of Muslim belief in divine unity, alludes to both aspects of this essential *tawḥīd*; as regards the first, in the verse "There is none like unto Him" and as regards the second in the verse, "Say: He is God the One." In the light of what has been said, it will be clear that the Christian doctrine of the Trinity—God the Father, the Son and the Holy Spirit—is unacceptable from the point of view of Islamic logic. . . .

Article 29

The second degree of *tawḥīd* pertains to the oneness of the divine attributes. We know that God is the possessor of all attributes of perfection: both intellect and revelation indicate the reality of the attributes within the essence of the Creator. . . . These attributes are distinguished one from another as regards meaning. . . .

The essential attributes of God are in reality eternal and everlasting, partaking of the absolute unity of the divine essence. The view of those who regard the attributes of God as eternal and everlasting but somehow added to the essence is erroneous. This is an opinion derived from a false analogy between the attributes of God and man. . . .

Imam Ṣādiq explains: "God shall never cease to be our Lord. And knowledge is His essence—and it cannot be known; hearing is His essence—and it cannot be heard; seeing is His essence—and it cannot be seen; power is His essence—and it cannot be dominated."

Imam ʿAlī has said: "Perfect sincerity in *tawḥīd* is that we negate all attributes from Him; for every attribute testifies to its being other than the object to which it is attributed and every such object in turn testifies to its being other than the attribute."

Article 30

The third degree of *tawḥīd* pertains to the oneness of the source of creatorship. This means that there is no creator but God, and that whoever or whatever dons the robe of existence is of necessity His creature. . . .

Say: God is the Creator of all things and He is the One, the Almighty (al-Raʿd [13]:16). . . .

In addition to revelation, the intellect also bears witness to the oneness of creatorship. For all that which is other than God is a possibility, as opposed to a necessity, and thus stands in need of something other than itself, in order that it be translated from possibility into actuality. Naturally this need for existence can only be fulfilled by God. . . .

Article 31

The fourth degree of *tawḥīd* pertains to the oneness of lordship and of the governance of the world and man. . . .

Article 33

Oneness in worship is a principle that is held in common by all the divinely-revealed religions. . . .

There is no doubt that the worshipping of one's parents, of the Prophets and of the saints is polytheism, and thus forbidden; on the other hand, bestowing veneration and respect upon them is necessary and indeed forms part of integral *tawḥīd*: "Thy Lord hath decreed that ye worship none save Him, and show kindness to parents" (al-Isrāʾ [17]:23).

Now we must focus on the element that distinguishes worship from veneration, and ask the question: How can a given act in certain circumstances—such as the prostration of the angels before Adam . . . be at one with *tawḥīḍ* while the same act in different circumstances—such as prostration before idols—be an expression of shirk and idol-worship? The type of worship which is directed to what is other than God, and which is therefore rejected and forbidden, is that whereby the person humbles himself before a relative, engendered being, in the belief that this being possesses independent power to change the destiny of man and the universe, wholly or in part; in other words in the belief that such a being is the lord or master of the world and of men.

On the other hand, if humility is manifested before a person who is himself a righteous slave of God, one who is blessed with virtue and nobility, and is, moreover, a model of piety and righteousness for mankind, then such humility is an aspect of proper respect and reverence for that person and not worship of him.

Notes

In this chapter, dates are given as AH/CE.

1. See *Encyclopaedia of Islam, THREE*, s.v. "Abū Zurʿa al-Rāzī," by Claude Gilliot, accessed May 20, 2017, http://dx.doi.org/10.1163/1573-3912_ei3_COM_23454.

2. Translated in Binyamin Abrahamov, *Islamic Theology: Traditionalism and Rationalism* (Edinburgh: Edinburgh University Press, 1998), 55–57.

3. See Hassan Ansari, Sabine Schmidtke, and Jan Thiele, "Zaydi Theology in Yemen," in *The Oxford Handbook of Islamic Theology*, ed. Sabine Schmidke (Oxford: Oxford University Press, 2016), 474.

4. Translated in Abrahamov, *Islamic Theology*, 64.

5. *Encyclopaedia of Islam, THREE*, s.v. "Creed," by Jon Hoover, accessed May 20, 2017, http://dx.doi.org/10.1163/1573-3912_ei3_COM_25587.

6. Translated in W. Montgomery Watt, *Islamic Creeds* (Edinburgh: Edinburgh University Press, 1994), 48–56.

7. Ibn Sīnā, *Ibn Sina's Physics and Metaphysics: Remarks and Admonitions, Parts Two and Three*, ed. and trans. Shams C. Inati (New York: Columbia University Press, 2014), 125–31.

8. al-Ḥaramayn al-Juwaynī, *A Guide to Conclusive Proofs for the Principles of Belief: Kitāb al-irshād ilā qawāṭiʿ al-adilla fī uṣūl ali ʿtiqād*, trans. Paul Walker. Used with permission of Muhammad Bin Hamad Al Thani, Center for Muslim Contribution to Civilization.

9. Al-Ghazālī, *Moderation in Belief: Al-Iqtiṣād fī-l-iʿtiqād*, trans. Aladdin M. Yaqub (Chicago: University of Chicago Press, 2013), 73–77.

10. These excerpts of *Al-Futūḥāt al-Makkīya* (hereafter cited as *FM*) are taken from William C. Chittick, *The Self-Disclosure of God: Principles of Ibn al-ʿArabīs Cosmology* (Albany: State University of New York Press, 1998).

11. Chittick, *Self-Disclosure of God*, 5, providing *FM* 3.148.10.

12. Chittick, *Self-Disclosure of God*, 30, providing *FM* 1.716.16. The poet Abu Aqil Labīd ibn Rabīʿa, a contemporary of the Prophet Muḥāmmad, was a respected member of the nascent Islamic community.

13. Translated in Norman Calder, Jawid Ahmad Mojaddedi, and Andrew Rippin, eds., *Classical Islam: A Sourcebook of Religious Literature* (London: Routledge, 2003), 156–58.

14. See biographical comments by James W. Morris and William C. Chittick in John Renard, ed., *Islamic Theological Themes: A Primary Source Reader* (Oakland: University of California Press, 2014), 205, 395.

15. Ṣadr ad-Dīn Shīrāzī, *The Wisdom of the Throne*, trans. James W. Morris (Princeton, NJ: Princeton University Press, 1981), 109–13. Brackets around words or phrases are the translator's.

16. English translation by Sajjad Rizvi, of Fayḍ Kāshānī, *al-Kalimāt al-maḍnūna*, in *Majmūʿa-yi rasāʾil*, ed. Mahdī Ḥājiyān (Tehran: Madrasa-yi ʿālī-yi Sihpahsālār, 1387 Sh/2008), 251–53.

17. Translated in Christian W. Troll, *Sayyid Ahmad Khan: A Reinterpretation of Muslim Theology* (New Delhi: Vikas, 1978), 257–64. Used by permission of the translator.

18. The text here is excerpted from Jafar Sobhani, *Doctrines of Shiʿi Islam: A Compendium of Imami Beliefs and Practices*, trans. Reza Shah-Kazemi (London: I. B. Tauris, 2001), 18–32. Used by permission of Institute of Islamic Studies. The ayatollah's name is sometimes transliterated *Subḥānī*.

PART V

Reflections

Dialogue in Northern Virginia

Reflections on Building Bridges Seminar 2016

LUCINDA MOSHER

The tone for discussion of monotheism and its complexities was set during the opening plenary by a reminder that the Building Bridges Seminar is always about Christians and Muslims extending theological hospitality to each other. Participants theologize together. Not only is the goal to gain better understanding of each tradition; the project's aim is (as Rowan Williams used to put it) to improve the quality of our disagreements. Participants are not working toward agreement, not trying to resolve questions that have divided Christians and Muslims for centuries. Neither are they hiding behind absolute statements of faith. Rather, participants let each other in on the complexities they have discovered.

Thus, during four full days at the beautiful Airlie Center in Northern Virginia, the 2016 assembly of thirty-eight scholars—eleven women, twenty-seven men; seventeen Muslims, twenty-one Christians—searched for keys to positive, productive relationship as they explored how each tradition has tried to make sense of the many possible meanings of Christian and Muslim texts about God's unity. As has always been the procedure of the Building Bridges Seminar, four discussion groups had been established in advance—each with its own meeting room and moderator. This essay is based on notes taken by two staff observers, amplified by notes taken by two seminar participants. As is always the case in Building Bridges Seminar reports, the "Chatham House Rule" is observed here: ideas are unattributed; participants are quoted or paraphrased anonymously.

As discussion began, it was assumed that the seminar would be addressing Muslim curiosity about what sorts of questions the Christian doctrine of the Trinity tries to answer, but it was also clear that it would be necessary to ponder the meaning of the whole story of creation, the way we are to understand the unity of the divine economy, the relation between "the One" and "the many," and the status of the divine name, its relation to divine essence, and whether name and essence are "meaningfully" distinct. In short, it was assumed that this seminar would be an extended exercise in complexifying and complicating the question of monotheism.

The Oneness of God in the Bible

On Saturday morning, the four groups were at liberty to discuss any of the dozen Bible passages included in the notebook of seminar study materials.[1] One group began with Deuteronomy 6:4–15, which begins, "Hear, O Israel: The LORD is our God, the LORD alone." The Muslims in this group were quite comfortable with this passage. One noted that, in it, "oneness has to do with how we live." Another found it interesting that it expressed God's oneness in positive terms, rather than the negative of the *basmala*'s "There is no god but God." One noted that this is a liturgical text: called the *Shema*ʿ by Jews, recitation of Deuteronomy 6:4–9 is a prominent part of Jewish daily morning and evening prayer. Thus, the participant said, liturgy brings monotheism's implications into focus; it brings monotheism into practice. Another suggested that Muslims could read this passage and feel that God is talking to them—in that it accords with the Muslim understanding of the way God speaks in the Qurʾān itself. Christians responded that the passage is a reprise of the whole of the Torah: God is identified in terms of what God has done; God makes Godself present.

The significance of the Tetragrammaton (YHWH)—which appears many times in Deuteronomy 6:4–15—was another theme of this conversation. Several Christians declared it a proper name in and of itself—a way of saying that God is unnameable, that no name can contain God. When asked whether the four letters indeed stand for something, as in an anagram, one of the Christians argued against this notion, explaining that what we have now is Aramaic Hebrew; earlier manuscripts would have used Canaanite script. During discussion of the Jewish custom of writing the Tetragrammaton but saying something else in its place, a Christian noted that giving a name creates a relationship; referring to a name without speaking it acknowledges that the name is still there in the text. Another Christian mentioned the Jewish custom of referring to God as Ha-Shem (The Name)—which, in a sense, names God as "the nameless one."

In turning to Proverbs 8:22–31, in which "Wisdom" is personified as female, a Muslim requested more information about "Wisdom" as presented in this passage. One Christian responded by noting the importance of this passage in the theological debates associated with Arius, since Wisdom is claiming to have preceded creation. A Muslim asked how Jewish commentators read Proverbs 8. While endeavoring to answer would have taken the discussion beyond the parameters of the seminar, the Christians of this group applauded it as an important question—and said that a Jewish reading would be notably different from that of any of the exegetes of the Christian patristic era. During the theological debates of the second century CE, Christians had already concluded that Proverbs 8 was about Christ. From here, this group explored resonances between the description of Wisdom in Proverbs and the Qur'ān's mention of *al-Hikma* (Wisdom) alongside the Torah and *Injīl*.

Study of Jeremiah 10:6–12 and Zechariah 14:9 led one Muslim to note that these passages are telling a creation story for a particular purpose. A Christian agreed, noting "hints" of the notion of *creatio ex nihilo* in those verses. Expanding on this, another Christian asserted that God's creating is different from any other sort of creativity, and that—from the standpoint of Christian doctrine—all acts of creation are acts of the triune God. In summarizing his group's conversation about these passages from two Old Testament prophets, one Muslim asserted that themes of creation—its authorship and purpose—are at the heart of our understanding of monotheism.[2]

The prologue to the Gospel of John was at the center of another small-group conversation. One Bible scholar noted that this passage may have floated independently as a poem or hymn; it was a "community text" that eventually came to be attached to the gospel account—similar to Genesis 1, with which the prologue to John resonates and which also seems to have been an independent hymn later attached to the collected narrative. When asked what word or phrase most grabbed their attention, the emerging list included "glory," "Word," "light." A Muslim was intrigued by the repeated mention of "light." One Christian replied that light is a theme throughout John's gospel. Another Muslim noted that, in John's gospel, Word seems to be both part of and distinguished from God. She noted similarity to Islamic theology's definition of God's attributes as "He, but not He." A Christian, pointing to John 1:1 and 1:14, in which the term "logos" occurs four times, called this something of a high point in the New Testament way of speaking of God. Four times here *logos* (word) becomes *sarx* (flesh)—and usually, *sarx* is negatively used in John's gospel; but here, *sarx* is something positive. After, the prologue, he continued, the author of John's gospel makes few other references to *logos*; other ways of talking are much more prevalent throughout the remainder. Yet so much hinges on this passage: its language was picked up by the Church and incorporated into liturgy and hymnody more so than "Spirit-language." Why that happened is an interesting realm of conjecture. A Muslim wondered how Christians understand the economy of what John describes: when "the Word became flesh," she pressed, did *all* of the Word become flesh—or just part of it? A Christian replied that John 1:3 is about instrumentality in creation. The Word is God's instrument.

Taking up the study booklet's excerpts from various epistles, one group explored the relationship between 1 Corinthians 8:4–6 and elements of the *Shema*ʿ—and the relationship of both to the *shahāda*. One Christian recalled a Jewish scholar's warning against having a too-linear view of Jewish monotheism: among Jews, there have always been multiple streams, multiple ways of talking about God. In looking at Galatians 4:4–7, the phrase "the fullness of time" caught a Muslim's attention: What might that mean? Muslims were intrigued by the phrase "God has sent the Spirit of his Son," recalling other biblical mentions of the "Spirit of God" and the "Spirit of Christ." Similarly, they were struck by the mysticism and powerful imagery of Philippians 2:5–11. One Christian explained that, probably, this was an old Christological hymn that Paul then inserted into his letter to the church in Philippi. Philippians 2:7 mentions "in the form of God"—which provoked a Muslim to inquire, "What is God's 'form'?" Another Muslim replied that it had to do with Jesus's taking on the fullness of humanity. As the conversation ensued, one of the Christians emphasized the ways in which this hymn reinforces the salvific narrative intrinsic to the New Testament. Calling attention to 1 John, another Christian mentioned the notion of Jesus as an icon of God. Many Muslims would find that an acceptable notion, said one of the Muslims in this circle, because of their understanding of the Islamic notion of the human as the mirror of God's attributes.

During Saturday evening's plenary reflection on issues that had arisen during the day's small-group work, one Christian outlined five issues he thought had bound together the texts studied during this day's small-group sessions: eschatological finality, thus the ultimacy of God; "fullness" (in New Testament Greek, *pleroma*)—a term used often in reference to grace and truth, used here in a qualitative rather than a quantitative sense, having to do with sufficiency rather than comprehensiveness—which, he argued, could refer to "all we need to know in order to be in communion with another faith"; directness—that is, the way in which the rational principle becomes historical experience; Spirit language; and prior experience—for example, the importance of knowing Genesis 1 in order to make sense of John 1.

Another Christian observed that, when looking at biblical texts, "we sometimes acted as if the texts were the first step in the development of the doctrine of the Trinity. We needed to remind ourselves that a process led up to these texts. The penning of these texts was preceded by a community's experience of the Risen Christ, a community who said, 'We saw his glory!' That is, they believed that they had had a true encounter with God. John then expresses that in his text. John's gospel is not the origin. The experience originates in community; the text expresses the meaning of the experience." A Muslim admitted that recalling that the New Testament texts are preceded by the Jesus event caused him to think about what precedes the Qur'ān. What, that is, would be the "mother of the Qur'ān"? Creation? When Muslims formulate doctrine, the Qur'ān is always the starting point.

Some Muslim participants remarked that the Trinity was not apparent to them in the biblical texts studied. A Christian suggested that this might be because Muslims approach the Qur'ānic texts as "the first thing," coming to the texts with an expectation that is different from that of Christians. In short, she suggested, what we saw today was that the relation between scripture and doctrinal statement is quite different in the two traditions. In the Christian tradition, the transition from New Testament text to authoritative, written creeds is extremely complex.[3]

A Christian suggested the need to recognize that, as the texts push toward theologizing, they also pose questions. They may continue to generate reflection, raising new questions without resolving the old ones. Concurring, another Christian pointed to the openness of the biblical texts: they invite interpretation, and the complex and elusive relationship between divine speech and human speech. "Both lead to questions about epistemology and ontology—that is, to the grammar of theology itself."

A Muslim observed that the day had begun with the *Shema*ʿ—the second part of which is about pedagogy. As participants in the Building Bridges Seminar, she suggested, "We are 'away,' doing what the *Shema*ʿ calls for!" A Christian again reminded the group that Christians read the Hebrew biblical texts differently than Jews do. Christians see themselves standing in these texts, standing in a long story. Particular words, like "tabernacle," are saturated with meaning. Christians are aware that the New Testament is preceded by a long history of God's capacity to "be with," a long history of God being named as Word and Wisdom. To understand these texts requires "formation." Meaning does not just "come off the page." Rather, it is the product of an inductive process.

The Oneness of God in the Qurʾān and Ḥadīth

Sunday's attention was given to thirteen selections from the Qurʾān and five ḥadīths.[4] As is often the case when studying Sūrat al-Fātiḥa interreligiously, a Muslim wanted to know what about this core element of Muslim prayer resonates for Christians. He asked: Can Christians pray it? Most in his circle replied that they could—but could not say that their understanding of its key terms would align with those of a Muslim.[5]

Moving to engagement of the other passages, one group pursued comparative understandings of divine grace. Another turned its attention to Sūrat al-Furqān's use of the term *walad*—which led to exploration of the difference in nuance between *walad* (child) and *ibn* (son)—and by extension, assertions by the Christians at the table that the relation of Jesus to the Godhead is as *ibn* rather than *walad*. Another Muslim stressed the importance of the distinction between the literal and the metaphorical (the nonliteral), saying, "If we understand the mention in Sūrat al-Furqān (25):2 of 'He who . . . has no offspring' as 'nonliteral,' then Jesus as 'son' could be the reflection of the Glory of God." A Christian responded that the divinity of God is not exhausted by Jesus. The glory of God is not exhausted by Jesus either.

Still another group took up the concept of *shirk* (idolatry; polytheism). Having acknowledged its being a distinctive concern within Islamic monotheism, a Christian noted that there is no equivalent in the Bible to this Qurʾānic preoccupation.

A Muslim responded that *shirk* was common among the pagans at the coming of the Qur'ān. "The Qur'ān is clear that People of the Book are not among the *mushrikūn* [idolaters; polytheists]," he insisted. "The Qur'ān never calls Christians *mushrikūn*, and there are even ḥadīths indicating that it is all right for Muslims to eat Christian and Jewish meat!" Yet, a Christian pressed, "Why is *shirk* unforgiveable?" A Muslim replied, "Think of it this way: if you die in a state of *shirk*, to which god are you calling out?"

The notion of the divine names (or attributes) was a recurring theme throughout the day. Christians had many questions about how Muslims think about the oneness of God and the manyness of the names. One wanted to know more about the Islamic notion that God's attributes are neither identical to God nor other than he. "It raises the question: Is God the sum total of his attributes? Is God's unity a unity in plurality?" God in his essence is *simple.* God's essence transcends gender—a Muslim asserted. But, another Muslim countered, "language creates reality. God may not have a gender, but if we constantly use male language, we risk thinking of God as male." As the uniqueness of the divine names are explored, said one Muslim, the discussion can indeed become quite esoteric. "The names are there for us so that we can call upon certain dimensions of the essence," another Muslim explained. "They are the prism through which we see God, not in his wholeness, but insofar as we need him and he relates to us. The names are for the purpose of identification. They enable address, and fit the address by way of analogy of eminence. The essence concerns predicates, not identification. The Qur'ān criticizes those who blaspheme God's names by using names not worthy of him."

One group focused on the meaning of the divine name al-Ṣamad. How best to translate it? In discussion, it was agreed that "Eternal" is not quite adequate, nor is "Self-Sufficient." It implies that God does not need sustenance; God is "solid," "full." In this sense, it has similar meaning to the Greek term *pleroma* (fullness). As al-Ṣamad, a Muslim offered, God is not contingent, thus contains his own principle. Pickthall renders this Name of God as "Eternally Besought of All," meaning "needs nothing, but everything needs it." However, many find this an unhelpful English construct. A Christian noted that finding "Eternal" in the sacred text raises questions of how a timeless entity relates to temporal beings. After all, "saying that God 'is' is not on any scale of comparability; God is beyond 'being.' Even to say 'God is' is problematic."

In the Qur'ān, al-Ṣamad occurs only in Sūrat al-Ikhlāṣ (112)—and that chapter itself received considerable attention during small-group discussion. A Muslim explained that, as Sūrat al-Ikhlāṣ uses it, "He" is a proper name. It indicates that God is exclusively one, self-subsisting, definable only by what he is not. In response to a Muslim who remarked that Sūrat al-Ikhlāṣ is "simple," another Muslim noted that it can be understood on more than one level. "We all have idols in our life! Sūrat al-Ikhlāṣ reminds us that there is nothing comparable to God." "No comparison necessary" is a difficult concept to grasp, said a Christian; a Muslim concurred, saying, "Transcendence is difficult to grasp. Philosophers embrace being bewildered!"

Eventually, consideration of al-Ṣamad led to questions about the Trinity. That is, Muslims wondered whether Christians affirm Sūrat al-Ikhlāṣ. In response, a Christian recalled that Louis Massignon had found words very similar to those of the sura in a decision of the Fourth Lateran Council in reference to the nature/essence of God. Another Christian agreed that some Christians could. The grammar of the Trinity is such, said one, that "we can't collapse all of God back into the Father." Some thought it possible to say that Father-Son-Spirit *is* the Ṣamad. Metaphorically, Father-Son-Spirit are "the fullness." However, Christians use "begotten" only adjectivally rather than chronologically. A Muslim interjected that "Ṣamad" is understood as solid throughout; it means there is no differentiation of substance throughout. So, how could the Trinity be "Ṣamad"? A Christian responded that God has one substance, concretely realized in revelation—one story, one being, not dependent on creation.

In short, said one Christian, "Whether Christians can affirm Sūrat al-Ikhlāṣ depends greatly on what the Ṣamad is." "Another issue is this: Christians don't always watch their theological language. We use lots of internal shorthand. We know what we mean, but our language raises lots of questions for non-Christians. Qur'ān texts like Sūrat al-Ikhlāṣ press Christians to look at, clean up our theological language." That said, it was interesting to hear a Muslim point out that, according to early *tafsīr* (exegetical literature), Sūrat al-Ikhlāṣ does not have Christians in mind. He went on to point out the persistence of the internal Muslim conversation in which some Muslims say that other Muslims are unbelievers.

As would be expected, the seminar's discussion of Islamic monotheism engaged the doctrine of *tawḥīd.* Muslims acknowledge four different types of unity of God, one Muslim asserted, and in some conversations, challenges arise between these types of *tawḥīd.* The first, he explained, is unity of the divine essence—which all Muslims concede. The second is the unity of God in worship (*ʿibāda*), and all Muslims concede this as well. The third is the unity of God in his attributes—and on this, not all theological schools agree. (Ashʿarites and Shiʿites take different approaches to addressing this, he pointed out.) The fourth is the unity of God in action—which has to do with the freedom of God and thus leads directly to the problem of evil. Who is the agent of evil? Whichever way you answer, you raise other problems. When we compare Muslims and Christians around questions of *tawḥīd,* the participant cautioned, we need to be clear which of these four types of *tawḥīd* are on the table.

One group wrestled with the way the Qur'ān represents Christian beliefs—particularly with regard to the oneness of God. As one Muslim put it, "The Qur'ān represents Christian beliefs in ways Christians recognize—but not in the way Christians speak. What are we to do with this? Are we to say that the Qur'ān is talking about nonorthodox Christians? Are we to say it is a polemical text meant to show the opponent as illogical and unsustainable—or meant to provoke constructively? The latter is what *A Common Word* is seeking to do.[6] The Qur'ān does see itself as a corrective."

The Oneness of God in Christian Thought

After two days of dialogue on scripture explicitly, the seminar now turned to close reading of the Nicene and Athanasian Creeds, plus excerpts from works by Christian theologians from several eras.[7] In his paper, Christoph Schwöbel had differentiated between Trinitarian doctrine (which took centuries to develop) and Trinitarian discourse (which can be discerned throughout the New Testament). He had identified four key functions of the latter: to express the identity of God in Christian worship (i.e., by using the triune name in liturgy); to provide, via Trinitarian worship, a frame for the whole story of redemption of the world; to explore the relation between divine action and divine being—how the temporal fits into the being of God; and to safeguard Christian worship from idolatry.

Many participants found this outline helpful. However, a Muslim admitted that she struggled to understand the complexity of the doctrine of the Trinity. "We Muslims ask, 'Why go for the complexity rather than the simplicity?' For you Christians, the story of God is based on 'redemption,' but we Muslims don't talk so much about redemption. You seem to be saying that for God to save, God must be God—but must also be 'us.' For Christians, being pointed on the right path is not enough; for Muslims, it is!"

A Christian responded that the relation between identity and otherness is crucial. The doctrine of the Trinity says that unity and particularity are foundational for one's personal particularity. "Redemption is necessary," he continued, "because sin has lasting effect; but redemption is not enough. There must also be transformation of the heart. In the Muslim texts, being pointed on the straight path also requires transformation of the heart. So, it will be interesting to explore further the 'grace versus works' contrast."

As one group pursued deep discussion of the Nicene Creed and its development, one Christian described it as an effort to express biblical truths in non-biblical terms. Muslims wanted to know why the words "under Pontius Pilate" had been added. "Why get so specific?" All Christians agree that the crucifixion happened "under Pontius Pilate," one Christian explained; another added that mentioning that fact in the Creed "anchors the event in history, in the interaction of real human beings." Pushing further, a Muslim asked why the Creed asserts that Jesus "*suffered* under Pontius Pilate." Why not simply say that he died? This led to a lively exchange about what issues mattered to fourth-century Christians.

While one Muslim declared that, for him, Gregory of Nyssa makes the Trinity understandable, the excerpt from Gregory's *On "Not Three Gods" to Ablabius* generated myriad questions: Could God the Father become incarnate? Does God pray to God? When Jesus speaks from the cross to God the Father, what is the Trinity in that moment? To this last question (from a Muslim), responses included: "The reality enfleshed in this world was already in eternity"; "The man Jesus, transformed by hypostatic union with God, shows us how to pray"; in the Incarnation, "God joins himself perfectly to a fully human life." One Christian pointed out that Jesus's praying from the cross is not unlike the overlay of subjects in some prophetic speech. The Old Testament blurs divine and human speech in a way that the Qur'ān does not (although the Ḥadīth Qudsi might). In the prophetic texts of the Bible, it is often grammatically difficult to tell who is speaking: the prophet, the people, or God. In fact, God can lament with the people. Jesus's prayer in the Garden of Gethsemane is a lament in which divine and human speech mingle. When Jesus on the Cross says what he says, we have a moment of extreme paradox followed by divine solidarity: into the place of utter abandonment, God enters. A Muslim wondered: "Where was the Holy Spirit at the Cross?" One Christian described an icon depicting the Father holding up the Son on the Cross, with a dove (representing the Holy Spirit) hovering over both. Another Christian answered by pointing to Thomas Aquinas's notion that the Holy Spirit is moving Jesus's prayer heavenward. This connects with Paul's assumption that all prayer comes from the Holy Spirit.

The theme of redemption intrigued one group. One Muslim wondered whether the Qur'ānic account of Adam and Eve might be read as a story of immediate redemption whereas in the Bible, it is a story of redemption delayed. Someone else wondered whether "redemption" was the right term here. "Redemption is associated with the notion of 'buying,'" he said. "There is cost involved." A Muslim replied that the Christian notion of deep empathy is very different from Islam, in which God stands exalted. "Redemption for Muslims comes via total submission. So," she surmised, "we have two different models of redemption."

A Christian reminded his group that creation is not just about bringing things into existence; it is the beginning of a drama. In the Bible, God's blessing on Adam and Eve says that humanity is meant to have a future in communion with God. Humans have no ability to get their own orientation. They accept the orientation that is offered by revelation and temptation. They are always victims of the fallibility of relying on themselves. The promise is maintained, but with humans who now know that they have been dislocated and can't relocate themselves. It is not enough for Adam and Eve to beg forgiveness from God. If that is an event in God's life, how do we find language for that? The doctrine of the Trinity is one way. God does not cease to be God but does envelop our situation. As Christians read the New Testament, to fix the problem, divine intervention is needed. Within the Christian tradition, there are various answers as to what sort of intervention that is. In Orthodox understanding, redemption focuses less on the cross than is the case for Roman Catholics. But always with the doctrine of the Trinity, the whole point is to tell us that there was a need for the Father to send the Son and for the Son to get back to the Father. In short, "We Christians are Trinitarian theists because the Bible tells us so!"

Of the day of complex dialogical thinking about the Christian doctrine of the Trinity, one Christian could only say, "Wow! All of this was generated by the need to be truthful to tradition!" Another Christian had noted, "This thing called the doctrine of the Trinity: we Christians receive it and believe it—and then strive to understand it." As one group's conversation came to an end, a Christian had asked, "Does the Christian account of God make any sense? Even if you still do not buy it, can you see an internal logic?" A Muslim recalled having heard a mid-twentieth-century Christian say that the Trinity is "a riddle wrapped up inside a puzzle and buried in an enigma."[8] That is, the doctrine is more about faith than about speculation. The best way to understand it is as "faith that helps Christians understand God." This Muslim went on to say that "God tells me that Jews and Christians are monotheists. The Building Bridges Seminar has affirmed that Christians are monotheists. It doesn't matter whether the doctrine of the Trinity makes sense!" Another Muslim replied that his questions about it are sharper now. Perhaps that is enough. Said another Christian: the doctrine of the Trinity does not make sense alone, on its own. We must remember that it was received by the Church as a solution to a problem. In summary, the group agreed that there are different types of rationalities, rooted in different sets of practices, that shape us. Bridge-building between religions is not easy, but it need not be superficial.

The Oneness of God in Islamic Thought

Texts under consideration for the fourth (and final) day of the seminar included creeds (in whole or in part) and a range of other Islamic texts.[9] Much of this material was quite unfamiliar to the seminar's Christian participants; in fact, some of the Shiʿite texts were new to many of the Muslims in the circle. Undaunted, the small-group discussions were lively—and most of these items were indeed given their due. We shall hear how groups handled a few of them.

Given the uses of the Nicene Creed in the Christian tradition, Christians wanted to know how an *ʿaqīda* functions in Islam. One Muslim replied, on the whole, an *ʿaqīda* is a theologically elaborate document that Muslims "know but have almost no need to recite." Another Muslim added that scholars might indeed memorize them, however. Another characterized an *ʿaqīda* as an effort at coming to truth through rational argument. Someone else said that the ḥadīth of Gabriel is the closest thing Muslims have to a creed in the sense that Christians use the word: vast numbers of Muslims are able to recite this summary of Islam's core beliefs and practices from memory.

Having surveyed the items in the study booklet, one Muslim called his group's attention to Ibn Sīnā as a prominent, influential representative of ethical philosophy. In his "On Being and Its Causes"—the portion of his *Remarks and Admonitions* being studied by the seminar—Ibn Sīnā is not trying to spell out doctrine, this Muslim explained; only occasionally is there direct engagement with the Qurʾān in his process here. Rather, he is digging into the notion of a first cause, issue by issue; he is working through a concept logically, trying to "get it right" as he discusses "existence." As a Muslim in another breakout group stressed to his colleagues, the fundamental point of the portion of Ibn Sīnā's writings under study is that "God *exists,* is *one,* and is *simple.* We can't reduce God to what is able to be experienced. There is being; how can we analyze it? Some 'being' is necessary; some is contingent. A feature of distinction between necessary and contingent being is essence versus existence."

In short, a Muslim explained to his group, Ibn Sīnā wants to establish a proof for the God of Islam. Thus, he turns the cosmological argument on its head: where others have argued that, because the cosmos exists, therefore there is God, Ibn Sīnā argues that, because God exists, therefore he can demonstrate that the cosmos exists. This approach was largely successful in Islamic thought. It also influenced Christianity, as Thomas Aquinas worked with a Latin version of this work. However, this Muslim emphasized: "Ibn Sīnā was not just a rational empiricist channeling Aristotle. When he didn't understand something, he'd go to the mosque and pray . . . and the answer would come. The role of prayer in this philosopher's life is important!"

Turning to al-Juwaynī's *A Guide to Conclusive Proofs for the Principles of Beliefs*, a Muslim explained that this author exemplifies Ashʿarī legal scholarship. "He's a member of the Shāfiʿī school of jurisprudence, an Iraqi, a teacher of al-Ghazālī. His title means he leads prayers in both Medina and Mecca. He is a very important theologian." His group engaged in considerable exchange about Juwaynī's piece, particularly his remarks on *messiah.* One Christian wished that he had been clearer about the relationship of the person "Jesus" to "the eternal Word of God"—conceding that Juwaynī is just describing the tension in the wider Christian community. As another Christian quipped, Juwaynī "is delightfully well aware of the Christian theological positions in his milieu." Another Christian appreciated the distinction Juwaynī makes between *division* and *difference.* "The divine attributes are *different*, but not inseparable. For example, Power and Wisdom are different, but they always go together. You can have *difference* within God, but God is an inseparable whole." A Muslim asserted that for Juwaynī, there is no division within God. The Christian replied that there is a coherent view of simplicity that excludes divisibility—so this participant pressed, why does Juwaynī use *difference*? The conversation continued. Later, a Christian reported that the value of the Building Bridges practice of having a significant number of scholars return to the seminar year after year was on full display in the intensity with which her group had engaged Juwaynī. "Repeat attendance fosters trust. The trust among us was evident as Muslims were able to press Christians as to whether Juwaynī got Christian theology right!"

For one group, the most fruitful part of their afternoon studying these examples of Islamic thought was spent considering Mullā Ṣadrā Shīrāzī's *Wisdom of the Throne.* A Muslim characterized Mullā Ṣadrā as a philosopher who is heavily influenced by Ibn Sīnā but who criticizes him, one who is heavily influenced by Ibn ʿArabī but who goes beyond him and rarely criticizes him. Mullā Ṣadrā has strongly monistic tendencies, but not starkly so. Clearly intrigued by Mullā

Ṣadrā's ideas, a Christian noted, "What God communicates is Godself, which might be more like a song in which we participate." As the last small-group session neared its conclusion, one Christian urged her colleagues not to overlook "the unusual thing that in the Abrahamic religions, God creates by speaking and writing."

Conclusion

As the seminar drew to a close, one participant stressed that the debate over monotheism and its meaning is a discussion by no means limited to Muslim-Christian understanding. It is much broader, including concerns about dualism, Aristotelianism, and other philosophies and theologies. It includes exploration of the "radical monotheism" introduced into the world in late antiquity through Judaism. It recognizes that the dynamic of transcendence and immanence is central to radical monotheism. The sequence of divine self-naming in human speech through revelation, through signs in nature, and through the human self is a disclosure of the ultimacy and intimacy of God. God is nameable—and names himself. We humans need the names to be in relation with God, the unknowable. Thus, the divine names tradition is a mode of reflection on God, but also on what it ultimately means to be human. And since theology is a practice, not a purely analytic exercise, the seminar concluded by asking what ethical commitments are raised by monotheism. Indeed, said one of the Christians, "during our discussions, I've been touched by the way systematic theology bears on our spiritual and ethical functions. These are linked!"

What had been learned? A Muslim admitted discovering that among Christians, there is more plurality in understanding of principle dogmas than she had assumed. She was impressed by the way Christian theologians articulate the complexity of the Trinity while being concerned for maintaining the boundaries, respecting the oneness. As a Christian asserted, "The 'une' in 'triune' is really important!"

One Christian said that his group experienced in depth what the process of dialogue can be. "We Christians and Muslims were thinking together!" he exclaimed. Another Christian concurred, saying, "I came hoping to learn more about Islam—and I did, but during this seminar, Muslims taught me as much about my own tradition! My Muslim colleagues pulled me closer to Christian orthodoxy." A third Christian said that it taught him to speak more intentionally about the "various understandings" of Christian doctrine, to be more sensitive to the varieties.

One Muslim asserted that, for her, it had never been a question of whether Christians and Muslims worship the same God, but she had not been aware of the breadth and complexity of the formulations of the doctrine of the Trinity. Another Muslim recalled the moment when one of the Christians had asked whether the

Trinitarian formula is intelligible to Muslims. "I was impressed by the fire-power of Christian theologians in this room! Christian doctrine is much more complex than I thought. I used to think that a lot more Christians subscribed to the position of Meister Eckhart or Nicholas of Cusa—whose positions make sense to Muslims—than apparently is the case. I now want to know more about what is at stake, about what would be lost, if Meister Eckhart's point of view were embraced."

Upon reflection, one Muslim suggested that the 2016 seminar had yielded three outcomes. The first, he said, had to do with refinement in mutual understanding. "Differences remain within and between us—and we continue to struggle. However, we Muslim participants now have a much more sophisticated understanding of the Christian position, which is helpful in identifying Christianity as monotheism." Second, participants have now reached a new threshold at which "to think about whether the differences ultimately matter," since questions about our respective understandings of God will indeed persist. Third, we adjourn reminded that, for all our differences in interpretation and understanding, "it is God who measures our worship!"

Notes

1. See "Texts from the Bible" in this volume for the complete texts of the items available for study.
2. For more on this topic, see Lucinda Mosher and David Marshall, eds., *God's Creativity and Human Action: Christian and Muslim Perspectives* (Washington, DC: Georgetown University Press, 2017).
3. Close reading of Christian creeds was part of small-group work on the third day of the 2016 seminar.
4. See "Texts from the Qur'ān and Ḥadīth" in this volume for the complete texts of these thirteen items.
5. This topic is explored in depth in David Marshall and Lucinda Mosher, eds., *Prayer: Christian and Muslim Perspectives* (Washington, DC: Georgetown University Press, 2013).
6. *A Common Word between Us and You*, signed by eminent Muslim leaders and promulgated in November 2007, called for robust interfaith dialogue.
7. For the complete texts of the items studied, see "Texts from the Christian Tradition" in this volume.
8. Indeed, said by Christopher A. Hall (reapplying a remark made by Winston Churchill regarding Russia during a 1939 radio broadcast) in his, "Adding Up Trinity," *Christianity Today*, April 28, 1997, 26.
9. These texts can be found in "Texts from the Islamic Tradition" in this volume.

Index

About the Editors

Lucinda Mosher is assistant academic director of the Building Bridges Seminar; faculty associate in Interfaith Studies, Hartford Seminary; and Center for Anglican Communion Studies Fellow in World Anglicanism, Virginia Theological Seminary, Alexandria, Virginia.

David Marshall is academic director of the Building Bridges Seminar; senior research fellow of the Berkley Center for Religion, Peace, and World Affairs; and associate professor in the Theology Faculty of Georgetown University, Washington, DC.

CPSIA information can be obtained
at www.ICGtesting.com
Printed in the USA
JSHW022114180523
41941JS00003B/81